Praise for *Full Alignment*

"A true masterpiece! The strategies in Full Alignment *have been invaluable for me both personally and as the leader of a large company. Silard's principles of personal and organizational leadership, when internalized, will unleash tremendous power and deep commitment toward powerful, compelling goals to which you and those around you aspire. I can't recommend this book enough. It's one of the best investments you'll ever make in both your own personal growth and the growth of your organization."*

—Tien Wong, CEO, Opus8 Corporation

"This wonderful book makes the vital link between personal leadership and organizational leadership. I highly recommend it to aspiring business managers, CEOs and others who want to get more out of their personal and professional lives. Filled with practical, highly effective strategies for bringing your day-to-day actions in line with your evolving vision, this book will help you discover what you truly stand for and how to manifest it every day to yield both tremendous results in the workplace and a nurturing, supportive environment in your home."

—Tim Kime, CEO, Leadership Greater Washington

"Anthony Silard is both talented and wise. His book Full Alignment *is an affirmation of the beauty and higher calling within each of us. It will help the reader firmly ground him or herself in values*

that spring from deep within, and then embark mindfully on a path toward meaning, joy, and unconditional self-acceptance."

—*Tara Brach, Author of* Radical Acceptance

"Ten years ago, my partner and I started a company with only an idea and a vision of what could be. It's not easy to bootstrap a vision into a great company. Even harder is dealing with its success—to paraphrase AA, first you own a company, then the company owns a company, and then the company owns you. Instead of thinking of yourself as a leader, you begin to think of yourself as a victim. Full Alignment *helped me realize that by changing my viewpoint I could once again lead both myself and others. The fascinating anecdotes, stories, and practical applications reawakened my deeper values and the optimism needed to regain control of my life. There's leadership potential in all of us. Tony Silard has dedicated his life to helping us realize that potential. I believe his book can help us all transform our despair into hope and then into the marvelous future we all deserve."*

—*Ashok Khosla, Chief Technical Officer and Co-Founder, TuVox Corporation*

"Silard provides compelling insights, real-life examples, practical do-it-yourself exercises, leadership lessons ranging from Dell and Sony to Churchill and Bono, philosophical insights from Galileo and Goethe to Hilary Swank, Muhammad Ali, and Gandhi, and a reader-friendly style that make this book a true gem. Full Alignment *is a beautifully crafted tapestry of wisdom, personal anecdotes, and extremely useful models that are easy to apply to your own life. Silard has proven himself the new master of the personal leadership genre."*

—*Jessica Teisch, Senior Editor,* Bookmarks

"Whether you want to be an effective CEO, a caring parent, a compassionate partner, a driven person who can tap the creative spirit

within, or all of the above, this is the book that lays down the road map for you to get there! Silard's timely advice is as incisive as it is fun to read. I have made tremendous changes in my life since reading this spectacular book. I recommend it to anyone ready to embark on the inner journey that is the foundation of true leadership."

—Octavio Hinojosa, CEO, The Congressional Hispanic Leadership Institute

"Full Alignment *is fun, dynamic, and a joy to read. Its unique approach combines meaningful content with memorable anecdotes to help you identify and remember the concepts. In one small book, Silard has created a one-stop resource with more substance than a whole shelf of self-help books—and in a busy world, that's what I need. Many readers will make life-changing transformations from reading its pages. Make this investment in yourself; you won't regret it."*

—Francesca Dea, Principal, Gordian Solutions, LLC

"Full Alignment *is the fundamental authority on taking stock of your innermost feelings, doubts, and desires, and channeling them toward compelling goals. It systematically challenges you to develop a roadmap for realizing your own leadership potential. This book is a must-have for anyone searching for optimum effectiveness!"*

—Cary Hatch, President & CEO, MDB Communications

"Tony is a natural leader who guides us on our most important journey: to rediscover our life's passion. Full Alignment *is a powerful and practical step-by-step guide aimed at focusing and balancing our lives. It achieves a unique balance between the heart, mind, and soul unlike any other book I've ever read. This book is a must-read for us action-oriented people!"*

—Jonathan Berkey, Professor, Monterey Institute of International Studies

"Which do we choose: (1) rushing through life to the finish line or (2) slowing down to discern what a meaningful life looks like and then making it a reality? If we choose the latter, chances are we'll need some help! In Full Alignment, *Anthony Silard inspires us with his own journey and the wisdom of ancient traditions, sharing enlightening exercises and lucid models that amount to a how-to guide for discovering and achieving a life of purpose and balance.*

—KLIA BASSING, PRESIDENT AND CEO, VISIT YOURSELF AT WORK

"This book is a dazzling, practical guide to personal change. The strategies outlined in Full Alignment*—from goal-setting and risk-taking to self-discipline and the discovery of one's passion—have fundamentally transformed the way my employees and I lead our lives from day to day, both at work and at home. I learned something invaluable from every page. I couldn't put it down, and when I finished I voraciously hungered for more. Anyone who aspires toward personal fulfillment and business success should read this book!"*

—FERN BARRUETA, CEO, THE HISPANIC COLLEGE FUND

"Anthony Silard, a man who walks the walk and the talk, combines a disarming humility with a confident, penetrating wisdom into who we are and what motivates us, at our core. Anyone interested in developing their self-mastery, interpersonal and communication skills should read this valuable book!"

—SANDRA CROWE, AUTHOR OF SINCE STRANGLING ISN'T AN OPTION... DEALING WITH DIFFICULT PEOPLE—COMMON PROBLEMS AND UNCOMMON SOLUTIONS

"Phenomenal! Professionally, I've read many self-help books over the years...however, Full Alignment *stands above the rest. Author Tony Silard gives exceptional insight into human motivation and the world. Reading this book was like getting an education in the secret of life and success.* Full Alignment *reveals a simple truth: the secret to enduring success—both individually and professionally—rests in creating a life*

where your daily actions are aligned with your deeper values and vision. Silard draws a clear and concise map toward inner fulfillment, enhanced purpose and directedness. This book will cause anyone who reads it to reflect more deeply on what truly makes their life worth living!"

—DEBORAH J. MITCHELL, TELEVISION PRODUCER

"Full Alignment *is a true roadmap to leadership success. Tony Silard shares his insights from many years of founding and leading companies and organizations and his unique way of encouraging all of us to find our own individual style as leaders. This book is not only a valuable resource for all readers but is also a fun book to read!"*

—RICHARD WALKER, VICE PRESIDENT, FBR CAPITAL MARKETS CORPORATION

"Full Alignment *tackles the age-old issue of why are we here and what are we supposed to do with our time to make it worthwhile. Of all the books written on self-development and leadership, this is without a doubt the most accessible and clear. If you want a gift to your family and friends that is based on profound and perennial truths that will inspire them to clarify what they stand for and value—and how to live it every day—look no further: this is your book. It has changed my outlook on leadership and my own personal development. I have bought it for the people I love and care about the most. Silard has left us a priceless gift!"*

—KHARI BROWN, CEO, CAPITAL PARTNERS FOR EDUCATION

"This book touched me to the core and brought out potential I never knew I had inside. It's the first book I've read by a modern author that has profoundly affected the way I think. I consider Tony my leadership guru because he helped me to realize that while I'm a servant to the mission of my organization, I'm actually working against the mission I'm striving so hard to achieve by not rejuvenating myself regularly. I realized while reading Full Alignment *that it is more than just a book—it's a paradigm shift in self-help. While turning its pages, I had the ineffable*

sense of history being made. It will be the go-to personal development book for the next decade. Read this book and be transformed!"
—MARY BROWN, CEO, LIFE PIECES TO MASTERPIECES

"Full Alignment *offers a practical methodology of how to translate your dreams and passions into action steps to move your life in the direction you determine. Every day we make many choices, and this stunning book clearly shows—thanks to Silard's take-no-prisoners, stop-BS'ing-around-and-confront-your-true-self writing style—how to strategically keep moving towards a more aligned life and become the person that you want to be."*
—ROBERT WALKER, EXECUTIVE DIRECTOR,
THE FRANK H. AND EVA B. BUCK FOUNDATION

"Reading Full Alignment *is like holding a mirror up to yourself. Tony is an exceptionally wise tour guide—Destination: You—and once you read the first few pages, you can't help but get swept up in the voyage he takes you on. I have been inspired to make some positive changes in my life since reading this wonderful book. I recommend it to anyone who has the courage to embark on this inner journey. Once you are ready to take the leap—for you may never be the same afterwards—prepare to be transformed!"*
—SUSIE KAYE, CEO, HOOP DREAMS

Full Alignment

A Practical Guide to Transforming Your Life Vision into Action

Anthony Silard

Full Alignment: A Practical Guide to Transforming Your Life Vision into Action

For information about this title or to order other books and/or electronic media, contact the publisher:

Five Spheres Press
1050–17th Street NW, Suite 520
Washington, DC 20036
www.fivespherespress.com
info@fivespherespress.com

ISBN: 978-0-9817853-0-1

Printed in the United States of America

Book design by Michele DeFilippo
Cover design by Randy Mays

This book is dedicated
to my mother and father.
You each taught me
the resilience of the human spirit,
and to believe.

Vision without Action is a daydream.
Action without Vision is a nightmare.
—*Ancient Japanese proverb*

Contents

Foreword

I first met Tony sixteen years ago when he took one of my courses while studying for his master's degree at Harvard University's JFK School of Government. Tony was curious about everything related to organizational development, and we spent many long sessions together in my office discussing how companies and organizations evolve. After Tony left the Kennedy School for the real world, he called me periodically to share his stories from the front line. Tony went through startups and transitions of a number of companies and organizations with remarkable resilience. I was always struck by how—regardless of what he was going through—he never lost his bold willingness to innovate, think out of the box, and continue developing and piloting new models of organizational change.

I was pleased to see his career as a leadership development trainer flourish, and to see him in action a number of times when he invited me to co-teach in his executive leadership training programs. Tony has a way of reaching people that is truly unique and exceptional. He has developed a solid framework of personal and organizational learning that combines his own experience with keen observation and solid research on the commonalities among people who have been tremendously successful. In *Full Alignment* he addresses personal leadership and organizational leadership in a way that enables the reader to own their own development and experience deep, transformative learning.

Tony exposes an exceptionally revealing fallacy about success: people sometimes think that success is the sum of their good experiences as opposed to their bad. He proves throughout this book that it's not. Our experiences are what they are, and I finished *Full Alignment* realizing that it's precisely the cumulative nature of our experience that makes us strong. Tony shows us that we don't need to think we have to exorcise our bad experiences, and that some of these aren't actually as bad as we think because they pave the way to our success—through the passion (poignantly described in the *Discover Your Passion* chapter) to learn from what went wrong and why it has affected us so deeply, and apply this learning toward our future growth.

Tony brings this to life by sharing examples of people whom we might perceive as having it made or having it all, and how they struggled to get there—people like Bono, Hilary Swank, *America's Most Wanted* director John Walsh, and others who we all just assume began with immense natural talent and then experienced overnight success. Reading about the struggles of these and many other very successful people—and the strategies they used to focus on their goals all the way until they made it big, and then afterwards—is both illuminating and inspiring. Tony vividly reminds us, no matter how successful we are, of our essential human qualities—such as fear, insecurity, and resentment—and how acknowledging them is the first step toward freeing ourselves from their control.

I came away from reading *Full Alignment* feeling reenergized and rejuvenated. I think *Full Alignment* is an essential book for CEOs, middle managers, entrepreneurs, rising stars, self-starters, and others who want to embrace change and create and achieve more compelling goals in their work or life. Within the following pages are the keys to personal mastery that lay the foundation for high-performance companies and organizations. This is a book you and your employees cannot go without if you are truly committed to organizational learning and change. I hope you enjoy it!

—Christine W. Letts
Senior Associate Dean for Executive Education
John F. Kennedy School of Government
Harvard University

Acknowledgments

To Karla: thank you for your unswerving patience and support, and for all the times—many more than I can number—when you listened to my ideas, questioned and shot holes through some of them, and helped me to refine this book.

To my sister, Julie, and my brothers, Danny and Andrew: it means a lot to me that we've always been there for each other over the years. Thank you for being such wonderful friends.

To my editor, Ingrid Busch: your eye for cutting unnecessary words and tightening up the book was both uncanny and superb. I couldn't have done it without your caring eye and compassionate help.

To my copyediting team, Sheridan McCarthy and Stanton Nelson: your eye for detail was truly exceptional, and I learned a lot from you about esoteric grammar rules I didn't know existed. You were a delight to work with.

To my designers, Randy Mays from *The Washington Post Magazine* and Michele DeFilippo from 1106 Design: thank you for creating the beautiful images that bring *Full Alignment* to life.

A special dedication to Jo-Lynne Worley: you believed in me as a writer before just about anyone else did—perhaps even before I did. This book wouldn't exist without you. You are a model of honesty and integrity and I have learned a lot from you. Thank you.

To my "Ideal Readers": Scott Brandes, John Derderian, Rachel Goodman, Tim Gray, Mary Gregory, Harriet Lerner, Nick Sales, and Joan Soncini: thank you for your painstaking work on the edits and many revisions of *Full Alignment.* Because of your tireless efforts, other people like you will feel heard in this book and keep reading.

To Sameer Abraham, Bill Adams, Lucia Casaravilla, Kathy Deboe, Andrew Giordano, Tom Golsen, Francis Kihanya, Cedric Laurant, Erika Lopez, Andres McAllister, Azita Parsarad, Scott Pitchford, RC Saravanabhavan, Cheryl Steele, Saira Sufi, Lisa-Joy Zgorski, and all my other team members, too numerous to mention but all deserving of my heartfelt gratitude, at The Center for Social Leadership, The Executive Leadership Institute, and Five Spheres Press: thank you for joining forces with me for so many years, and for giving so much of yourselves to make this world a better place.

To Ina Bechhoefer, Johnny Clibbon, Roberto Dragonieri, Sam Frumkin, Norma Garcia, Maritza Guttridge, Laura Marquez, Pedro Marquez, Russell McClymont, Anthony Muiru, Aditya Narain, Alison Ormsby, Don Roberts, Scott Shermer, Monique Silard, Mario Soncini, Clark Wilson, Anthony Young, and Edward Yu: thank you for bringing so much joy into my life for so many years.

Introduction

Los Angeles Dodgers manager Tommy Lasorda had just lost the National League pennant race. A journalist, eager for an interview, was surprised to find him cheerful, humorous, and in overall good spirits. Curious, the journalist asked how he could be so happy after losing the most important game of the year. Lasorda replied, "The best day of my life is when we win a game. The second best day of my life is when we lose a game."

When you find your purpose in life, the day-to-day ups and downs become almost insignificant. What you value most is that you are living your dream; your daily reality is aligned with your Vision for what you know it can be.

Vision. Dreams. Purpose. Meaning. The larger picture—something at your core that you want so much there are times you would rather work toward attaining it than eat. Something about the world that, in your gut, you need to change as much as you need air to breathe. Have you ever experienced this feeling? There is an old saying: "I'd rather be the person who loses himself to passion than the person who loses his passion." What is your passion? How do you find it?

Full Alignment is a guide to achieving complete Vision-Alignment. Vision-Alignment means:

1. The Visionary within you can paint a clear picture of your life goals and what you want your most important relationships to look like.
2. The "Actionary" within you knows how to commit actions that transform (and avoid actions that do not transform) this picture into your present reality.

Life is a series of choices. Every day, every hour, every moment you make choices—from coming home and choosing whether to turn on the television or read a book to choosing which jobs to apply for to deciding whom to date or marry. Whatever your situation, *Full Alignment* will help you check in with yourself, uncover your deepest values and priorities, and integrate them into the way you are living your life *now.*

Full Alignment is a collection of practical, easily adaptable tools designed to help you consistently move your life in the direction you determine. The strategies that fill these pages will enable you to become not just the actor, but also the director of your own life.

Fasten your seat belt. This is where we're going:

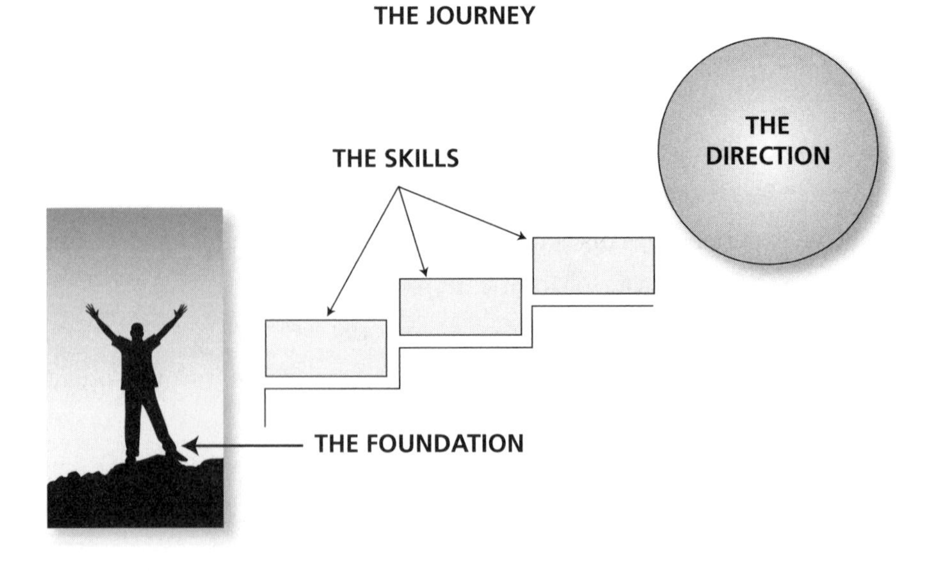

Picasso once said, "Every act of creation is first of all an act of destruction." The first chapter, *Dream*, will help you clear away all the "stuff" that's clogging up your life. By freeing up the space for new thoughts and feelings, you'll be poised to make a breakthrough. This chapter asks you to stop being a "human doing" and to become a human *being* again. It encourages you to take a step back from your busy schedule, to reflect on what you truly value, and to decompress. When you take time out of your life for thoughtful contemplation, you get more from the time you put in.

Your Vision is a mental picture of your desired life and how you want to live it. Your core values guide you as you paint this image of what your life can become. Developing a clear sense of Vision is one of the most important components of *Full Alignment.* In *Part One: The Direction*, you will develop your own personal Vision. In *Part Two: The Foundation*, you will build the inner foundation of self-confidence you'll need to transform your Vision into your present reality.

We start with *The Direction* because once you create a mental image of where you want to go, it's easier to build *The Foundation*—you have a purpose for building it. Self-change becomes a priority once you realize it's not optional if you want to transform your life into what you know it can become.

You cannot develop your Vision for how you want to live your life until you discover what motivates you—which, as you will learn in *Chapter 7—Discover Your Passion*, is most likely rooted in the suffering you've experienced. This is hard work. It requires some soul-searching and the willingness to confront your inner demons.

An understanding of your most challenging moments is a necessary step toward determining your life's direction. Chapter 7 is one of the most critical for finding the right path; for many it will also be the most difficult to read. While *Part One: The Direction* provides the tools for developing your Vision, the profound feelings Chapter 7 generates within you will give you the extra push you need to discover and refine the content of that Vision.

Developing your Vision without identifying strategies to actualize it yields "analysis paralysis" and the daydream in the Japanese proverb you read after opening this book. *Part Three: The Skills* is about how to choose actions on a moment-to-moment basis that are congruent with your deepest values. What actions? You will learn the art of self-discipline, how to take risks, and how to jump-start yourself into action when your mind has become stuck pondering the options.

Full Alignment contains a revolutionary new goal-setting system that will enable you to transform your lofty dreams into concrete, deadline-driven goals. In Chapter 4 you will create your own Vision Statement: a timeless summary of your core values and what you want to be remembered for in this lifetime. In parallel, in Chapter 10 you will design a time-sensitive Action Plan that you will use to transform your Vision Statement into tangible goals with the guiding theme that "A goal is a dream with a deadline." Your Action Plan will contain goals that are SMART (Specific, Measurable, Aligned with your Vision Statement, Realistic, and Time-based). This goal-setting system will enable you to choose daily, everyday actions that are consistent with your long-term Vision. In so doing, you will achieve the ultimate goal of this book: Full Alignment.

Every chapter in *Full Alignment* contains a set of concrete tools and strategies—from learning how to take risks and handle disapproval to how to trust your instincts and hold yourself to task—which you can integrate into your daily life. Each chapter also includes dozens of entry points where I challenge you to apply the strategies to your life. I strongly recommend you read *Full Alignment* with a notebook or journal handy. Be ready to write down your thoughts, or your responses to the thought-provoking questions the book poses to you, or to create an entry in your Vision Statement or Action Plan inspired by the theme of the chapter you're reading.

Most of the chapters also include at least one "Make It Happen" exercise, which provides yet another opportunity to make the strategies your own. If you feel that working through the "Make It Happen" exercises interrupts the natural flow of the book for you, an alternative is to initially just read them through so your subconscious mind can begin pondering how they apply to your life, and then return to them later when you feel ready. I have included some blank pages at the end of the book for you to work on these exercises as you see fit.

The final chapter, *Discipline—Cultivate the Actionary Within,* is about how to continue using the strategies after you've learned them. While the first ten chapters will help you to achieve Vision-Alignment, this last chapter is about how to remain in this exalted state where your life just feels "right." It's about how to align your life continuously, even and especially after you get off-track.

We will conclude with a brief section, *The Player and the Spectator,* which will review *Full Alignment* and revisit how you can create alignment in your life.

CULTIVATE THE BEGINNER'S MIND

Many of us like to think of ourselves as "experts" who have all the answers for how we should live. Ironically, it may be better not to be an expert. Experts do not feel they have anything else to learn—that's why they call themselves experts. If you can instead cultivate what Japanese Zen master Shunryu Suzuki calls the beginner's mind and think of yourself as a beginner, you will enable your mind to recover its original, natural state of wonder and curiosity. You will then be ready to embark on a lifelong courtship with learning. You'll understand that the only moment in which you know you haven't arrived is when you think you already have.

If you want to make a personal transformation while reading this book, you can't just read it with your mind. You must also use your heart and feel how each page applies to your life. You have to open up the tender part of yourself and allow yourself to be vulnerable. This includes asking yourself difficult questions to confirm what's relevant for you and what isn't. It also means being willing to plumb the depths of what you truly value when working on your Vision Statement and the "Make It Happen" exercises.

My work with CEOs, executives, and many other individuals seeking to improve their personal and professional lives has taught me that there is only one way to truly learn: by doing, by participating, by giving of yourself to a self-initiated process. That involves risk. You may go to great lengths to avoid risks because you fear if you stand upright and reach for something even higher you will have much farther to fall than if you cower close to the ground. Yet as you will learn in *Chapter 9—Develop Your Capacity for Risk,* taking risks is the only means of securing a high return in your career, your relationships, your efforts to meet the right person, or any other area of your life.

FULL ALIGNMENT: A CONFLUENCE OF LEADERSHIP DEVELOPMENT, PHILOSOPHY, PSYCHOLOGY, AND SPIRITUALITY

A few years ago I realized the most successful CEOs I've coached are not just amazing leaders—they're also amazing people. I also noticed that the executives who were constantly struggling to keep their companies above water or to gain influence in their positions had difficulty communicating with others, inspiring and building trust among their constituents, and setting a direction for their companies. The need for personal leadership as the basis for organizational leadership became very clear to me. A Harvard study that discovered 85 percent of a leader's success is attributable to personal character confirmed my observations.

Once I could no longer separate personal leadership from organizational leadership, I began integrating personal development themes into my leadership conferences. The executives' level of participation and interest skyrocketed. I was happy to discover most of the leaders I worked with also recognized that personal development skills such as speaking with an authentic voice, leading with empathy and "meeting their employees where they are," building a collective Vision that inspires their constituents, and balancing work and life are the most critical factors in their success. The thousands of individuals who have attended my leadership conferences have been my greatest teachers. By sharing their personal stories and challenging moments, they have enabled me to develop the strategies for personal leadership in *Full Alignment*.

In addition to coaching leaders, my own leadership roles—eight years as CEO of a forty-employee international organization with six offices around the world and presently as president of three global companies—have taught me more invaluable lessons about personal development and relationship-building (the kernel of leadership) than any research or set of theories.

Yet the foundation on which I write this book has not been constructed in any office. It's been built from the intense personal interest I've always had in what motivates people and how they think. Throughout my life, I've been blessed to have never lost my curiosity. My interest in how people think about life's larger questions and my own search for meaning launched me on a spiritual path when I was studying for a master's degree fifteen years ago. A good friend in graduate school from Tamil Nadu, India, exposed me to the writings of Swami Vivekananda, which led me to ashrams in India and spiritual centers in Indonesia,

Nepal, Vietnam, and Burma, and generally to a fascination with Eastern forms of spirituality such as Buddhism, Hinduism, and Taoism.

The four years I lived in rural villages in the developing world—first as a Peace Corps volunteer in Kenya and later while setting up community-based education programs in Guatemala, India, Indonesia, Tanzania, and Zambia—provided the experiential context within which I could begin to understand Eastern spiritual principles. The resilience, compassion, and interconnectedness that are the essence of Eastern spirituality enabled me to interact well with people and live harmoniously in more challenging and less predictable environments where, as John Lennon once said, "Life is what happens to you while you're busy making other plans."

Many years later, my research and coaching of executives in leadership and organizational development led to my forming a philosophy that blended Western organizational practice, personal initiative, and resourcefulness with Eastern (and Southern, e.g. African) detachment, humility, and resilience. The philosophy that underlies *Full Alignment* is an interwoven tapestry of East, West, and South, and those who have lived in each region will feel its influence in the strategies that fill these pages.

Full Alignment will help you look deeply into the beliefs that form the roots of your values. A diamond surrounded by layers of rock need not be told how to be a diamond—it already knows that. Yet it does need to be scraped and polished to remove the layers of rock until only the diamond remains. The tools in this book will challenge and provoke you to rid yourself of the layers of false perceptions and negative habits that surround you so you can refine what you already know, deep within you, to be true.

While I do care what you believe, I care more that you believe in *something,* and that you align your actions with whatever that is. When you align your actions with what you value, you will feel like your life is cohesive—that it "holds together." The goal of this book is Vision-Alignment because every single interaction I've had in over fifteen years of helping people work through their critical life issues has taught me—without fail, without a single exception—that this alignment is the Number One make-or-break ingredient for living a life filled with meaning, success, and happiness.

Writing this book has given me a sense of purpose I never imagined I would find. I hope it will help you to do the same. Let's embark together on the journey to Full Alignment!

—Anthony Silard
Washington, D.C.

The Roadblock

The least initial deviation from the truth is multiplied later a thousandfold.
—Aristotle

It all started way back. As a child you took cues from your parents and other adults who wielded power in your life. You internalized what *you thought they thought* into your self-view. When people who don't love themselves or have low levels of self-esteem become parents, they don't know how to convey love to their children since they didn't receive much of it themselves. They are critical because when we are critical of ourselves we also criticize others, and vice versa. Their criticism, whether overt or indirect, roughly translates as follows: *I don't love you the way you are. You cannot be your true Self if you want my love—you must change.*

As a result, you may have begun at a very early age to believe that receiving love depends upon meeting certain conditions. You may have adopted the belief that you are unworthy of love and must mold yourself into someone else to obtain it. You probably learned how to act well enough to win an Oscar, and then used your acting skills for years. You may still be using them. In fact, you have very likely refined them into an art form.

Why did you become such a good actor rather than stand up and object to such tyranny? Because when you were a child, your parents were so large in your mind that *they were your world.* If they criticized or acted in an unhealthy way toward you, you couldn't disagree with them, because to believe that they were misguided would be to entertain the thought that *your world* was misguided. That would have been too painful and would have swept the rug from under your feet.

Accepting their beliefs may have wreaked devastation in certain areas of your life. If your parents told you that you were wrong to speak up about something, you most likely believed you were wrong, because if they were wrong then your whole world would be wrong. If you sought your parents for love and they were irritable, angry, or depressed and could not give it to you, or if you sought their attention and they withheld it because they grew up without receiving much attention from their own parents, then you probably learned that it is wrong to seek love or attention from others—or, even worse, that you are unlovable. Over time, these deficient self-perceptions may have become entrenched within you. To cope with a world you could accept, you most likely co-opted your parents' behaviors into what you came to define as "normal."

Then something even worse may have occurred as you grew older: their voices may gradually have become your own. Their criticism may have become your self-criticism. Their view of you may have become your self-view. The conditions they set for loving you may now be your own conditions for loving yourself. Most likely, you then spent years upon years filtering through events, circumstances, and comments directed toward you from others to find evidence to substantiate this view, and discarded anything that didn't. You in effect became a lawyer with a limited jurisdiction—yourself—and spent your life building a case. This case, with the tremendous archive of information you have collected to support it, has become your habitual patterns.

Let me now define what I call a habitual pattern. A habitual pattern is a belief or way of acting that you continuously repeat in your life. At first, your habitual patterns created the lens through which you view yourself. Then you started projecting them outward to create the lens through which you view others and the world.

This is the story of how the values and opinions of others came to control you.

But your story does not have to end this way. Ever since the dawn of time there have been some people who break these negative patterns and stand up for their unbridled truth.

This book is about how to become one of these people.

Part One

The Direction

Chapter One

Dream

Those who dream by day are cognizant of many things which escape those who dream only by night.
—Edgar Allan Poe

I was going through the motions. Rather than taking my usual two- or three-week vacation for the holidays, I worked up until the day before Christmas setting up a leadership conference in Mexico, and then started up again the day after New Year's. By mid-February I was cutting with a dull blade. As much as I love my work, little things were starting to irritate me and I was losing my motivation. I needed a break.

I planned a trip to Argentina and Chile with one of my best friends. A week before departure, he reunited with his ex-girlfriend and canceled. I had two options: stay home or go it alone. I went. The highlight was a five-day trek in Torres del Paine, a national park in southern Chile filled with spectacular glaciers, mountain peaks, and lakes. Long days of walking alone gave me a lot of time to think. At first I didn't feel comfortable with myself. I was ashamed of how I had acted over the previous year. I had worked too much and dated without wanting to get serious with anyone. Yet deep down I knew I wanted something more meaningful in my life.

While walking through the beautiful landscape each day and writing in my journal in log cabins each evening, I kept asking myself one question: *Why*? Why had I allowed my life to become so shallow? I felt I had been losing myself. When I thought of all the women whose hopes I had raised but ultimately kept at arm's length, these words kept returning to my mind: "If you destroy what is sacred, you destroy the sacred within you."

Then on the third morning, while hiking up the *Valle Frances*—the middle of the "W" trek that begins at Gray Glacier and ends at the mystical "blue towers" that give the trek its name—my internal landscape came into view. I had never admitted to myself the extent of the hurt I felt from a previous relationship. I thought I had finally found "the one"—and then it all fell apart. I had subordinated my feelings of rejection and emotional distress by diving into work and dating casually. I hadn't wanted to become vulnerable—and potentially hurt—again. I had subconsciously trained myself not to want so I wouldn't be disappointed anymore.

Yet I had not been fully alive. I had not lived up to my potential. I felt like a hypocrite. My actions in the intimate part of my life were not aligned with my spirituality or the values that guide my writing and leadership work.

The day after the trek, I took a bus to Punta Arenas, a small industrial town in southern Chile with a large Croatian immigrant population. After a day of walking around town and eating *congrio,* the best fish I'd ever tasted in my life, I took a taxi to the airport. I started a conversation with the driver, José, who had been married for twenty-one years.

"What have you found is the secret to making your marriage work?" I asked.

"Simple," he replied. "You have to know how to do two things: listen and shut up."

I sat in the back seat pensively, remembering some of the times I had done neither very well.

"You see," said José, "when my wife is upset, it's not worth trying to make my point. It just ends up becoming a back-and-forth until we want to kill each other. It's better to just leave it. Once the anger is gone, she always comes back and hugs me."

"You have a lot of wisdom," I said. "That sounds like a good philosophy to make a relationship work."

José smiled at the compliment, paused for a few moments as if to consider whether I was worthy of hearing his next level of wisdom, and then said, "Do you know about *Memento Mori*?"

I shook my head.

"Hold the palms of your hands in front of you facing toward you," he said. "Point your fingers toward each other and look into your palms. Do you see the two Ms?"

I had never noticed them before, but sure enough, there were two Ms traced into my palms.

"They stand for *Memento Mori*. In Latin, this means 'A reminder that you will die.' You don't have much time in this world, so you must make the most of it. Figure out what's important and leave the rest."

THE WAKE-UP CALL

Ever since the day I stepped into José's taxi, I stop a few times a week and look at the palms of my hands until I see the two Ms. I have become more open and honest in relationships, and I have been hurt. Yet I no longer exist in a self-created fantasy where I preclude any possibility of real connection. I risk, I accept the consequences of those risks, and I feel alive.

Not only do I take vacations, but I also take long weekends more regularly to decompress and prevent myself from overworking. Sometimes when I'm sitting in my office at six, debating whether to keep working for another hour or to leave the office and go for a long walk, to the gym, or to a meditation, I look at my palms, close my planner, and get up from my chair.

Your awareness of death can wake you up to life. Being conscious that your time is limited can bring you to purpose *now* while you can still do something about it. I have coached more than a few people who left dead-end jobs after the attacks on September 11, 2001, to pursue careers that really matter to them. I've observed many others make significant life changes—moving to a quiet rural town, traveling the world, reducing their work schedule to part-time—to spend more time with their loved ones.

One of the deepest ironies of life is that it's not until you're at risk of losing it that you give it the value it deserves. Most people look at life as a high school student looks at a term paper: they procrastinate and don't think about it until just before it has to be handed in. Time and again I observe that the people I know who have stared death in the eyes—struggling with cancer and going through chemotherapy, or being hit by a car, or even one friend who was on a plane that ran out of fuel, plummeted out of the sky and miraculously landed—are the same people who best know how to live each moment, pursue long-held dreams, and get the most out of the time they have left.

Take Carl, a guy I used to work out with at my gym in Washington, D.C. Carl was a bus driver until he was caught in a cross fire between two gangs while driving his bus and shot in the arm three times. In his own words:

> I was never the same after those bullets went through my arm. It humbles you, you know. It takes you down on one level and raises you up on a whole other level. I've come much closer to God. I don't take my life for granted anymore. I used to look in the mirror and see my clothes, how I look. Now I see something much deeper. It made me realize the important thing in life isn't money. The important thing is living. Today I just appreciate being alive and able to walk on this beautiful earth.

Are *you* aware of how limited your time is on this earth? As long as you think the time you have left is infinite, there's no need to start doing what really matters. The eighteenth-century English writer Samuel Johnson once said, "Depend upon it, sir, when a man knows he is to be hanged in a fortnight, it concentrates his mind wonderfully." Until you realize you may not have the time you think you do, you won't know how to truly live today. Before you hit your big deadline, or get married, or your kids go to college, or have their own kids, you will always be in this position: with no guarantee that you have any days remaining; capable only of enjoying today.

Internalize this awareness of your mortality and let it focus your mind *now* on what you truly value. Why? Because *you have no future.*

"What do you mean I have no future?! What kind of book is this?!" you may be thinking. Let me now dispel one of our most common myths: *the future does not exist.* Any moment in which you arrive at what you consider your future will still be the present. Present moments and nothing more—today, tomorrow, in three weeks, always: the *only moments* you will ever experience in your entire life.

MAKE EVERY PICTURE MEANINGFUL

It's difficult to think about death when your culture sweeps it under the carpet. America's aversion to death (and anything else that symbolizes weakness) is not universal: in many developing countries, death is more integrated into life. On the first two days of November, Mexicans celebrate *El Día de Los Muertos* ("The Day of the Dead") by having a party at the local cemetery with their ancestors. In Teotihuacan, the center of the Aztec empire near Mexico City, the ancient marketplace was located next to the mausoleum. To visualize how different this is from U.S. or European culture, picture a cemetery across the street from the shops at Covent Garden, along the Champs-Elysées, or on Fifth Avenue.

In America we are taught to think about money, position, consumption, power, fame—and to avoid any talk about weakness, including death. Yet as we grow older we realize the only things that truly matter are love and truth. The problem is by then it may be too late. By then we have missed out on so many opportunities: so many times when others needed our love but we were too busy thinking about our material or professional gain.

Opportunity doesn't usually knock twice. To live a fulfilled life, you have to begin thinking *now* about the end so you can make each moment count. A motion picture comprises still frames—literally, "pictures in motion," one after the other. The best way to ensure the motion picture that is your life will be meaningful when you're lying on your deathbed is to get busy now making each and every picture meaningful.

THE ANCESTOR OF EVERY ACTION

Touch your nose with your right index finger. To perform this action, you first sent a thought to your hand to move in the direction of your face. After you lifted your right hand, you sent another thought to your hand to outstretch your index finger toward your nose. The poet and philosopher Ralph Waldo Emerson wisely observed: *The ancestor of every action is a thought.* Touching your nose, like every other action you've ever carried out, is actually a "second action." The "first action" was its ancestor—the thought that preceded it.

Everything you see in the world besides nature and human beings—a bridge, the paper this book is printed on, a movie, your house or apartment—is the physical manifestation of a thought someone once had. Just about anything you can conceive in your mind you can make tangible and real. But you have to conceive it first.

Consider all the actions you commit every day—giving a presentation, bringing up a difficult issue with someone you care about, avoiding a conflict when your emotions are running on overdrive—that are much more complex than touching your nose. How will you effectively perform even a subset of the challenging actions life requires of you if you don't spend any time thinking about how you want to perform them?

It stands to reason that if you don't take time out to think, you'll only perform actions that don't require new thoughts. Like Bill Murray in *Groundhog Day*, you'll act out the same day and get the same results over and over again into oblivion. You'll lose your edge. And why would you do this? Because you're afraid to slow down, leave opportunity on the table, and accomplish less than the next guy.

There is a constant race between your actions and your thoughts. Your actions are almost always far ahead and winning the race. One of your greatest life challenges is to give your thoughts the regular opportunity to catch up. Framed in this way, your life is a continuous two-tier process of thinking and acting. You're either thinking about what you want to do, doing it, or thinking about what you've already done. Thought, action, thought, action—thoughts and actions fill your entire life, one after the other!

Since your thoughts will enter the scene at some point, the real question becomes whether they will come before your actions or after. Ask yourself this question: "Will I take the time out of my life to set its direction, or will I allow my actions to leap so far ahead of my thoughts that I cease to recognize them?" If you take the time to dream, your thoughts will precede and guide your actions. If you don't, they will follow your actions and yield guilt and remorse—as mine did on that long trek in Chile. Direction or regrets—which will you choose?

YOU WON'T RISE HIGHER THAN YOUR AIM

Your dreams set the ceiling for your existence. You can only achieve what you first conceive. Think about it: How could you possibly rise higher than your imagination, or exceed your self-perception? Where will you find the determination or internal compass to navigate through obstacles and keep pushing on toward a destination unless you instinctually know what the destination looks like and have faith in your ability to reach it?

Yet somewhere along the way you may have lost your courage to dream. Are you afraid of having hope and wanting something again? Going for what you really desire in life means putting an end to keeping your dreams at bay and your ceiling low. It means no longer saying: "If I aim too high and don't get what I want, I won't be able to live with myself. It's safer for me to just stay where I am and not think about something greater. This way, I won't be disappointed." If you insist on living this way, get ready for a life you don't have to get ready for.

Here's how your actions translate when you refuse to take the time away from your daily tasks and interactions to reflect on your innermost values, hopes, and longings: "I can robotically do the right thing, all the time. My actions are so perfect in execution that I don't need to take the time to consider them beforehand, nor to ponder how they measure up against what I deeply value." If this is true, can I hire you?! Please write to me at ... OK, you know as well as I do that perfect execution is impossible. Yet taking the time to dream brings you much closer to it because you sharpen your axe before you lift it over your shoulders.

HOW DO YOU DREAM?

What unique strategies can you design to integrate time to dream into your daily life? I've asked thousands of people in my leadership workshops over the last ten years to share what they do and where they go when they want to dream. Here are some of their responses:

Some Ways to Dream ...

Watch the sunset	Meditate	Sit in front of a fireplace
Take a walk in nature	Practice yoga	Visit an art gallery
Light a few candles and take a long bath	Sit by a creek and listen to the sound of the water flowing	Watch the snow falling outside
Look at the stars	Travel	Listen to music
Climb a mountain and look at the view	Talk with friends about ideas	Go away for the weekend
Drive in the countryside	Look at the city lights at night	Walk by the ocean
Sit in a quiet room at home	Visit a church, synagogue, temple, or mosque when there is no service and just sit quietly	Listen to the sound of the rain
Go for a long run	Go to a bookstore	Work on the garden

American poet Wallace Stevens wrote, "Perhaps the truth depends on a walk around the lake." What does your truth depend on? Where do you go to decompress and think through life's larger issues? Where is the special refuge that enables you to clear your mind and ruminate on why your significant other has become more distant, or why your father told you he's "surprised" you haven't given up on an important career goal you've been struggling with, or to manage the anger and insecurity that began welling up within you when your boss hinted that your performance has suffered ever since you made a significant change in your personal life?

There is no *right* way to dream. Each of us has different ways of tapping into our Vision. Discover what *you* need to do to become tranquil and centered enough to think deeply about what gives your life meaning. Don't rely on just one strategy. Depending on your situation, what works one day may not work the next. Going for a walk in a local park may be an excellent choice on Thursday evening when it's warm out, but if there's a torrential downpour on Saturday, have a Plan B to go to a yoga class or a museum. Be open to finding new, creative ways to dream.

Taking time to dream does not mean neglecting your career, family, or other responsibilities. Your self-time is a refueling for your everyday life, not a departure from it. Many of my clients make complete life transformations by implementing such simple changes to their schedules as stopping work an hour earlier to go to the gym, or taking a thirty-minute walk during their lunch break, or leaving their laptop behind on family trips, or not checking their emails on weekends. Here's the principal take-away of this chapter: the only way to build your relationship with yourself (as is the case with your other relationships) is to make yourself a priority.

Does this rub you the wrong way, or make you feel self-indulgent? I know it's challenging to schedule time for yourself. Yet this is precisely why making even a moderate change to your daily routine holds such tremendous leverage and will immediately transform your life: it yields a "spillover effect." Once you step over this self-imposed hurdle and make it a priority to nurture your own well-being—even in a small way—you begin to feel loved by yourself. This love makes you feel worthy of happiness in even greater forms and capable of loving others more completely. This great journey really does begin with a single step!

RETURN TO THE FIRST CREATION

I often find time to dream by taking walks alone in the early evening and watching the sunset. For me, the limitless colors of the sky are the most sublime form of art that exists. I stand in awe of the unique canvas painted across the sky every evening. The great expanse above gives me a feeling of spaciousness that helps me put my life back into perspective. The sunset has even provided me with a feeling of stability at various times in my life. I remember how anxious I felt about the idea of leaving Washington, D.C. to live in an African village. My awareness that the sun would also set there every evening gave me the solace that no matter where I was in the world, I would still be able to watch the sunset and reconnect with my higher Self.

It is no coincidence that most (but not all) of the ways you dream involve a deeper connection to the earth and its elements than your normal day-to-day life affords. If you believe God created nature and human beings, you could consider them both a "first creation." You could then view the concrete, plastic, glass, fiber optics, and other products human beings have in turn created in the technological society that surrounds you in a new light: as a "second creation."

When you step out into nature, you (literally) return to your roots—the first creation. The tranquil lakes, flowing rivers, and shady trees urge you to reconcile with your higher Self. Perhaps this is why the German philosopher Friedrich Nietzsche said, "All truly great thoughts are conceived by walking," or why most people are more easily able to reconnect with God and their inner truth when they're strolling on the beach, biking, kayaking, or climbing mountains in the great outdoors.

I often hear people say how quiet it is in nature. Yet it's really not that quiet. It's just the noises in nature are not the same as those you hear in your daily life, so you associate them with silence. Nature certainly offers a respite from the car horns, police sirens, cell phones, blaring radios, screeching truck brakes, and other noises that continually derail your attempts to find peace and quiet in your daily life. Yet you don't *have* to be in nature—or doing anything at all for that matter—to dream. Your dreams come from only one place: within you.

This couldn't be more true. Neither the sunset, the mountain, nor the cool running stream enable you to dream—*you* enable you to dream! It's not nature, after all, that makes the decision to open up your mind to your dreams. In the words of author Robert Pirsig: "The only Zen you find on the tops of mountains is the Zen you bring up there." Even in the middle of a bustling city surrounded by people, you can close your eyes and walk to the top of a mountain, watch the sunset, or hear the sound of the ocean.

Imagine you are stuck in a traffic jam, watching an elderly man step off a bus and meander along the street with his cane. You start to ruminate on what his life is like and soon you're envisioning what's important to you and are reconnected with your deeper values. Alternatively, envision yourself sitting on the sofa in your living room. You pick up a magazine and see a picture of a blind elderly woman struggling to protect her granddaughter from raiding militants in Darfur, and the look of helplessness and fear in her eyes etches a permanent imprint in your mind. You feel both indescribably moved and utterly disgusted at the tragedy she's experiencing, and think: "Hasn't history taught us anything?" You look down at your iPod and then out the window at the house next door, and contemplate how mass genocide can still exist side by side with all the technological advances in today's society.

DON'T JUST DO SOMETHING, SIT THERE

The best way to connect with your inner purpose is to take time alone to consider what you truly want out of life. This isn't as easy as it sounds. Everyone around you reinforces your activity and steers you away from inactivity. Your parents, teachers, and other role models taught you how to *do*, but not how to *be*. Yet you are a human *being*, not a human *doing*. You were probably told over a thousand times as a child: "Don't just sit there, do something!" Yet why didn't anyone ever say, "Don't just do something, sit there!"? If no one else ever told you it was OK to just *be*, how will you feel telling yourself?

The Lebanese poet and philosopher Kahlil Gibran sagely observed, "In order to endure the tests of everyday living, one must respect that zone of privacy where one retires to relate to the inside instead of the outside." How do you handle the times when your life isn't progressing as you'd like it to? Do you take time to relate to the inside, or do you continue acting out the same dysfunctional patterns on the outside, even when the writing on the wall is signaling you need to take a break and reassess? If both inner contentedness and effective action are among your priorities, simply begin scheduling "self-meetings" to loosen up and ponder life's larger questions alongside the scores of meetings you so effortlessly schedule with everyone else.

You will not be effective at what you do until you first become effective at how you dream. It is within your power to re-engineer your internal voice by discarding thoughts like "I don't have time to disengage, there's just too much to do," and replacing them with new, more holistic thoughts that recognize you as a complete human being, such as "While

I do have a lot to do, I must disengage regularly or I'll lose track of why I'm doing it and how to do it well."

Refuse to take time out of the game and you'll only win until those who slow down enough to contemplate not where the ball is, but where it's going to be next, render you obsolete. If you design clothing, your styles will soon fade as designers with more creative Vision steer consumer tastes in other directions. If you teach children, your lessons will lose their edge as other teachers discover methodologies that kids relate to better. If you run a company, you will lose market share as other companies rapidly innovate while your products designed for yesterday's consumers make their way to the back of the shelf.

ALONENESS VERSUS LONELINESS

Ask yourself this question and try to answer it with brutal honesty: "How do I feel about being alone?" Do you embrace being alone, or do you go to great lengths to avoid yourself? Consider the ancient wisdom of Confucius: "Silence is a friend who will never betray." As with a friend from whom you've become estranged, it can take a while to reestablish your comfort with silence. Yet it's important that you do. Just as music would lose its soothing quality if there were no periods of silence between the notes, your life will become an unbearable cacophony of noise if you refuse to give yourself time to relax, recover, and process what life has sent your way.

No matter where you are, you can access these moments of silence that transform the noise of your life into a beautiful symphony. One strategy I practice daily is to pause for a few moments before entering a house, building, or car. I stop for five or ten seconds, look at the sky, and take a few deep breaths. After I walked in the front door of my building the other day, the receptionist, Janet, asked me, "Tony, why do you always do that? You stop and look at something, but you're really not looking at anything."

This simple practice reminds me to not take myself too seriously, to breathe, and to appreciate the beauty of life. The vastness outside reconnects me with the vastness inside. While this may sound minimal, these few seconds of silence interspersed throughout my day make it easier for me to also pause for a few moments in more difficult circumstances—such as when someone puts me down or lashes out at me in anger, and I'm feeling a strong emotion like insecurity, anxiety, or resentment and need to reconnect with my higher Self before acting.

Here's the essence of this chapter and the reason it precedes all the other chapters in this book: inactivity, in the right doses, will yield more results in your life than any form of activity. Studies have shown that most people do not make their most significant work breakthroughs when they're in the office. Ironically, their most creative work ideas come to them when they're hiking in nature, walking on the beach, or just enjoying a relaxing vacation. You may conceptually believe this to be true, yet in practice find it difficult to free yourself from your ultraviolet productivity chamber.

You may complain that society doesn't give you enough time to disengage, yet not realize it's you who contribute to making society what it is. You may surround yourself with people, possessions, tasks, television, electronic leashes that keep you perpetually connected with others—anything to avoid yourself. Then you may wonder why your life has gone in the wrong direction. Developing a Vision for what you want to create in your life and then following it is the only highway that leads to success. Learning how to comfortably spend time alone is the toll you pay to travel.

Until you discover the joys of aloneness, loneliness will result. You breed loneliness when you constantly surround yourself with people. You are on a perpetual train ride with many companions, yet you may not truly know any of them nor where the train is heading. Your cabin is full, but you may be empty. You may fall prey to the words of the French philosopher Rochefoucauld: "When we are unable to find tranquility within ourselves, it is useless to seek it elsewhere." The more you distance yourself from your higher Self—which you connect with most easily when you're alone—the lonelier you feel.

YOU WILL NOT INSPIRE UNTIL YOU ARE FIRST INSPIRED

A friend once told me why she prefers not to take long trips: "If I travel, I worry about all I'll miss out on at home." You may also fear if you take time out to dream you'll be "out of the loop" and will miss precious time with family and friends, or reaching a sales target, or meeting the right partner. Take time to reconnect with your higher values and you'll discover that widening this inner space is precisely what makes your moments with others so precious.

It's my experience that the most successful leaders integrate regular recovery time—whether it's throwing a ball around with their kids, or going to the spa or gym for a few hours, or taking the afternoon off to go fishing with their buddies—into their daily schedule. This is not to say I haven't seen people achieve great things while ignoring themselves during a "crunch" period. Yet any leader I've ever coached who has *consistently sustained their performance* has discovered how to strike this balance and maintain themselves as a priority.

Think about the people you look up to as leaders. Are they workaholics who emanate nothing but stress to others? I don't think so. Are they unwilling to take time away from the grind to envision something greater than themselves? I doubt it. They take time for themselves because they know that if they want to inspire others, they must first be inspired.

You always have the choice to complain about your busy schedule or to take a bold stand for yourself and make your self-time a priority. When you go hiking by yourself for the day, or go for a long run, or take off for a weekend retreat in the country, the message you're sending others is not, "You're not important to me." Rather, it's "I'm important to me. By giving to myself, I expand my capacity to give to you."

SLOW DOWN TO THE SPEED OF LIFE

At lunch earlier this week my eyes became transfixed on a high school couple holding hands. I started to wax nostalgic about how my relationships used to seem so innocent and magical. Shifting my attention from what I still had to get done that day long enough to recall some warm, heartfelt memories enabled me to dream again about what I want to create in that part of my life.

You can connect with your Vision throughout the day as long as you're willing to slow down long enough to catch a glimpse of it. Even while brokering a peace accord during the civil unrest that followed India's independence and partition, Mohandas Gandhi took time daily to sit at his cotton loom and spin clothing. The nonviolent social activist reminds us: "There is more to life than increasing its speed." When you get into your car, let your mind drift instead of making a call on your cell phone. When you have dinner plans at eight, don't work until seven-thirty. If you want to enjoy your dinner, or to be good company, or to maybe even make others laugh, take time to wind down and reflect on your day before making the transition to social time.

The most formidable obstacle to taking time for yourself is yourself. If you want to make yourself a priority, my advice is simple: get out of your way. When you have thoughts such as, "Work is my only priority at this point in my life. I can't think about anything else," or "I'll take time for myself once I have more experience. I have serious responsibilities now and can't be a slacker," or "I have to keep active to feel good about myself," mark those thoughts as "Spam" and send them back to wherever they came from.

Go deeper to understand the roots of your ignore-myself-and-get-it-done-ism. Ask yourself, "Where did those thoughts come from?" and "Why do I focus only on achieving and allow my life to pass me by?" You may fear if you take time alone you'll lose touch with others and lose ground in your career. Put yourself as a priority and you will discover that the decrease in quantity to your time with others is more than compensated for by the increase in quality.

You may have an inescapable image entrenched in your mind of a parent or family friend who sat around the house and did nothing with their life, and this image may keep you working constantly so you never become like them. Alternatively, you might worry that if you don't occupy every waking moment you'll hit a lull in your schedule and become bored, anxious, or lonely.

I realize what I'm asking you to do isn't easy. We all have a natural propensity to want to get things done, hit all our goals, and enjoy the feeling of accomplishment. But if we don't take time out to dream, all of the above becomes impossible.

As the Taoist philosopher Lao Tzu reminds us, "To the mind that is still, the whole universe surrenders." If you are running all day long from one meeting to another, arrive early enough to your next meeting to walk around the block a few times before entering the building. You will end up using this time to reflect on the purpose of the meeting and the key points you want to emphasize. The outcome of this simple act? The world will surrender to your calm, directed energy. You will become both more confident about what you have to offer and more empathetic to the needs of the person you're meeting with, and will be more likely to obtain the results you desire.

The same is true for any task you want to complete. If you are pulling a four-hour stretch writing a proposal or crunching out a spreadsheet, take a fifteen-minute break halfway through and go for a walk or pull out a yoga mat and do some stretching exercises in your office. Let go of the task at hand, relax your mind, and you will be pleasantly surprised to discover how much more effectively you finish your work.

EXPERIENCE MIRACLES EVERY DAY

"But I'm so busy," you may be thinking. "I agree taking time for myself is important, but I just don't have enough time to do it right now." You don't have time *not* to do it. If you don't periodically step offstage and onto the balcony to observe yourself onstage, you will lose your ability to perform. Whether you are reading a book, listening to music, writing poetry, climbing a mountain, or just sitting in a quiet corner of your room, these everyday activities enable you to recover from the tasks you concentrate on so intensely—which ironically enables you to get them done more quickly and effectively.

Make a commitment to introduce a healthy portion of self-time into your daily schedule and you will see lightness, confidence, and directedness replacing confusion and anxiety in your life. If you are unwilling to take this time out, don't expect to enjoy what you're doing for any length of time. How will you enjoy what you're doing if you've lost sight of *why* you're doing it? As the opening story of this chapter illustrates, while one person is just driving a taxi, another is philosophically transporting passengers to where they need to go. Which would you rather be doing?

Albert Einstein once wrote, "There are two ways to live your life. One is as though nothing is a miracle. The other is as though everything is a miracle." If you don't take the time to dream, your life will operate on the dull, mundane plane where nothing is a miracle. You can instead choose to give your mind the periodic time it needs to discover the meaning that nourishes it. In so doing, you will transform everything you experience into a miracle.

Neglect this need to disengage and neither will you be able to engage. Instead, you will feel low on energy, or as if you are "running on empty." Taking time to dream is the only way to consistently experience the wonderful feeling of being calm rather than stressed, and purposeful rather than irritable as you carry out your daily responsibilities. Once you begin scheduling time for self-nurturing along with your other priorities, you will become adept at integrating this practice into your everyday life. In fact, you won't be able to imagine how you ever did without it.

OK, forget for a moment all the reasons you've read in this chapter to give yourself time to recover, to reconnect with what you value, to relax, and to enjoy life. Here's one that's much more compelling: *you're worth it*. Take time out of your busy schedule to dream simply because you deserve nothing less. Give this practice a try and you will be pleasantly surprised by how much more capable you become of both giving to others and embracing the irreplaceable beauty of each day you have left on this planet.

MAKE IT HAPPEN:

1. Write down two or three ways you have integrated time to dream into your daily schedule in the past.
2. Consider some new ways to dream you haven't tried before that you could get excited about—such as practicing yoga, or waking up early to bicycle to work, or learning how to canoe, or walking in a nearby park during your lunch break. Write down a few of them.

3. Imagine you are eighty years old and looking back at yourself right here, right now, with this book in your hand. How much of your time will you wish you had allocated to building your relationship with yourself? How much time out of your schedule to decompress, to relax, and to just enjoy being alive? To figure out what you truly want out of life and what gives it meaning? Write down a percentage of your time you want to allocate to your Self based on this mental projection.
4. Multiply this percentage times 168 hours (the number of hours in a week). Get out your planner and schedule the activities you listed in questions one and two to fill the resulting number of hours for the coming week. Be creative.
5. At the end of the week, check how successfully you aligned the Vision you just developed for your self-nurturing with your daily schedule. Give yourself a rating for the week, from "Needs Improvement" to "Excellent."
6. Based on your results, commit to a specific number of hours of self-time for the following week. Be ambitious yet realistic in your projections. Continue to evaluate how you perform in this vital area of your life. Save what you write so you can integrate your specific commitments to everyday self-nurturing into your Vision Statement and Action Plan in chapters 4 and 10.

Chapter 2

The Timeless Power of Vision

Most people ... are like a falling leaf that drifts and turns in the air, flutters, and falls to the ground. But a few others are like stars which travel one defined path ... they have within themselves their guide.
—*Hermann Hesse,* Siddhartha

A few years ago I was watching the Winter Olympic freestyle ski jump competition, and was amazed at the number of flawless flips, twists, and turns these athletes pull off in midair before landing on the ground with unbelievable poise facing perfectly downhill. It's like watching art in motion. After seeing the jumps replayed a few times, I noticed that each skier did a few acrobatic flips and twists, looked down to where they were planning to land, did a few more stunts, glanced at the ground again, and so on until they landed.

Have you ever driven to a party without good directions? Can you remember trying repeatedly to find the house, pulling over, and feeling lost and frustrated? Locating a physical address is easy compared to discovering your Vision. When it comes to your Vision no one can give you accurate directions. You can't click on MapQuest and, in the box that says "Destination," type in "Vision." While it would certainly simplify the process to receive a printout that reads, "Go to medical school for 3.4 years, then meet Jennifer and go out with her for 2.6 years, then take a trip to India for 1.2 months …," to develop a Vision you have to write your own directions. You do this by putting into practice the same strategy ski jumpers use to land in the right position. You look beyond what's directly in front of you to determine where you want to go.

DEVELOPING YOUR VISION

If you want to develop a Vision that will guide you through the twists and turns of your life, you have to ask yourself some tough questions about your core values and what you stand for. Start by visualizing what kind of son, daughter, parent, friend, partner, manager, or coworker you want to be, what you want to be remembered for, what you want to accomplish in your life, and what you want your relationships to look like in the future.

Many avoid this process at all costs. You hear this all the time: "I'm too busy living to stop and think about lofty ideals. I'll figure them out naturally along the way." This is like saying you'll take care of your health without periodically going to the doctor for a checkup, or that you'll build a house without a blueprint. If you don't take the time to clarify what you stand for, you will feel listless, unmotivated, and conflicted, even when you are busy—which will become an end in itself to help you avoid the difficult work of looking within.

Time to create your Vision does not come out of thin air, but out of your schedule. Before you say "Yes" to one more meeting or social obligation, ask yourself, "What am I saying 'No' to by saying 'Yes' to this?" You will only learn how to move toward your life goals if you first learn how to avoid moving in other directions. Recognize that every time you say "No" to something, you are saying a deeper "Yes" to something else. Until you develop your Vision, you will not know what this "something else" is, and you will say "Yes" to just about anything.

YOUR EYE IN THE STORM

Your Vision is timeless. It doesn't change because of the ups and downs you experience from day to day, or because of what happens "out there" in the environment. Your Vision provides a basis for all your decisions. To put it into practice, before you turn on the television, or make a phone call, or go on another date, or stay late at the office for another hour, or make any other decision, simply ask yourself, "Is this action in line with my Vision?" and "Are there other actions that would better help me realize my Vision?" When you consider your actions in this context, you choose what is referred to in Buddhism as "right action"—action that's right for *you* because it's consistent with what you value.

Unlike your job, an argument you're embroiled in, today's headlines, and everything else in your life, your Vision is timeless and permanent. It provides something stable to hang on to, come what may. Once you develop a Vision for your life, you will finally be able to confront your fears because you will view them in a new light: as nothing more than obstacles to the attainment of your goals. You will become a part of something larger than yourself, a greater purpose. Held in this light, your fears will pale in comparison.

When you have a compelling Vision, even the most dire circumstances become bearable. Nietzsche put it this way: "He who has a *why* to live can bear with almost any *how*." Once you paint this long-term picture of what you want to accomplish in your life and how you want to treat others, you will have your *why*, your direction. You will then be able to steer toward this North Star rather than allowing yourself to be distracted by the negativity around you.

Viktor Frankl, an Austrian survivor of the infamous Nazi concentration camps Auschwitz and Dachau, provides a poignant example of the power of Vision. According to Frankl, those prisoners who maintained their belief in a greater purpose for their lives—whether to return home to care for a child or to complete a series of scientific books they had started writing before the war to advance humanity —were the most likely to survive. Conversely, Frankl writes:

> Woe to him who saw no more sense in his life, no aim, no purpose, and therefore no point in carrying on. He was soon lost ... he let himself decline and became subject to mental and physical decay. ... Only the men who allowed their inner hold on their moral and spiritual selves to subside eventually fell victim to the camp's degenerating influences.

In contrast to the life of a prisoner in a Nazi concentration camp, you have grown up with immense luxury and privilege. Yet you may still feel lost and confused and find little purpose in your life. What your life most likely lacks is not the means, but the *meaning*.

LET GO OF HAPPINESS AND SEEK TRUTH

All the possessions in the world won't give you as much to live for as one ounce of purpose. The Swiss psychiatrist and founder of analytical psychology, Carl Jung, astutely remarked: "The least of things with a meaning is worth more in life than the greatest of things without it." Do you allow yourself to become obsessed with drugs, alcohol, sex, money, food, or vain arguments that squeeze out any time to truly relate to others? You may unwittingly transform your life every day into a quest to experience short-term pleasure and avoid pain without *assessing* that pleasure or pain with respect to anything.

If you are unwilling to put your short-term needs for intimacy, sexual pleasure, an assuring nod from your parents, or bringing in those dollars on the back burner, then don't expect to move toward your long-term goals. How can you reach your destination if you're heading in another direction, or in no direction at all? I know it's not easy to shelve what feels in the moment like a burning desire. Yet it's even more difficult to live with the consequences of decisions that transform you into someone you don't want to become.

The society you live in impels you to fixate on short-term pleasure. It sends you packages of information every day—from television ads to advice columns to Hollywood films—laced with values that are not your own. These messages encourage you to seek immediate fulfillment and avoid anything that causes you to feel difficult or complex emotions. You are encouraged to seek happiness and avoid whatever makes you feel sad. I am proposing something radically different: *forget about happiness and sadness and seek truth.*

A central theme of this book is that you become what you give your attention to. Fixate on short-term pleasure and you (may) become someone who experiences occasional short-term pleasure. Alternatively, determine what you've been put on this earth to do and then pursue it with everything you have and this is what you become: someone who lives an aligned, values-driven life.

THE PURSUIT OF HAPPINESS?

Your definition of happiness is precisely what makes you unhappy. You create an ideal state in your mind, attach the word "happiness" to its attainment, and then refuse to allow yourself to feel happy until your current reality agrees with this mental image—which it rarely does. Swami Vivekananda's insightful words break down popular misconceptions about happiness: "Happiness is a gold chain; misery is an iron chain. Both are chains." When you seek happiness or comfort, you may obtain it for a fleeting moment, but it will soon fade and leave you feeling vacant and unfulfilled.

Your concept of happiness—status, a vacation home, a promotion, an orgasm, perfect health, recognition, affection—glitters like gold, but you become shackled by it because most of the time when you steer toward it, you steer away from your Vision. You move in with someone you quickly become passionate about because it makes you feel happy now, but ten months later you realize that being with them is not aligned with your Vision of finding the person with whom you want to start a family. You drop out of college to pursue music because playing the guitar fulfills you and Sociology 101 doesn't, and years later you realize you ignored one of your core values: to have an education—a value you learned from watching your father, who never went to college, spend his life shifting from one low-paying job to another. When you seek truth, be prepared to feel very *un*comfortable at first. Yet know in the long term you will feel more comfortable, solid, and authentic.

"Now wait just a minute!" you may be thinking. "The American dream is the pursuit of happiness! It sounds masochistic not to make happiness my primary goal!" Pursuing short-term pleasure is certainly more fun. I can find dozens of people on very short notice who would be willing to confirm this for you. It's more fun to take the first apartment you see and enjoy the immediate fulfillment of having a place to live than to couch-surf for a month. It's a lot easier to jump into another relationship than to go trekking in Nepal for three weeks and eat *dal bhat* (rice and beans) twice a day with a sherpa guide who asks your advice on the virtues of arranged marriage versus "love marriage" while you gaze at the peaks of Annapurna and Everest and contemplate why your previous relationships didn't work. The problem with allowing happiness to be your guiding light is it prevents you from making the more difficult Vision-aligned choices that, in time, will bring what you truly want into your life.

NO MORE "GOOD" OR "BAD" DECISIONS

I recently drove past a billboard in Northern California showcasing a sleek red sports car with a black background. The caption read: "Faster than therapy." There's no question about it: you can access short-term pleasure much faster than a deeper understanding of what you truly value. So which is more important to you—happiness or truth?

My work with a woman in her late twenties revolved around her need to ask herself this question. When Laura wasn't buried in work at a Boston marketing firm, she felt that her boyfriend of two years, Greg, didn't treat her very well. Greg belittled her frequently by telling her she was too sensitive and needy. He constantly commented on her weight, and took to calling her "CBF," which he deciphered for her as "Chunky But Funky." Laura tried to improve their communication but felt only she was willing to make an effort. Whenever she brought up a sensitive issue, Greg refused to talk about it and often stormed out of the room. If they were out on a date and he became upset, he would take her home without a word. She knew she could do much better.

Yet Laura feared being alone. She wanted to avoid the short-term pain she knew she would experience if she broke up with Greg. Have you ever been in Laura's situation? Aware that a relationship wasn't working, yet wanting to avoid the pain and loneliness you knew would come with separation? How did you move forward in your life?

I urged Laura to develop a Vision for the kind of partner she wanted to spend her life with. Laura decided she was looking for someone who is giving, who is committed to her and also wants to have a family, and with whom she can communicate openly about anything—including deeper emotional issues.

"I know I have to be realistic about it," Laura told me. "It's unlikely I will find the 'perfect' man. I mean, I'm not perfect—so how can I expect him to be? I'm prepared to not get exactly what I want in terms of other compatibility issues—the music he listens to, the books he reads, even where he wants to live—provided the core qualities I'm looking for are there."

Once Laura etched an image in her mind of what she was truly looking for, the issue of being alone or with someone in the short term fell by the wayside. Greg either had the potential to become aligned with her Vision of a life partner or he didn't.

"If you don't feel Greg is currently aligned with your Vision, you're doing the right thing to ask yourself whether he has the potential to become aligned over time," I shared with Laura. "Another question you can ask yourself is whether your Vision of a life partner can evolve to appreciate his qualities and accept him as he is. This is the more likely option, as people almost never change to fit our desired image of them. Consider how the relationship is most likely to evolve, and if the likelihood of Greg and your Vision coming into alignment is enough to keep you engaged in it."

Two months later, Laura ended the relationship. As was the case for her, once you develop your Vision—whether it's for an intimate relationship, or your career, or how you will treat your family members, or the types of friends you will spend time with, or how you will make an impact in your community—your path forward will become more visible.

You only know what darkness is because you've seen light. Had you never caught a glimpse of the sun, you would consider it normal to fumble around in the dark all your life. When you develop your Vision, you create the light that illuminates your path. From this day on, you will never allow yourself to live in darkness again.

"OK, this Vision thing is sounding very lofty and pie-in-the-sky," you may be thinking. "How does this work in practice?" Your Vision becomes your guiding light by providing a benchmark against which to measure all your alternatives. You will not give in to pressure from your so-called friends to take drugs or engage in other self-destructive behaviors for one simple reason: those decisions are incongruent with your Vision for your health and well-being. You will not get involved with someone who is married—not because anyone else tells you it's wrong, but because it's a decision that's inconsistent with your Vision of both how you want to treat others and how you want to go about finding the right person. You will ultimately come to a life-changing realization: *Decisions are not good or bad—they're Vision-aligned or not Vision-aligned.*

GOT MEANING?

I have been fortunate enough to personally witness on many occasions what most people call miracles—and what I call the power of Vision. When I met Carla I was immediately struck by her radiant, friendly personality. I could never have imagined what she'd been through. The mother of two young sons, she was diagnosed with terminal cancer at the age of twenty-five. Her husband couldn't handle it, and left her. In Carla's words:

> All my ex-husband could say was: "Why is this happening to me? Why is my wife sick?" Yet it was me, not him, who had to go to the hospital every week for two years.

As the cancer worsened, Carla left her sons with her father and was taken to the hospital.

> They told me twice while I was in the hospital that I would die by the morning. At one point the entire left side of my body was paralyzed. I thought: "I will not die. No. I won't. I can't. I have two children to take care of. I lied to my kids and said I was going on a trip. I can't leave them like this, nor can I leave my father with all this responsibility. He would never be able to handle it."

Seven years later the cancer is in remission and Carla is remarried. She goes to the gym four days a week and looks absolutely stunning. After Carla told me her story I asked her how she was able to handle such devastating hardship. Her words are a lesson to us all:

> During the worst of it, my friends kept looking at me and saying "poor thing"—which I detested. I told them not to pity me. I was not willing to be a victim. The truth is if I had started crying, I never would have stopped. Now I look back at what I went through and think "Oh my God." At the time, I couldn't be afraid. I just had to handle it.

Stop and think for a moment about your underlying purpose. If you had a terminal disease like Carla did, would there be anything you value so highly you would will yourself to live for it? What makes you want to hold on to the days you have left with everything inside you and make each one count?

Alternatively, do you stand for anything so strongly you'd be willing to undergo extreme discomfort or even die for it? Would you die to prevent women from being raped, or children from being abused, or innocent people from dying from starvation, or families from receiving no medical care and perishing from routine illnesses? Would you make it your personal charter to ease the suffering of those less privileged than you? Well, guess what: these atrocities are afflicting millions of people right now as you read these very words!

The more revealing question is *what do you feel compelled to do something about while you're still alive*? Your home offers you *luxury*, but it will not provide *comfort* until you start living your purpose. You won't appreciate all the locations in your house where you can access hot water until you realize that the vast majority of your fellow citizens in this world live without even one source of hot water in their entire village. If you want to make peace with your relative affluence and live a life where you feel you merit all the benefits and resources you've been taking for granted, there's no way around it: you must find your purpose.

"Now wait a moment," you might say. "I have no interest in moving to Africa and saving the world, but I do want to make a difference in my own home." You may have grown up with parents who couldn't buy you the things your friends had, or take you on vacations, or send you to a better college, and your Vision may be to become a successful investment banker so your children can grow up the way you always wished you could have. We will delve much deeper into the connection between the suffering you've experienced and the construction of your Vision in *Chapter 7—Discover Your Passion.*

LET GO OF WHAT?

A popular mantra in psychology and spirituality is to "learn to let go." Less attention is given to what you're supposed to let go of. After feeling a negative emotion such as anxiety, insecurity, or resentment, it's a necessary characteristic of healthy human functioning to be able to move past it (usually after trying to understand why you felt the emotion). But consider this question: What *don't* you want to move beyond? What do you want to create that—unlike the emotions, people, events, and circumstances that swirl around you every day—you will go to great lengths *not* to let go of?

A core characteristic of many forms of meditation is to detach from your thoughts so you can relax the mind. This detachment can bring sublime inner peace and fulfillment. Yet if you haven't created a strong set of core values, how will you construct the inner security to let your mind drift in other directions? It stands to reason that you will find it much easier to "let go" and enjoy your life once you become secure in knowing you can always return to the core values that anchor you.

To develop a Vision is to create an image in your mind of your most magnificent achievements and how you will act toward the people you care about—including yourself. Paint this picture of your envisioned future, refine it periodically, and, most importantly, let it guide you. If you take the time to create your Vision and then measure all your future actions against it, you will be amazed at how much more *meaning*-full your life will become. Even the most mundane tasks and interactions will have value once you perceive them as steps along the path toward your higher purpose.

Your Vision, like your education, is an investment in your future. Make this investment and you will expand many times over your capacity to bring the results you want into your life. The days of going through the motions and watching life pass you by will become a distant memory. You will have made the landmark shift toward the life you have imagined.

OK, it looks like you're getting it. You understand *why* developing a Vision is important. You're almost ready to descend from the mountaintop to the plains and determine *how* you can develop a Vision that will guide your life.

Before you learn how to transform this lofty concept into concrete strategies you can use to make real changes in your life—which you will begin doing in the chapter after next when you create your own Vision Statement—it's important to first understand *where* your Vision comes from.

Let's now turn to the source …

CHAPTER 3

THE CONFLUENCE OF HEART AND MIND

Inspiration is much higher than reason, but it must not contradict it. Reason is the rough tool to do the hard work; inspiration is the bright light which shows us all truth.
—*SWAMI VIVEKANANDA*

Would you describe yourself as a person who gets "lost in their thoughts" or as someone who gets "carried away with their feelings"? Which do you trust more—your mind or your heart? If you could only use one of these internal instruments to make your decisions from now on, which would you choose? The heart and mind can be so at odds with each other that you could imagine them fighting out their differences in a boxing ring.

Let's go to one corner and see how your heart feels about this perennial inner battle.

Neglect your heart and your mind may take you in the wrong direction. Civil rights activist Martin Luther King Jr. wisely observed: "Occasionally in life there are those moments of unutterable fulfillment which cannot be completely explained by those symbols called words. Their meanings can only be articulated by the inaudible language of the heart." The language of the heart understands what is not visible to the eye or perceptible to the mind.

Recall a moment in your life when you did much more than perceive—you *knew*. Have you ever met someone and left that first encounter completely transformed, thinking "I don't know what will happen, but I've never felt like this before"? If you do not include your heart's desires in the equation when you make key life decisions, you will live a life of "dis-ease" (a lack of internal ease that can easily lead to real sickness), rigid self-control, and adherence to a thought-based ideal that is not truly your own.

The heart is swinging hard and has the mind on the ropes ... This is what we're overhearing: You can "think your way into a corner," but have you ever heard of anyone "feeling his way into a corner"? You would probably rather be accused of making a "mindless" comment than a "heartless" one. You've very likely heard someone called a "prisoner of her own mind," but not a "prisoner of her own heart." While no one wants to be considered "crazy" or "mad," to be "crazy in love" or "mad about someone" are desirable qualities for a healthy relationship. For authentic communication, you "speak straight from the heart" and "take what is said to heart." Substitute the word "mind" for "heart" in these popular expressions and they no longer sound authentic.

Try this quick exercise: look straight ahead, point to yourself, and say with conviction, "This is who I am." Really, try it. I'll bet you just pointed to your heart, not your mind. This simple test demonstrates which part of your body you identify with more.

Rabindranath Tagore, the Bengali poet whose book Gandhi carried wherever he went, perceptively wrote: "Logic is sword, all blades and no handle. It bleeds the hand that holds it." If you go out with a person who hits all the marks on your "compatibility checklist" (which your mind, not your heart, creates) but leaves you feeling empty, loveless, and ultimately lonely, you will walk away with nothing but guilt and emotional scars. Similarly, if you study business because you *think* it will impress others, or bring up a sensitive issue because you *think* it's "due" even though you instinctively *feel* it's not the right time, or make any other decision based exclusively on logic, you will succeed only in bleeding the passion and joy out of yourself.

THE DIFFERENCE BETWEEN A MOOD AND A FEELING

If you are going to rely mainly on your feelings to select a career, spouse, or any other critical part of your life Vision, it's important to understand what *is* and *is not* a feeling. The most common mistake we all make time and time again is to confuse a mood with a feeling.

While there are limitless theories and books on the subject, I would like to make an important distinction between moods and feelings to help you better understand your emotions. Moods are brief. Their duration is usually a few moments, hours, or days—although occasionally they last for weeks. In short, moods are feelings in disguise. A mood can be the result of what you just ate, whether you exercised in the last day or two, your reaction to what someone said or didn't say, or a negative string of thoughts you've allowed to spiral out of control.

Feelings, on the other hand, last for weeks, months, years. They reflect how you truly experience your life. Your feelings consistently return to remind you of your innermost convictions. While moods are like small waves constantly shifting direction and stirring up the water, feelings are like a continuous swell of water moving in a specific direction.

Moods are driven by short-term emotions such as pain, pleasure, anxiety, and anger. Feelings are driven by the heart. Feelings do change direction over time, but at a much slower, more stable rate than moods. You can choose to have a conversation with yourself before you act impulsively based on a current mood such as edginess, anxiety, depression, or anger. A simple reminder such as "I'm experiencing a mood. I will let it pass so I can return to a more stable, long-term feeling." Then stop yourself from acting on your mood and you have created Vision-Alignment right in that moment!

Imagine you just met someone for the first time and are starting to have romantic feelings toward him or her. Moods are like those first rushes of emotion you're not sure if you will act on. A protracted mood that can last for weeks or even months is similar to infatuation. You think about the other person all the time, yet there's a voice deep inside telling you to slow down.

To understand how feelings work, on the other hand, imagine you meet someone and get acquainted at a slower pace. Each time you see the person you share a little more of yourself, and he or she reciprocates. Over time, you feel more comfortable, strong, and passionate in the relationship.

Feelings are like love. They resonate deeply within you. They are congruent with and become a part of your Vision. Even if your mind initially questions them, your feelings can feel so "right" and become so deeply entrenched in your heart that your Vision evolves over time to accommodate them.

Pick a situation and ask yourself whether a mood or a feeling is driving your actions. If a comment from your partner causes you to feel jealous or insecure, sit with your emotion and try to determine if it's a temporary mood. Let it go, knowing if it's a long-term feeling it will consistently return. If you feel worried about your child's performance at school, or indignant because your spouse has returned home late from work three nights in a row, or anxious because you're about to go on vacation and there are still so many loose ends to tie up at work, let go of your emotion so the mood can pass and the feeling, if it exists, can return.

Your judgment in differentiating between a mood and a feeling will determine your ability to bring success and happiness into your life. Why? Because while feelings are a make-or-break factor in developing a viable Vision, moods disguised as feelings often steer you *away* from your Vision. Your moods go up or down depending on the pleasure or pain you associate with any decision—rather than the decision's alignment with your larger life goals.

YOU ARE WHAT YOU THINK OTHERS THINK YOU ARE

As a child, Albert was classified by some as "retarded." He ignored subjects in school that bored him and instead focused intensely and exclusively on what interested him. Ironically, over fifty years later his name is used as a synonym for genius—"OK, you're right, Einstein!" The German-born father of quantum mechanics (the basis of modern physics) surprisingly revealed, "I never came upon any of my discoveries through the process of rational thinking." Which method do you use? Do you rely on your thoughts, or do you step back and trust your feelings to guide you—often toward the breakthrough you've been seeking?

While neurologists dispute how clear-cut this dichotomy is, it's commonly understood that your left brain and frontal lobes (including the neocortex) think, analyze, and logically process information while your right brain and amygdala reign over your intuition and feelings. Although this is an oversimplification, you can consider your rational left brain to be the medium that further entrenches your habitual patterns—which, too often, allow the values of others to control you.

To understand how your left brain can lead you in the wrong direction, envision what you'd like to become in your career. Picture yourself as a lawyer, a doctor, a ballerina, a lion tamer, or whatever. Imagine you already are now what you want to become. Which feeling comes to your mind more quickly—happiness or pride?

If you imagine yourself feeling *happy*, this career warms your heart and emanates from your true inner purpose. If, alternatively, you envision yourself feeling *proud* of your career, it's because you're doing what *you think others think* you should be doing. Not what others think, which you never truly know, but what *you* think they think. Building your life on such far-fetched speculation is like trying to build a castle on sand. Not only will this "should" path not lead you to where you want to go (since you're walking toward a destination you can't accurately describe), but it will transform you into a shell of a person. Your life will become nothing more than your (most likely incorrect) interpretation of what others think it ought to be.

"However," you might say, "at least my family and others in society will accept me if I choose a respectable career." The irony is that others will not ultimately accept you if you saunter along the path they cut for you. People accept people who accept themselves. As soon as you start using the term "respectable" to describe your career, partner, car, or house, be assured you are steadily progressing toward a life that will never fulfill you. You are the only person who has to live with your choices, so my advice to you is simple: make choices you can live with.

DON'T BECOME A PRISONER OF YOUR OWN THOUGHTS

In Hermann Hesse's fictionalized account of the Buddha's spiritual journey, *Siddhartha*, the main character, an Indian man, does not develop a true compassion for human beings until he feels a tremendous sense of loss when his son leaves home to live his own life in another town. Until that point, Siddhartha has a detached philosophy about humanity that does not truly comprehend human emotion and love.

Here is a well-known fact about philanthropy: the single event in a person's life that renders him or her most likely to become a donor is having a child. A first child, like a first love, can bring a torrential rush of emotion into your life and turn everything you once valued upside down, or right side up. If you rigidly follow your thoughts without paying attention to the direction your feelings are steering you in, your life goals will become sterile and unappealing once your feelings inevitably surface.

Kahlil Gibran admonishes us of the dangers of not balancing thought with feeling: "Keep me away from the wisdom which does not cry, the philosophy which does not laugh and the greatness which does not bow before children." If the path you're walking on doesn't *feel* right, you will eventually reach a point where you don't have the energy to go any further.

Your thoughts set you on a path but they don't sustain you during the journey. When you stop to rest you need nurturing, which comes from your heart. If you feel it's too late to change course because you've already finished graduate school, or have a mortgage to pay, or have made commitments you don't feel you can get out of, your undetected heart will eventually make its desolation known in the form of stress, dramatic episodes, periodic illnesses, unexpected anxiety, or depression.

Your thoughts are like an endless computer program. They entice you because they always provide more to do. Neurological research suggests you have over fifty thousand thoughts per day. If keeping yourself busy is one of your goals, thinking is an attractive option: you will never run out of thoughts to pay attention to, flesh out, and expand upon. Many people, especially men, get locked up in (and by) their thoughts because they're only comfortable when on an action-planning mission.

When you have to be doing something active to feel content, thoughts fill the void.

Feelings are fewer and simpler. Recall the feelings you've already experienced today: they probably number less than ten, and possibly even fewer than five. You may have felt happy in the morning, irritated and angry and then depressed in the afternoon, and then joyful again in the evening. Your feelings, while fewer in number, drive you in a more sustainable way than your thoughts.

Aristotle's famous words were "Know thyself," not "Know *about* thyself." Mapping out all the facts, data, calculations, and projections you run through your mind—with all their inherent permutations—is like trying to solve a puzzle that expands by five pieces every time you put another piece into place. This mind-dominated process is unlikely to lead you to where you want to go.

If you want to find your path, get out of your way. Be aware of the potency of your thoughts to mislead you. Recognize the mental formations you've inherited that pressure you to become the one among your siblings who is the apple of your mother's eye, or the one to fulfill the legacy of your father's work. Become conscious of your left-brain thoughts that impel you to pursue a "safe" or "socially prestigious" career even though your true calling (which you emotively understand in your right brain) is to teach yoga, ride horses, or lead expeditions. Never stop paying attention to your feelings: they're the only warning bell God lodged into your inner circuitry to remind you of your higher purpose.

FEELINGS TAMPER WITH THE EVIDENCE

Before we give the ultra-welter-weight crown to the heart, let's hear from its opponent. While it has admittedly been taking a beating, it's not yet down for the count. Let's step into the other corner and hear what your mind thinks about this long-standing rivalry.

Galileo understood the importance of what's upstairs. In fact, he believed in the power of thought so strongly he received a sentence of condemnation from the Vatican and was confined to Siena for publishing books that rejected blind allegiance to either authority (including the Church) or the accepted philosophers of his time (such as Aristotle). In the words of the seventeenth-century Italian astronomer and philosopher: "I do not feel obliged to believe that the same God who has endowed us with sense, reason, and intellect, has intended us to forgo their use."

God endowed humans with more highly developed thoughts than other animals, but not with stronger feelings. If you doubt this statement, observe any dog, cat, or warthog when it's angry. This will confirm very rapidly that you do not have stronger feelings.

Your feelings can mislead you. Simply following your feelings can result in blind belief and behavior that harms others. It can lead you to say, "I will do whatever I please regardless of how it affects others because I *feel* like doing it!"

Your mind performs two key roles. First, it serves as a Visionary that sees beyond the here and now to the horizon and helps you define your long-term goals. Second, it acts as a regulator that provides your heart with parameters to operate within so you consistently move toward these goals.

Your mind keeps you in check. If it weren't for your mind, you might end up with someone who makes your heart skip a beat but who is abusive and manipulative and doesn't share your values. Your mind informs you that although your love for singing is admirable, you should buy a karaoke machine rather than make a career change (considering the dogs in your neighborhood start howling every time you break into song).

Your thoughts remind you to become conscious of negative feelings before allowing them to guide your decisions. You may have a long-entrenched fear of public speaking, or a deep anxiety about confronting your boss, or an obsession with what might go wrong if you were to travel abroad or break your daily routine in any significant way. Your thoughts enable you to override these negative feelings and say, "I will not allow this fear of public speaking I've had since childhood, or this anxiety about speaking openly with people in positions of power I picked up from my dictatorial father, or this fear of the unknown I've had ever since the day I came home and received that phone call, to prevent me from pursuing my goals in life." You can use positive thoughts like these to replace long-held negative feelings that *no sirven* ("don't serve you" in Spanish) with positive feelings—such as self-confidence, resilience, and strength.

The German poet and philosopher Johann Wolfgang von Goethe knew the dangers of unchecked feelings: "Whatever liberates our spirit without giving us self-control is disastrous." While feelings can be liberating, a court of law requires due process because they can also be unreliable. Would a jury always make the right decision if they only trusted their feelings? If so, we wouldn't need fingerprints, arrest records, blood samples, or any other hard data.

Thoughts are necessary because feelings tamper with the evidence. If a man on a jury deciding an assault case was recently assaulted himself, he may be more likely to ascribe negative motivations to the defendant, especially if the accused is the same ethnicity as his assailant.

Your feelings also distort the evidence in more mundane and unseen ways. If you are a manager, your feelings can compel you to hire someone like you because you *feel* comfortable around her, even though if you were to *think* about it you might realize she lacks the skills needed for the position. If you are a student, your feelings can impel you to take the class your friend signed up for so you won't have to go it alone, or the class you're comfortable in because the subject comes easily to you, rather than the class where you will learn what you need to know to advance in your career.

YOUR MIND CAN HELP—IF YOU USE IT IN THE RIGHT WAY

Imagine a couple sitting on a park bench in a passionate embrace as the brightly colored autumn leaves gently float down to the ground around them. What feeling does this image evoke within you? Now picture this scene again, but this time imagine that the man is your father and the woman is not your mother, but one of your former teachers who never liked you. What do you feel now? The scene was the same both times, but your feelings changed based on your mental perception of what you beheld.

With the exception of some physical feelings such as touch, smell, and sound, your feelings are a reaction to earlier thoughts. Even most of your physical feelings are derived from your mental "historical record." If you close your eyes and a good friend whom you trust tells you he is handing you a gummy bear or a piece of Play-Doh, but then places a dead slug in your hand, you will be perfectly comfortable with how it feels. You will only feel disgusted when you open your eyes, look down, and think, "I'm holding a dead slug!" This means that, contrary to popular notions, your feelings aren't something out of your control that just "happen" to you, but are directly related to your long-held perceptions.

You don't just feel insecure, then, for no reason. You *think*, "Something must be wrong with me because my last two boyfriends broke up with me," and *then* you feel insecure. You don't just feel envy in a vacuum. You *think*, "Why don't I have a car like that?" and *then* you feel envy. This is a groundbreaking realization with far-reaching implications. It means your personal power and self-control hinge on the capacity of your mind to replace negative feelings with positive ones. It means *you can exercise more control over your feelings by choosing which of your thoughts to empower and which to ignore.*

RE-ENGINEER YOUR FEELINGS

The mind has bounced back and come out swinging … It just landed an incisive blow with a statement it appears has, well, hurt the heart's feelings. Here it is: *A feeling is nothing more than an entrenched thought.* Here's the mind's reasoning: while you allow most of the thousands of thoughts you have each day to float out of your mind as easily as they floated in, there are a few thoughts you choose to empower by concentrating your mind on them over and over again until they ossify and become feelings. If you feel fat, it's because you had "repeat thoughts" about your weight—reactions to opinions directed toward you from others or yourself that you gradually assumed to be truth. If you lived in an African culture that values weight as a sign of nutrition, wealth, and status, you wouldn't have had those thoughts, and you wouldn't feel fat.

The heart is taking a pounding against the ropes and says it feels "crushed." The mind isn't letting up … it just said your thoughts, which are conditioned by the thoughts of the people around you, *determine* your feelings. If you feel jealous because your husband is having a lunch meeting with a female client, it's because you *choose* to feel jealous based on what your mind associates with his actions. Your father may have very skillfully documented for you that if a man is alone with a woman, it's for only one reason. If you had a different father, you would have different habitual patterns, different thoughts and, consequently, different feelings. The real question is whether you will allow someone external to you (in this case, your father) to control the most core, intimate part of your being—your feelings. Make a pact with yourself now to live an original life, not the one you inherited.

The mind is no longer content just taking shots at the heart, and is now debunking this whole book. Its latest comment is that although habitual patterns have become a four-letter word in this book, they're not all bad. Some exist for a reason: you feel it's bad for your health to smoke because your habitual pattern derived from hearing about or witnessing people die of lung cancer reminds you that smoking is dangerous. Your feeling of fear derived from various observations over time that tells you it's better not to look a barking dog in the eye also serves a purpose in your life.

The key words here are *serves a purpose*. Therein lies the secret: if a feeling helps you move toward your Vision, it's worth incorporating into your repertoire. It's to your advantage. Living a healthy life—which includes not contracting lung cancer or rabies—is hopefully a part of your Vision. The problem, then, occurs only when those feelings that do *not* move you in the direction of your Vision become permanent fixtures in your internal landscape.

It's probably not a part of your life Vision to become paralyzed with negative feelings such as remorse, anxiety, or self-doubt. Recognize if you feel remorse after thinking, "I shouldn't have been so critical when she asked me what I thought of her painting," and replace those thoughts with others such as, "I learned from that experience and in the future will balance constructive criticism with praise for what others have done well." Make the connection between feelings of anxiety and thoughts such as "Maybe I won't be fully prepared for my meeting today" or "Why do I have to go through with this? I hate these get-togethers—they're so artificial" and let those thoughts slip out of your mind as easily as they entered. Link self-doubt to thoughts like "I can't believe they have me making these client calls. Somebody must realize I don't know what I'm doing" and gracefully bid those thoughts farewell.

AND THE WINNER IS ...

I was given two tickets to see the sneak preview of the movie *Syriana* a few years ago and went with an Italian friend, Paolo.

As we walked out, I asked Paolo what he thought of the film.

"It was interesting but not involving," Paolo replied. "I liked that it showed some new perspectives on issues in the Middle East. But there were so many characters and plotlines I didn't feel connected with any of them."

I have since evaluated a number of movies based on how they score on Paolo's Interesting/Involving Scale. *The Da Vinci Code* struck me as much the same as *Syriana*—so much going on I couldn't immerse myself into any of the characters and really experience what they were feeling. As for movies that were involving but not interesting—I can't remember any! I enjoy watching them, but then forget about them within a few days.

How about your Vision? Does it contain so much information that it overwhelms rather than motivates you? Alternatively, does it feel good yet lack substance? How does it rate on Paolo's scale? Does it hold your mind's *interest*? Does it *involve* your heart? To develop a sustainable Vision, you must paint a picture that will keep you engaged for a lifetime. Compare this process to seeing a movie—another kind of "picture." Just as a movie director can create character after character and plotline after plotline, your mind can create thought after thought after thought until you're thoroughly confused and no longer have the faintest clue what's going on.

Nineteenth-century romantic poet Walt Whitman put it this way: "The words of my book nothing, the drift of it everything." Words aside, what is the *drift* of your Vision? What is it *really* guiding you to achieve? If it's like a book or movie filled with too many words but not enough feeling, your Vision will be interesting but not involving—and will not captivate you.

The feelings your heart produces make you feel empathetic, engaged, involved. They make you feel good about what you're seeing, while you're seeing it. Yet without the thoughts your mind creates, you will ultimately become bored and uninterested. Like a movie that's involving but not interesting, your Vision will not hold your attention for any length of time.

Your Vision for how you want to live your life will only be sustainable if it both piques your mind and engages your heart. The person you want to spend your life with—they must be interesting and involving. Your heart and mind must both give "Two Thumbs Up—Way Up." The right career: interesting and involving. Heart and mind must both be attuned or you won't sustain your motivation to grow it and grow in it. The books you read; how you spend your weekends; the friends you hang out with: interesting and involving, or you won't keep showing up.

So who do you think should win the title—your heart or your mind? The results are finally in and ... the judges have declared a tie! They are applauding both the heart and the mind for putting up a good fight, and are insisting the only way to develop a sustainable Vision is to balance your left- and right-brain mental activity and determine a life direction that you both intellectually *think* and instinctively *feel* is right for you.

SYNCHRONIZE

Take a moment to consider an important decision you've made in the last year. Which was the key agent in your decision making—your thoughts or your feelings? If you want to find the right career, life partner, place to live, or pet ferret, ask yourself both "How do I *feel* about this?" and "What do I *think* is the right way to go?" Sometimes your mind and heart will respond differently, and that's OK. It's the internal conflict in the protagonist that makes for interesting (and involving!) literature and theater.

Discovering this intersection between heart and mind is to the individual what compromise is to the couple. If he wants to live in San Francisco and she wants to live in New York, moving to Wisconsin is not the right solution. As a couple, they have to assess how strongly each person feels about his or her preferences. Similarly, acknowledge how strongly your thoughts and feelings are both declaring their preferences, and how each is affecting you. Then incorporate them into your Vision so they can *codirect* your actions. Like a healthy couple resolving complex issues in their relationship, your *thoughtful* and *heartfelt* decisions will enable you to live in a state of internal harmony.

Just as every healthy couple has its difficult moments, the dissonance between your heart and mind will become a source of tension at certain times in your life. You may feel attracted to a person with whom you have very little in common, or not attracted to a friend whom you think is perfect for you. You might feel deeply offended by how your sister has been acting since her recent promotion, and upon further reflection realize it's your envy speaking. Recognize this inner tension between your heart and mind and you will be pleasantly surprised with your capacity to hold it in your arms like a mother holds her child. Sit calmly with these conflicting thoughts and feelings and view them (and the struggle they elicit within you) with compassion. Be patient yet steadfast in your efforts to understand this internal conflict until you see through it to the right solutions for how to live your life.

WILD HORSES ... COULDN'T DRAG ME AWAY

Your feelings can be compared to a stable of horses. After you let them out and watch them roam, learn how to respect their unique attributes and let each one inspire you. Yet simultaneously use the power of your mind (which, after all, is what separates you from the horses!) to rein in those that will run in other directions if left to their own devices. Also use your mind to determine how to cultivate, train, and breed those with the potential to run gracefully in the direction you want to move in. Know that if you hold the reins too tightly, the feeling, like a horse, will lose its passion, yet if you don't hold them tightly enough it may give in to its baser instincts.

You will not train your horses, or bring your feelings under control, overnight. Be patient. You will go through thousands of "almost" moments before you locate the space within where your heart and mind simultaneously flourish. Once you locate it, it's only a matter of time before a horse becomes wild, lurches out of control, and throws you off again.

Developing a Vision that fuses the yearnings and deeply felt emotions that emanate from your heart with the beliefs and ideals your mind holds dear is a continuous process which, like your Vision itself, is unattainable. Nonetheless, maintain your focus on coalescing your heart and mind into a sustainable Vision and you will make spectacular progress.

I realize I'm issuing you a formidable challenge. I know it's not easy to uncover the small space within where your heart and mind intersect. Yet it will be even harder in the long run if you ignore what your heart desires or your mind commands. I strongly encourage you to devote your energy to this inner search for the zone of agreement between your thoughts and feelings. It's one of the most potent strategies available to help you bring what you desire into your life, including a life partner and new friends whom you both love (with your heart) and respect (with your mind).

Your heart and mind, when heeded in concert, will yield a future in which the excitement and joy you feel every day are coupled with feelings of motivation and pride which come from a mental awareness that you're reaching your potential. While it's true that it will not be easy to find this intersection of heart and mind and you will stumble thousands of times, find your solace in knowing that each of your efforts is a necessary, invaluable step toward developing a Vision that will guide you for a lifetime.

MAKE IT HAPPEN:

1. Make a list of things you haven't yet done in your life that you really *want* to do.
2. Make a list of things you haven't yet done which you think you *ought* to do.
3. Circle the items that appear on both lists.
4. Regardless of whether there are items on both lists, make a third list of additional things you both *want* to do and think you *should* do in your career, personal relationships, and other areas of your life.
5. Consider your desired goals that fulfill both your heart and mind—both the items you circled in the first two lists and those you wrote down in the third list—as you write your Vision Statement in the next chapter and your Action Plan in Chapter 10.

Chapter 4

Create Your Vision Statement

The majority of us cannot see beyond a few years, just as some animals cannot see beyond a few steps. Just a little narrow circle—that is our world. ... This is our weakness, our powerlessness.
—Swami Vivekananda

Let's go on a journey into the future. First, step back from everything for a moment. Take a deep breath, and relax your body and mind. Imagine you are at your own eightieth birthday banquet. (If you are over eighty, imagine you are at your hundredth birthday banquet.) You are sitting at a long, beautifully varnished wood table in a warm, spacious, comfortable room. Around the table are the people you value the most in your life—such as your family, friends, partner, children, the people you have worked with over the years, and members of your community. Envision the people you would want sitting at the table with you.

They are going around the table, one by one, and talking about *you*. They're sharing what you have meant to them, how you've acted toward them over the years, and how you've influenced their lives.

80th Birthday Banquet

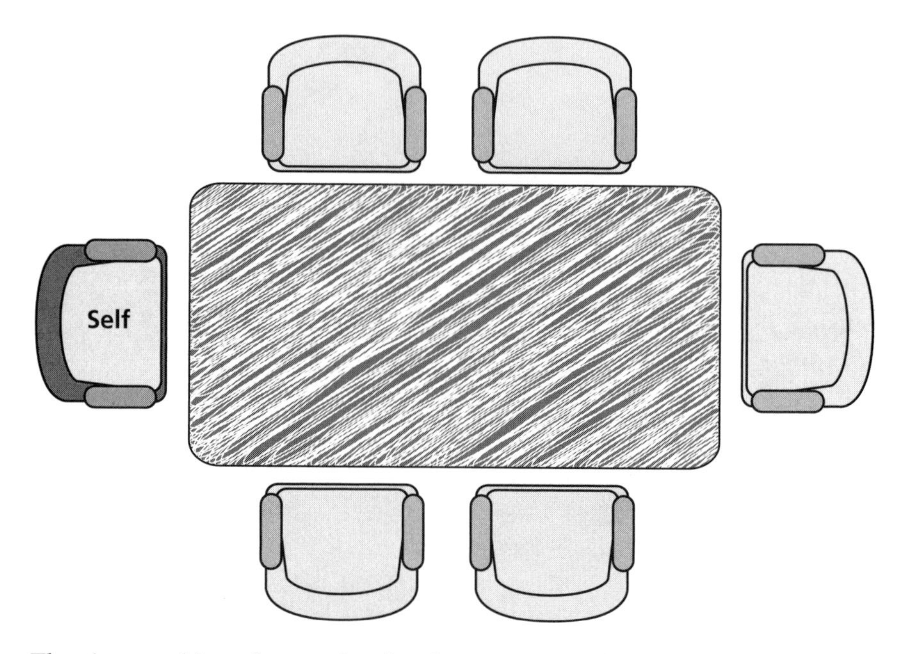

They're speaking about why they're so proud of you and what you've accomplished in your life.

After a few hours, the banquet is over. You go for a long walk alone in a place where you've always felt very peaceful and centered. Picture yourself walking on a beach listening to the sound of the waves crashing on the shore, or on the top of a mountain feeling a cool breeze caress your hair as you look out at the 360-degree panoramic view, or in a forest with the smell of fresh pine and eucalyptus filling your senses. As you stroll, you contemplate what you have achieved in your life. You ponder the *impact* of your life on the world. You consider what's given your life meaning. You think back to how you have acted toward the people who really matter to you. You reflect on what you want to be remembered for and what you've stood for in your life.

What do you want to remember? What do you want the people

around the table to say about you? What will give your life meaning when you go for your walk alone on your eightieth birthday?

When you visualized yourself at your eightieth birthday banquet, what came to your mind about the choices you made and how you lived your life?

The value of this exercise: to help you determine what's truly important to you *right now* while you still have the opportunity to do something about it.

THE VISION STATEMENT

A Vision Statement is to the individual what a constitution is to the nation. It's your life charter, or statement of purpose. It's the basis for your long- and short-term goals. A Vision Statement enables you to translate your dreams into concrete declarations that govern the way you live—every day, every moment.

Your Vision Statement is a written summary of the principles that will guide your life decisions. It's the core script that defines how you want to act toward others, how you want to act toward yourself, and what you want to accomplish with the limited time you have left on this planet. When you create your Vision Statement, you reclaim your life. You replace the voices projected onto you by others throughout your life with your own. It's the essence of the power available to you to determine your life's direction.

Your Vision Statement is your new gold standard. In the middle of an argument with your partner, or before an important work meeting, or when you're about to discipline your child, or when you feel frustrated because you've stayed at the office late every night for the last week … whenever you feel it's necessary, you can stop to review your Vision Statement and determine how aligned your actions are with your Vision. You can then figure out what you need to do—from that moment forward—to better align them.

GET STARTED

There's no better way to understand a new strategy than to observe how someone else has applied it to his life. Here are some entries from the Vision Statement of a good friend, Keith, a college athletic director in Florida:

- To get to know my student-athletes and recognize their accomplishments on a personal level
- To help my staff grow in their professional development
- To encourage the coaches and athletes to become involved in community service
- To always keep a sense of humor
- To maintain a positive attitude about life. As an African-American I know there will be obstacles in life, and I have to be positive when these obstacles occur and figure out ways to overcome them.

While your Vision Statement will hopefully still be relevant in another few years, don't think of it as etched in stone: you can amend, add, or delete entries whenever you want. Most likely, the frequency with which you change your Vision Statement will decrease over time as you become more and more comfortable with it.

MAKE IT HAPPEN:

Let's begin. Write down two or three entries to get your Vision Statement out of the starting gate. Don't worry how the words sound; just get down a few ideas to start the process.

Note how each entry in Keith's Vision Statement began with the word "To." Your Vision Statement is a picture you paint of where you are traveling *to* in your life, so beginning each entry with this word encourages you to be forward-thinking.

Also, please note that your Vision Statement does not have to be a set of bullet points as in the sample entries I provide in this chapter. You may choose to write a few paragraphs, or even to draw a diagram or a picture. It's *your* Vision Statement, so unleash your inner creativity and write or draw something that resembles your internal picture of what you want your life to become. You will know you're on the right track when you create a picture through words or images that speaks to you at your core and motivates you to move your life toward it.

Throughout *Full Alignment,* you will have many opportunities—including various "Make It Happen" exercises—to update your Vision Statement.

NEVER STOP WORKING TOWARD WHAT YOU'LL NEVER ACHIEVE

In the fourteenth-century epic poem *Inferno,* Dante Alighieri describes an allegorical trip through hell. The sign inscribed on the door as he enters hell is very telling: *"Lasciate ogne speranza, voi ch'intrate."* ("Abandon all hope, ye who enter here.") The Uruguayan proverb "Hope is the last thing we lose" reinforces the words of the Italian poet. When no hope remains, you pass through this door into a hell on earth no person merits.

To inspire you for a lifetime, your Vision Statement must never fail to provide hope. To do this, it must be *unattainable.* Your Vision Statement comprises your greater purpose, your guiding life principles, your core values—not your attainable short-term goals.

"This doesn't make sense," you may be thinking. "Why would I want to write down a Vision I can't achieve?" Have you considered how you would feel if you *did* attain your Vision? What would come next? There would be nothing left to hope for, nowhere to direct your aim. You would feel disoriented, deflated, and dejected. You would become living testimony to the construction of the word "despair"—from the Latin roots *de* ("without") and *sperare* ("hope"). When there is no light at the end of the tunnel, it becomes very dark.

Take another look at Keith's Vision Statement. Is it unattainable? It must be if it is to continuously inspire him not just today or tomorrow, but always. Will Keith ever finish getting to know his student-athletes? Not as long as he keeps coaching. Will he ever say, "I'm tired of maintaining a positive attitude about life, it's time to change things up"? Not from what I've seen.

Your Vision Statement never stops inspiring you because it always provides *something more to do.* One of life's greatest dangers is to not have the faintest clue what to do next. You've no doubt seen movies about celebrities who lose their way and succumb to drugs, self-destructive behavior, and even suicide. They achieve their goals beyond their wildest expectations, find themselves without anything left to aim for, and enter a personal hell.

Consider the trajectory of Johnny Cash's life as depicted in the movie *Walk the Line.* Celebrity brings a rush of excitement to the life of a door-to-door salesman from Arkansas, which is quickly followed by depression and an addiction to pills. What pulls him out of it? A compelling

Vision to improve the lives of prisoners and to love a woman. Did the Man in Black ever finish helping prisoners and then say, "Been there, done that. Time for a new goal"? No way. Did he run out of love to give to June Carter? Never.

I realize this is a hard sell. I'm asking you to buy a ticket to a destination you'll never reach. I know it sounds counterintuitive. So why buy your ticket? Because it's the journey—not the destination—that gives your life meaning. To step on board, ask yourself this question: "What will I never attain yet willingly pursue for a lifetime?"

SPIRITUAL ALIGNMENT

You may be thinking, "This is absurd. Why dedicate myself to goals I'll never achieve? That won't work for me. I need a sense of completion—and I need results!" I'm encouraging you to step away from short-term results and examine your underlying motivations for achieving those results. Why? Because it's not only your Vision that's unattainable. There is much in your life you will never reach, yet never stop seeking.

To name a few: God, love, and truth. You will never call up a friend and say, "Hey, guess what? I've found God. Glad I don't have to worship anymore." I doubt you will ever say, "It's great to have finally learned what love is. I can cross that one off the list." Nor will the words "I've discovered the truth. Whew! It's good to be done with *that* search" hopefully ever come out of your mouth.

The lawyer and civil libertarian Clarence Darrow described the unattainable nature of truth: "Chase after the truth like all hell and you'll free yourself, even though you never touch its coat-tails." The next time the holidays roll around and a close friend sends you a card that reads, "I wish you the fulfillment of all your dreams," after you bask in the warmth of their heartfelt caring for a moment or two, sober up and remind yourself, "That would be horrible! What would I have left to live for? I hope I *never* fulfill all my dreams."

I am now going to propose, through a series of rhetorical questions, that these unattainable entities—God, love, truth, and ... your Vision and your higher Self—are actually all one and the same. Let's get started. Do you believe God is greater than all, even truth? Gandhi didn't. In the words of one of our greatest spiritual thinkers: "There is no God higher than truth." Consider this revealing question: If God were no longer synonymous with what you believe to be true, which would you choose—God or truth? Would you say, "It looks like I'm giving up on truth and choosing God instead"?

An even more difficult question: If God ordered you to steal your best friend's hamster, or kill an innocent person, or shout at your mother when she irritates you, or covet thy neighbor's wife, or forgo what you know deep in your soul to be true, what would you do? If you would choose truth, then God is not higher than truth. What if what you believe to be true contradicted God? I would think if it contradicted God, you would no longer consider it true. This means God is truth and truth is God.

Now let's consider love. Is God greater than love? If so, you would be willing to say, "That was a close one. I almost chose love, but had to go with God"? What if God ordered you to neglect your child when she cries out for help, or to stop volunteering and helping people? How about if God told you to break up with your fiancée, who is the first person in your life to care enough to make light of your idiosyncrasies and truly understand you? Would you abandon love at God's request?

You may think, "That's ridiculous! God would never tell me to abandon love, and if He or She did, I wouldn't believe in God." In this case, God is not higher than love. What if someone you love said, "I want to marry you, but I have only one request: abandon God"? I doubt you would be willing to do so. This implies neither God nor love is higher than the other, so God is love and love is God.

Now let's get personal. What if God said, "Hey, enough of that. I want you to abandon your Vision for how you want to live your life." Alternatively, what would you do if your Vision urged you to leave God by the wayside? I don't think you would be willing to do either. This means God is not higher than your Vision nor is your Vision higher than God, so God is your Vision and your Vision is God.

And finally: What if God told you not to heed your higher Self, or your higher Self insisted that you stop listening to God? Would you take the advice of either? If you wouldn't, then neither one is higher than the other, so God is your higher Self and your higher Self is God.

This philosophical discourse provides the foundation for the core spiritual message of *Full Alignment*: God, love, truth, your Vision, and your higher Self are all one and the same. Believe in one and you will become acquainted with them all. The repercussions for your Vision Statement? To sustain your motivation over the long haul, your Vision—as described in your Vision Statement—must reflect what you consider love, truth, God, and your higher Self.

DESCRIBE YOUR FUTURE BEHAVIOR

Hopefully by now you're convinced *why* creating this cardinal document—your Vision Statement—is such a critical ingredient for living a life of success and happiness. Let's now drill deeper into *how* you can create a Vision Statement that will both reflect who you truly are and incite you to action.

Begin by concentrating your mind on an adjective that describes what you want to become: steady, generous, empathetic, calm, effusive, young-at-heart, confident, whatever. Picture yourself as already being that which you imagine. Envision what your relationships will *feel* like, and how they will evolve once you start acting in the way you've described. If you want to be steady, recall times in your life when others have put you down openly or behind your back. Remember how you used to respond, then visualize how you will respond now.

Imagine getting fired from your job or losing your most important client. How will you react? Picture a good friend standing you up and not calling to apologize. Will you shun her from your life? Alternatively, will you take the high road and learn how to both speak assertively for what you want in the friendship and accept that she will not always live up to your expectations? Reflect now on how to be the person you want to become and you will configure your path to get there. This mental clarity will prepare you to navigate the rough waters ahead—especially when you've lost your way—by providing an image to constantly move toward.

An entry in my own Vision Statement is:

- To be authentic, calm, caring, confident, empathetic, generous, humble, humorous, and reflective toward every human being with whom I come into contact

Those are nine adjectives that describe my Vision for how I want to act toward others. Keeping my actions consistent with these adjectives is the most significant way in which I give to the various people in my life.

Whether you're about to go into an important work meeting, or broach a sensitive issue with your partner, or visit your aging and increasingly irritable father for the weekend, review the adjectives in your Vision Statement that govern how you want to act toward others. (You will create these adjectives in the exercise below.) Choose to act based on these adjectives rather than react based on the adjectives governing how others treat you.

MAKE IT HAPPEN:

Which adjectives define how you want to treat other people? Meditate on how you want to act toward others, and also toward yourself. Picture yourself in your difficult moments, and allow the adjectives that best describe how you will exhibit "grace under pressure" and maintain your loyalty to what you value to float into your mind.

Give your thoughts the space to transmute into these essential adjectives. Discover your Vision in the place within where you feel an irrepressible love for others, where you care only for what is true, and where you connect with God and your higher Self. Then let the words that emanate from this sacred place flow from your hand onto the paper. Incorporate these adjectives into your Vision Statement.

REDEFINE YOUR REALITY

After losing the 2000 presidential election, Al Gore spent some time contemplating what to do with his life. Disheartened by the most questionable election loss in U.S. political history, Gore channeled his energy into lecturing and lobbying domestically and internationally for environmental causes. In 2006, Gore released the Oscar-winning film *An Inconvenient Truth* and placed global warming squarely on the U.S. political map (it was already on the radar of 169 countries around the world—the U.S. and Australia notably excluded—that ratified the Kyoto Protocol, which has reduced the emissions of carbon dioxide and other greenhouse gases worldwide) and in the consciousness of millions of people worldwide. The former vice-president won the Nobel Peace Prize for his groundbreaking environmental work. In his prescient words:

> Future generations may well have occasion to ask themselves "What were our parents thinking? Why didn't they wake up when they had the chance?" We have to hear that question, from them, *now*.

Compel yourself to wake up every single day and hear that question about the values guiding your life from the future generations who will live with the consequences of your decisions. Put how you will answer them in your Vision Statement.

If you read your Vision Statement each week and upgrade it periodically to keep up with your evolving values and priorities, it will become an increasingly solid reflection of who you are and what you strive to achieve in your life. Many of the entries in my Vision Statement are etched in my mind because I have read them every few weeks for over ten years. Here are three of my oldest entries:

- To create and communicate ideas for personal and social change
- To appreciate what I have rather than focusing on what I don't have
- To always compromise with family and friends. To think of the needs of others and try to be accommodating. To not become too rigidly attached to any preference.

At its rawest level, your Vision Statement is a means of "reprogramming your voice." It replaces the voice projected onto you by others with your own. It enables you to leave the person you have been behind and become the person you now want to be.

Your Vision Statement is at the core of leadership. The word "to lead" is derived from the Latin roots for "to guide" or "to travel." To understand what is required of a leader, imagine you are standing on a dock and many ships are setting out to sea. How will you decide which ship to board?

Certainly one of the most important criteria would be the ship's destination. If you want to go to Jamaica, you won't board a ship heading to France. Another factor would be the commitment of the captain to reach the destination. You probably won't select a ship with a captain who says, "We'll probably go to Jamaica. Well, let me think about it and I'll get back to you."

Your Vision Statement clarifies your destination and your commitment to reaching it. It's the first step on the great journey toward redefining your reality. While everything else in your life will fluctuate, your Vision Statement will be a constant, enduring source of stability—an eye in the storm—that will give you something to hold onto during times of change. Your Vision Statement will make you the indisputable captain of your ship, and will provide the necessary inner clarity to handle whatever comes your way.

IF YOU WANT TO GROW HEALTHY, BUILD YOUR OWN FENCE

Does this strategy feel too constraining? Does it feel too simplistic and self-limiting to attempt to narrow down who you are to whatever you can fit onto a few sheets of paper? Are you thinking, "Writing down guidelines for my life leaves no room for spontaneity. Besides, I trust myself enough not to need any "internal laws" to govern how I act. There are enough already on the outside restricting me!"? If you don't want your Vision Statement to constrain you, here's my simple advice: don't write one that's constraining. Simply write down the values you want to guide your life *no matter what*, and only proscribe those activities that are absolutely off-limits.

To grow up straight into a tree, a young sapling either needs to be tied to a firm piece of wood or to have a fence built around it. Once it's grown healthily for a few years, the wood or fence can be discarded. You are no different from that young sapling. No matter how impressive your accomplishments, I guarantee you there are areas of your life you need to contain if you wish to remain healthy.

Build this fence when necessary by setting parameters in your Vision Statement for how you will live your life. If you procrastinate on your most important projects every day by spending countless hours checking emails, add an entry to your Vision Statement that reads:

- To spend at least four hours each day working on important projects before checking my inbox

If a police order wouldn't get you to the gym, add:

- To go to the gym at least three times per week

If your intimate relationship has turned into one installment after the next of the long-running mini-series *The Same Old Bitter Argument*, add two entries that read:

- To be genuinely curious about why my partner feels the way she does and listen to her
- To try to wait until I am calm to express what I feel

Know this for certain: if you don't write down some guidelines for how you will and won't act, you'll have nothing to refer to when you are hijacked by those nefarious internal terrorists commonly referred to as your emotions. You'll have no baseline or benchmark to refer to, and will be like a sheep among wolves when you try to negotiate with these well-trained militants who are very up to speed on the latest indoctrination tactics to make you a believer in their cause.

You can either live your life like a highly-skilled soccer player—continually making minor deviations yet always moving further downfield toward the goal—or like a leaf blown about by the wind as it falls to the forest floor. Where the leaf will land—roll the dice. Creating your Vision Statement just may be the single most important decision you make in your entire life to set it on course.

A LESSON FROM A VISIONARY COMPANY

In their landmark study of business leadership, *Built to Last,* James Collins and Jerry Porras compared eighteen "visionary companies" such as General Electric, Hewlett-Packard, and Marriott with comparison companies like (respectively) Westinghouse, Texas Instruments, and Howard Johnson. Collins and Porras compared these pairings of companies based on the extent to which they had developed a Vision. The result of their findings:

> A fundamental element in the "ticking clock" of a visionary company is a *core ideology*—core values and sense of purpose beyond just making money—that guides and inspires people throughout the organization and remains fixed for long periods of time. ... A detailed pair-by-pair analysis showed that the visionary companies have generally been more ideologically driven and less purely profit-driven than the comparison companies in seventeen out of eighteen pairs. ... This is one of the clearest differences we found between the visionary and comparison companies.

Merck is a good example of a visionary company that chose purpose over profits during the period of this study. Merck described a key part of its Vision as:

- "We are in the business of preserving and improving human life. All of our actions must be measured by our success in achieving this goal."

Anyone can proclaim a Vision, but not everyone can back it up with aligned actions. Merck scientists developed a cure for river blindness that was afflicting over a million people in West Africa. Their market research indicated it would be unprofitable to sell the drug, Mectizan, because the rural people in West Africa who needed it couldn't afford it at the price the company would need to charge to turn a profit. So Merck elected to ship Mectizan to West Africa for free.

Merck made a similarly unprofitable decision to bring streptomycin to Japan after World War II to eliminate a tuberculosis epidemic. "But why would a private company make unprofitable decisions?" you may be asking yourself. The answer is simple. These were the only available options aligned with Merck's Vision of "preserving and improving human life."

Merck attracts some of the best scientists in their respective fields, who are loyal to Merck because of its ideology. Without these top-caliber scientists, Merck would lose its internal capacity to develop other drugs that *are* profitable. Due to its adherence to a set of core values its scientists and customers believe in, Merck has been extremely profitable as a company—growing to nearly $6 billion in profits and surpassing the general market by over ten times between 1946 and 2000. Now consider Merck's comparison company in the study, Pfizer:

> Whereas Merck has explicitly and prominently articulated a consistent set of high ideals for four generations, we found no evidence of similar discussions at Pfizer until the late 1980s. Nor did we find at Pfizer any incident analogous to the Mectizan or streptomycin decisions at Merck.

In fact, the president of Pfizer was quoted as saying, "So far as is humanly possible, we aim to get profit out of everything we do." Ironically, Pfizer was much less profitable than Merck over the same period.

WHEN IN DOUBT, CHECK OUT YOUR VISION STATEMENT

Whether you want to lead a visionary company or become a person with strong core values, the only way to reach your goal is to reassert those values daily. Just as Merck's employees need a sense of purpose that makes them feel good about walking through Merck's doors every morning, you need a sense of purpose that makes you feel good about the decisions you make every day.

"But I know what my life goals are," you might be thinking. "Why do I have to put them on paper?" First, if your Vision remains an amorphous concept because you refuse to write it down, you will have nothing to which you hold yourself accountable. Second, when you commit to the goals you put into writing in your Vision Statement, you increase your chances more than tenfold of actually achieving them!

Here's proof: if you had invested one dollar in a mutual fund consisting of the eighteen comparison companies in Collins and Porras's study in 1926, it would have been worth $955 in 1990, more than double the increase in the overall stock market. Had you invested that same dollar in a mutual fund of the eighteen visionary companies during the same period—companies that clearly articulated and then adhered to a Vision that inspired their employees, customers, and investors—it would have increased in value to $6,356, over fourteen times the change in the general stock market!

When you create a Vision Statement, you paint a picture of how you want your life to look and feel in the future. This image becomes the basis for the decisions you make today. When your friends say, "Come on, have a drink. Don't take life so seriously," how do you respond? Do you have a compelling reason not to drink, or smoke, or do whatever else they insist you do? Your Vision Statement provides the compelling reason, the standard you use to assess any possible course of action.

When you don't get the promotion you've been waiting for, or your brother calls you a hypocrite to divert attention from his own behavior, or you hear some dirt on a coworker, you can consult your Vision Statement before acting rashly and doing something you'll regret later.

The same holds true in your moments of glory. When you reach a major milestone such as receiving a marriage proposal from the man you love, or having your first child, or publishing a major article, or seeing your new company finally turn a profit, you can refer once again to your Vision Statement so you don't lose your way. Whether you're focused on building your career, bettering your relationships, or just finding more balance in your life, developing a Vision Statement to guide your daily actions is one of the best strategies I know of to help you achieve the results you desire, year after year.

MAKE IT HAPPEN:

Here's an exercise to help you distill your core values so you can integrate them into your Vision Statement:

1. Describe how you want to live your life.
2. Have a heart-to-heart with yourself about what you stand for, what you believe in, and what you want to be remembered for. Write down a few qualities that come to mind that you hope others will use to describe you in the future.
3. Write a letter to your (present or future) child. Begin the letter as follows:

Dear ...,

These are the values I've stood for in my life. I understand that you will make your own decisions and I want you to know I'll support you in whatever you do. Whatever choices you make, I at least want you to know the values that have come before you and guided me in my relationships, career, and life...

4. Go down your list and, for each value, ask yourself the following questions:
   - What would I do if I were losing friends because of this value?
   - What would I do if this value was putting me at risk of losing my job?
   - What if I had to pass up a business opportunity to maintain this value?
   - What if potential mates were losing interest in me because of this value?
   - What if I was frequently laughed at because of this value?
5. If your answer to any of the above questions is to get rid of the value, get rid of it now. Cross it off your list. It's not a core value. A core value will stand the test of time regardless of what comes your way.
6. Which values are still standing? These are your core values. Integrate them into your Vision Statement. Create new entries or update old entries to reflect your core values.

PAINT YOUR NORTH STAR

It was one of those hot, humid summer days that make me wonder if I chose to live in Washington, D.C. as some masochistic form of self-punishment. I was exhausted after staying up late and sleeping only five hours. I crawled out of bed with a singularly focused thought: returning to it. As I stepped out of the sweltering Washington heat ninety minutes later and opened the glass doors to my office building—an entry point to the leadership work that is my passion—two thoughts crossed my mind: "Thank God I have air-conditioning. Thank God I have Vision."

Loving your job doesn't mean loving it every moment of every day. To paraphrase the words of American inventor Thomas Edison, success is 1 percent inspiration and 99 percent perspiration. Sometimes I review a presentation or edit a chapter for the umpteenth time and think, "This is definitely the perspiration."

Your purpose is the motor that propels you through the most mundane of tasks. It enables you to glide through even the trite and the trivial because you perceive these tasks as no more than steps on your path toward building a loving family, or re-engineering how companies do business, or making an impact in the lives of others, or providing the person you love with a stable, emotionally resilient partner who is considerate of her needs. However you want to live, write it down in your Vision Statement so you will have the patience to endure the "perspiration" that awaits you on your journey.

In addition to the questions you asked yourself in the eightieth birthday exercise above, here are some additional questions to help you develop your Vision Statement:

How can I best serve humanity? What is the *impact* I want to make in the lives of others?	How will I make time for myself to just *be* and continuously refine my Vision?
What do I want to do with my life?	What are my long-term goals?
Why am I here? What gives my life meaning?	What is my calling? How will I realize it?
What kind of people do I want to surround myself with?	What will it take for me to consider my life a success?

What philosophy do I want to have with respect to my health? My continuous education? My financial sustainability?	Who am I? What makes me special and unique? How will I develop those talents and qualities?
How can I increase the happiness of my family? My friends? My partner?	What values will govern how I act toward my family? My friends? My partner?
How can I improve the lives of those less privileged, or others in my community?	What is my philosophy toward work-life balance? How can I ensure that when I look back on my life, I will see not just a career, but a *life*?

Put pen to paper or fingers to keyboard and start writing your Vision Statement. You will launch yourself into a new world of *conscious living*. Design and periodically upgrade this document until it becomes your perpetual benchmark, code of ethics, moral guidelines, self-imposed parameters, and desired-future-dream all wrapped up into one. It's my experience that the most successful people paint a picture of their desired future and then allow this image—rather than temporary emotions such as anger, envy, or insecurity—to be the point of reference for their everyday decisions.

I know you can make your Vision concrete by writing it down on paper so it will always be there to guide you. While it's true that when you sketch out your desired code of conduct you will have to face all the times you come up short, it's also true that committing to a goal and then building your get-back-up-and-try-again-ability when you fall short of reaching it is the only way to move closer to the life you know, deep within your soul, is possible.

Create a compelling Vision Statement and you will see inner clarity replacing confusion, and a burning internal energy replacing weariness in your life. You will also experience an exhilarating feeling of inner peace and self-confidence in knowing that—no matter what happens in your life—you can always refer to this personal constitution in moments of uncertainty to determine what to do next. Please give this strategy a try. It's the clear and present starting point for bringing your life into alignment.

MAKE IT HAPPEN:

Now it's your turn. Pick a few sample questions from the eightieth birthday banquet exercise, the core values exercise, and the above table, and try to answer them. Use your responses to create your Vision Statement.

Don't worry if what you write down isn't exactly what you want to say—it's more important that you at least put *something* down on paper to get started, which you can of course amend or delete later on if you want. Just draw a bullet, write the word "To," and see what naturally follows. Alternatively, create your own unique format. Whatever model you select, write down a few entries to jump-start your Vision Statement so you can upgrade it as you continue reading this book.

You do have an alternative: this book can become yet another of the many theoretical exercises you may already engage in that leave you with more to think about yet no further along your path than when you began. There is no other moment in which you can get started except the present moment! No other moment exists! Right here and now, initiate this new tool for defining your most important life goals. You will launch yourself on a journey of continuous self-renewal that will last a lifetime.

Any act of creative genius begins with the door closed and ends with the door open. Whether you are an author, a clothing designer, or a software developer, you begin a new project by closing the door and connecting with your creative Vision or original intention for what you want to produce. Once you have this inner clarity, you open the door and solicit feedback from others. Based on your calm analysis of this feedback, you determine how to adapt your book, clothing line, or software—without giving up your core intention—into a language others will understand so they can integrate it into their lives.

Up until this point I have been guiding you on a journey into your Self—into how you want to *be*. You have been looking inwardly to "dis-cover" (remove the layers covering something to detect what's underneath) your core values and Vision. The door has been closed. You have been determining what you want to create in the absence of any competing influence from others. You've been calibrating your compass and setting your *direction*. It's almost time to go public.

But not so fast. Before you export your creation to the world by opening the door and learning how to *do*, you must first build your *foundation* so you have something to fall back on no matter how many hits you take out there in the real world. The core themes covered in Part Two—believing in yourself, making peace with disapproval, and discovering the roots of your passion—will help you strengthen your self-identity. They will become the launching pad from which you exercise the *skills* you will learn in Part Three to propel yourself repeatedly in the *direction* you determined in the previous chapters.

Part Two

The Foundation

CHAPTER 5

BELIEVE

Faith is to believe what you do not see.
The reward of this faith is to see what you believe.
—SAINT AUGUSTINE

I loved living in Oakland, California, because it's one of the most racially diverse cities in America. I once went to a church there to listen to Les Brown, an African-American author and motivational speaker. I was struck by his words—"If you argue for your limitations, you just might get to keep them"—and by a story he told about growing up in Miami that he later published in Jack Canfield and Mark Victor Hansen's Chicken Soup for the Soul series.

Les was classified in his public school as "Educable Mentally Retarded." He failed both fifth and eighth grade, and so was much older than the other kids in his class. In eleventh grade, he went into a friend's classroom and the teacher asked him to work out a problem on the board. He told the teacher he couldn't.

"Why not?" Mr. Washington asked.

"Because I'm Educable Mentally Retarded." Les answered.

Mr. Washington stepped out from behind his desk. "Don't ever say that again. Someone's opinion of you does not have to become your reality."

One day later that year, Les overheard Mr. Washington giving a speech to the graduating seniors, telling them: "You have greatness within you. You have something special. If just one of you can get a glimpse of a larger vision of yourself, of who you really are, of what it is you bring to the planet … then in a historical context, the world will never be the same again."

Afterward, Les approached Mr. Washington in the parking lot and told him he heard his speech.

"What were you doing in there?" Mr. Washington asked. "You are a junior."

"I know," Les replied. "But I heard your voice coming through the auditorium doors. That speech was for me, Sir. You said they had greatness within them. I was in that auditorium. Is there greatness within me, Sir?"

"Yes, Mr. Brown." Mr. Washington replied.

"But what about the fact that I failed English and math and history, and I'm going to have to go to summer school? What about that, Sir? I'm slower than most kids."

"It doesn't matter. It just means that you have to work harder. Your grades don't determine who you are or what you can produce in your life."

The teacher then turned to walk away.

"Mr. Washington?"

"What do you want now?"

"Uh, I'm the one, Sir. You remember me, remember my name. One day you're gonna hear it. I'm gonna make you proud. I'm the one, Sir."

Many years later, Les had some friends call Mr. Washington when one of five television specials he produced—*You Deserve*—appeared on the educational channel in Miami.

He received a call soon after at his home in Detroit.

"May I speak to Mr. Brown, please."

"Who's calling?"

"You know who's calling."

"Oh, Mr. Washington, it's you."

"You were the one, weren't you?"

"Yes, Sir, I was."

THE FOUNDATION OF EVERYTHING YOU WILL EVER ACCOMPLISH

Self-esteem is the core of everything. All else flows from it. Your belief in your own worth will attract all you need in your life: caring friends and family members, an intimate partner, investors for your business ideas, career opportunities beyond your wildest dreams, and much more. Your relationship with yourself is the basis for all your other relationships and everything you will ever accomplish in this world.

I would venture a guess that you choose to spend as little time as possible with people you don't enjoy being around. If you don't like Frank, you probably avoid spending time with him. Here's a sobering parallel truth: if you don't like yourself, you'll avoid spending time with yourself. Yet, as you learned in *Chapter 1—Dream*, you must be capable of comfortably spending time alone to create a life Vision. This leads us to a staggering conclusion: you must first love yourself if you wish to develop a Vision for your life.

Yet developing a Vision requires more than just love. It requires hope. Hope is the anticipation of a desired state—for your family, the environment, your intimate relationship, anything—that is different from what you are currently experiencing. To feel hope, you must believe in the capabilities of a person or group to bring that desired state into existence.

It's difficult to hope for peace when you don't believe in the ability of existing politicians to bring it about. Similarly, if you don't believe in your own capability to make things happen in your life, you won't want to waste your time hoping for futile dreams, and you won't develop a Vision. No matter what you aspire toward in your life, the foundation for accomplishing it is self-esteem.

TAKE A LEAP OF FAITH

A woman in her mid-fifties asked me at a recent conference, "How do you do it? How can you always stay so positive and encourage others to believe in their potential?"

I put my hand on my chin for a moment as I often do when pensive, and gazed at a painting on the other side of the room. Then I looked back at her and asked matter-of-factly: "What's the alternative?"

You tell me. What's the alternative to believing in your abilities to bring what you want into your life?

The American poet Henry Wadsworth Longfellow astutely observed, "Not in the clamor of the crowded streets ... but in ourselves, are triumph and defeat." The key phrase here is *in ourselves*. It implies that anything you want to achieve in your life must first be born within you. If you want to sustain a healthy and happy marriage, or patent an invention that revolutionizes a key function of everyday life, or build on your career success while still finding ample time to spend with your children before they leave for college, look within yourself first. See if the kernel of what you want to create—your unwavering belief that you *can*—is there.

No belief, no creation—it's that simple. Hoping for what you want in life without believing in yourself is like waiting at the airport for the arrival of a flight that never had enough fuel to depart. It's like checking your bank account for interest on money you never deposited.

Self-confidence is born from self-acceptance and breeds self-actualization. It manifests itself in your personal relationships, your success in your career, and everything else in between in every possible way. You design art because you love to create. But your paintings are an expression of your inner self-picture. You write because you love to write. But your characters reflect your self-image and the filters you've constructed over a lifetime to understand others. You sell clothing because you love the daily interaction. Yet the way you approach customers reflects your belief in the quality of the dresses, sweaters, and shoes you sell, which is an even deeper reflection of your belief in your good judgment in selecting the right styles from many alternatives to enrich their lives.

FAITH IS ITS OWN PROOF

Although the world's greatest scientists preside over a field predicated on empirical studies, facts, and evidence, most acknowledge the importance of faith. Albert Einstein himself sagely remarked, "I cannot prove scientifically that truth must be conceived as a truth that is valid independent of humanity; but I believe it firmly." When you know something to be true, you accept it independent of constantly changing events or circumstances. This is what we call faith.

You can't say, "I have faith in Apple as a company," and then sell all your Apple stocks when a competitor takes on the iPod and the price drops. You don't tell your daughter, "I have faith in your ability to be a good student," and then come down on her like a ton of bricks when she brings home a C on her report card. Neither can your self-faith hinge on what you do or don't achieve at any given time in your life.

Your self-confidence is the Number One most significant factor in your success, your inner contentment, and your ability to implement any of the strategies in this book. So take a leap of faith: believe in yourself. No one else can do it for you.

"But how can I believe in my capabilities when the evidence is stacked up to the contrary?" you may ask yourself in your weaker moments. Does this mean you'll gain self-faith when you have "the evidence" to back you up? Let's destroy a common myth right here and now: you will never *prove* to yourself that you're a good and worthy person. Instead, heed the words of the ancient stoic philosopher Epictetus: "Seek not good from without: seek it within yourselves, or you will never find it." When you try to prove your value, you focus on how *others* value you. Your focus is external; you seek good from without. You examine the outcomes in your life—how much money you earn, the approval you receive from others, the potential mates who desire you—and pin your self-assessment to whether they're up or down.

Consider what you are signing up for when your self-perception hinges on the taste others have for you. Ben & Jerry's New York Super Fudge Chunk and Häagen-Dazs Vanilla Swiss Almond—like other premium ice creams—are made from high-quality ingredients. Yet while some people love these flavors, others can't stand them. Unless you want to be the Flavor of the Month one day and yesterday's news the next, don't base your self-perception on how you taste to others. Instead, develop an appreciation for the high-quality ingredients that make you a unique, dynamic, and lovable human being.

As Saint Augustine instructs in the opening quote of this chapter, the only way to see what you desire in your life is to first believe in it. Are you willing to take the mental leap to self-faith, or will you continue to allow your thoughts to steer you away from what you've always longed for—despite its always being right in front of you? If you *think* you're hopeless as an athlete, your thoughts will only find evidence to support and entrench your hypothesis. Decide instead to have *faith* in your athletic ability and you will transform yourself into a more talented swimmer, runner, or tennis player.

The primary reason you can accomplish anything that's important to you is not your God-given talent, but your belief that you can. I've seen this happen over and over again with the individuals I've coached and known in my personal life: the person who wins is not the one with the most innate ability but the one who believes she will win. Once you learn how to access the power of faith, you will realize that you win or lose the most important battles of your life before you even arrive at the battlefield.

LOVE BEGINS AT HOME

Many people confuse their lack of self-confidence with a consideration for others. William, a health care professional in his early forties, practiced this act of self-deception every day. Here's how William would ask a woman out: "We could have dinner on Friday if you'd like. Of course, I realize you're busy. If you have too much to do, don't worry if you can't make it." Is William being considerate? Hardly. He's trying to reject himself in his own words before she rejects him in hers. Why is he trying to soften a blow that may never be inflicted? Because rejection is what he expects.

How would you react if William were asking you out? You would probably consider him either unconfident or uninterested, but not considerate.

"But I'm just trying to be thoughtful about the other demands on her time," William argued in one of our early sessions.

"Is it thoughtful to ask her to dedicate her valuable time to a cause you don't believe in?" I asked rhetorically.

Imagine a laundry detergent commercial with a woman holding a box of powder and saying, "I know you're busy, and you're probably doing just fine with the detergent you're already using, but if you have a moment and would like to try a new detergent, perhaps you could try this one." If the company doesn't *believe* in their detergent and consider it an excellent use of anyone's resources, no one else will either.

Ask yourself this simple question: "Can I expect other people to believe in something I don't believe in myself?" There's an even greater philosophical question: if you don't trust what you have to offer, wouldn't it be unkind to ask others to trust it? Wouldn't that be asking them to build their castles on shifting sand?

ARE YOU QUALIFIED TO SELECT THE WINNER?

I'm sure you've heard the old expression "To love others you must first love yourself." Why is this true? If you don't love yourself, how will you value the love you have to give? After all, it comes from a person you don't love, so what could it be worth? And why would you want to give away something you don't value? That would be like saying to a friend, "Hey, I really don't like this shirt. It's a miserable excuse for upper-body clothing. Here, you have it."

There is a corollary that strikes to the root of violence and conflict in our society: if you don't value yourself, neither will you value anyone else. How can something that's worthless determine the worth of something else? In what contest does a judge with no value select the winner? He wouldn't have the inner wherewithal to perform the task since he has no personal experience with finding value. The prerequisite for the job of valuing another person is to value yourself.

Self-love is the gateway to other-love because love is actualized in only one way—giving—and you can't give away something you don't have. If you want to give a box of chocolates to someone you admire, you first have to be the proud owner of a box of chocolates. If you don't have any chocolates, you're plumb out of luck—and so is she. If loving others, building relationships, creating a family, or any measure of personal or professional success is high on your list of priorities, you simply must learn how to love yourself. This is the most important ingredient for building the high-quality, premium foundation that is necessary to bring anything you desire into your life.

Unfortunately, there's another side of the lack-of-self-love equation: if you don't feel worthy of love, you question and devalue it when it's given to you. When someone offers you that same box of chocolates, you ask yourself, "Why is she being so kind to me? She must want something"—or, even worse, you question the gift itself. You say, "There must be something wrong with these chocolates. They must be spoiled or of poor quality. Surely if they were good chocolates she wouldn't be giving them to *me*."

When someone agrees to meet with you, the meeting becomes the box of chocolates. You say, "She must be meeting me out of obligation," or "She must be tired of working and need a break, and no one else is around." Because you don't value yourself, you assume there must be a *reason* she wants to spend time with you since, after all, Time with You is in the liability rather than asset column of her life.

Trust me on this one. I know because I've been there. I spent the first half of my life second-guessing others because I couldn't believe they actually enjoyed being around me. Why? Because I didn't enjoy being around myself. I couldn't detect on the outside what I wasn't familiar with on the inside—no matter what the evidence objectively stated. Just as you only hate in others what's already inside you, the same is true for love.

What about you? In the workplace, does your self-doubt lead you to distrust your instincts and let opportunities to speak up and suggest important changes pass you by? Do you refuse to allow your creativity, imagination, and brilliance to surface for others to experience because you don't believe in what you have inside? In your personal relationships, do you push others away by questioning their motives since, after all, they can't genuinely love or care about you? Until you accept love from yourself, you won't accept it from others.

The comedian Groucho Marx once said, "I would never join any club that would have me as a member." If you want to form a special society of people who truly love you and want to make you a priority in their lives, you have to become the first card-carrying member. Without self-love, hoping for other-love is fruitless. Why? Because the only way to lead is from the front, by example. Otherwise you're expecting others to do what you're unwilling to do yourself.

DOUBT YOUR DOUBTS

I couldn't hold down food, and had lost over thirty pounds. I kept asking myself, "What am I doing here in Africa?" My mind flashed back to when I was twenty and traveled alone outside the U.S. for the first time. I spent a week in a decrepit budget hotel room in Portugal with a stomach flu so incapacitating I couldn't even lean up in bed without running to the toilet. I stared at the ceiling hour after miserable hour, wondering if I had what it takes to travel on my own.

Shakespeare refers to doubts as "traitors." Worse still, they're traitors that regenerate themselves. Like the government agents in the film *Men in Black*, your doubts effortlessly replace each other, one after the other, until you realize that trying to conquer them is a worthless endeavor. Just as faith in yourself generates more faith, doubting yourself generates more doubt. First you question why you can't get a date. Within an hour you've painted an ominous picture of yourself growing old alone. You wonder why you didn't get the promotion. Before long you're imagining yourself being fired and fruitlessly pounding the pavement because there's no need for your skills anymore. This really happens! The traitors at work!

If you have dug yourself into a hole in any area of your life through overthinking, my advice is simple: stop digging. The next time a negative thought enters your mind, question your motives for entertaining it in the first place. Here's a simple strategy to ward off that destructive "It'll never work ..." chatterbox inside your brain: *instead of doubting yourself, doubt your doubts.*

When the doubt train is inching out of the station and about to gain velocity, shut it down immediately. Pull it aside and launch a doubt interrogation. When the thought "You're not good at that" pops into your mind, ask yourself, "Now why would I tell myself 'You're not good at that'? That's certainly not going to help me accomplish anything!" When the thought "I don't know how I'll do that" enters your mental space, follow it up with a more positive thought such as, "If I think I don't know how to do it I won't be able to do it. Instead, I'm going to have faith in my ability to learn how to do it along the way—and I'm going to do it!"

While it's true that every opportunity you create in your life begins with an inner belief in your ability, it's also true that every opportunity you destroy has its roots in your questioning this ability. U.S. New Deal president Franklin D. Roosevelt once said, "The only limits to our realization of tomorrow will be our doubts of today." The voice of self-doubt is like a stubborn and angry spouse, or a dog in your neighborhood that won't stop barking at you. Once it starts yapping, you'll never shut it up by trying to argue with it on its own terms (although this would be quite entertaining to watch). Negative thoughts, like positive beliefs, only verify and regenerate themselves. So instead of trying to argue with your doubts, switch tracks and bring positive thoughts about yourself into your mind. Like a barking dog not getting the attention it desires, your doubts will go away.

THINK FROM A POSITION OF STRENGTH

Have you ever stayed home from work because you felt sick, and then—as I did in Africa and Portugal—spent the day doubting yourself and your ability to achieve your most important goals? While the voice of self-doubt can thrive in any environment, illness amplifies it. In *Chapter 1—Dream,* I reminded you that your actions are usually rushing way ahead of your thoughts. Often when you get sick, your body has been telling you, "Slow down already!" for some time—but you haven't been listening. All of a sudden, you're bedridden and have the time to process the huge backlog of past actions you've been stockpiling like dirty clothes in your laundry hamper.

This natural human tendency to wait until you're run down and pulled off the field before you examine how you've been playing plain and simply doesn't work. Here's why: when you're sick, your internal weakness creates a mental filter of self-doubt rather than self-belief. You fall into the same trap many couples get stuck in: you don't analyze the relationship until there's a crisis. An argument starts, negative emotions of fear, anxiety, or insecurity quickly follow, and you decide that now is the right time to wash the dirty clothes. This is like marching into a battle with the wrong ammunition. The filter you're viewing the issues through is stained with doubt and negativity, so the clothes just get dirtier.

To understand how dysfunctional this pattern is, imagine you are walking alone in a beautiful valley for a week. You coast along, feel relaxed and happy, and don't take the time to contemplate its spectacular beauty. Then one afternoon you fall, break your leg, and lie on the grass motionless for hours in indescribable pain. You look around and the valley doesn't look so mesmerizing anymore. You search for the negative—the fallen trees, the withered grass, the decaying soil, the erosion, the mosquitoes biting your ankles—that reflects how you're feeling inside. You think, "I hate this awful valley. I hope I never see it again!" Yet it's the same valley you thought was so spectacular only hours earlier!

This is why I encourage couples to schedule a time to check in regularly and discuss the relationship when it's going well as opposed to when they've hit a rough spot. This replaces the normal reactive something-is-wrong-so-let's-roll-up-our-sleeves-and-fix-it process with "Let's have a regular talk so we can discuss issues from a positive viewpoint and improve them before they become larger and more difficult to manage."

I urge leaders to use the same process to proactively check in with their employees on their progress. This enables them to give their staff the necessary feedback while they still have a chance to incorporate it and be successful. The alternative form of management, which is unfortunately much more common, is to wait for a crisis to hit and then react with harsh words and pointing fingers. As in any other relationship, this yields resentment, stress, and anxiety.

You can use the same strategy in your relationship with yourself. Sit up at the wheel and think about your larger life issues regularly when you're feeling positive instead of dozing until the next speed bump wakes you up. Schedule a time to go for a walk in a nearby park and reflect on your life as an integral part of your weekly routine. Use this time to catch up with yourself, to process what's transpired, and to consider how you want to move forward. Detect the negative habits and routines steering your life in the wrong direction before they become even further entrenched through repetition.

Here's the crux of this principle and the only way to consistently construct a solid self-image: *meditate on your greater life questions (only) when you're feeling strong.* Do your most important thinking from a position of strength. Make your inner voice so supportive and reassuring when times are good that your doubts are unable to hijack it when the tough moments arrive.

QUESTION YOUR ACTIONS ALWAYS, YOUR ABILITY NEVER

The month in India before my first international leadership conference for two hundred Indian executives was a difficult one. My voice of self-doubt was having a field day: "Who are you to be doing a leadership conference in India? You're not Indian … India has an intense culture of philosophical debate (in part because Hinduism, while classified as one religion, is in practice a complex assortment of gurus and spiritual philosophies) and has more intellectual capital than just about anywhere else in the world. How will you keep this conference from getting out of control? ... Most of the executives will be much older than you. What if they don't respect you? …"

While doubting your ability—to achieve your life goals, to love, to be a good person, to make a difference in the world—will never help you in any way, questioning the merit of your past actions or views (and those of others) is crucial to your self-construction. Why? You build faith in your own judgment in the process. As the Irish playwright George Bernard Shaw insightfully declared, "Skepticism is the beginning of faith."

Was it a good idea, then, for me to feel nervous and question my approach to teaching leadership before stepping up in front of all those

Indian executives for three days in New Delhi's most lavish hotel? Absolutely. The scrutiny I placed on *how* I taught leadership helped me improve my teaching techniques and deliver my best conference ever, with 97 percent of the executives saying they would recommend it to a friend. It's commonly understood among actors that some nervousness keeps you on edge and enables your best performances. Questioning *if* I was a good leadership coach, however, did not help in any way—and I had to root it out.

Self-belief is not something you agree to uphold as long as the evidence supports it. If you look hard enough, you'll find evidence both for and against any hypothesis you create about yourself—from "Am I intelligent enough to do this?" to "Do I have what it takes to be a good partner?" Questioning your intelligence will not help you. Considering *how* you approach your research or present your ideas will. Questioning whether you are a good partner will propel you into a downward spiral of self-doubt. Reflecting on *how* you communicate and give to your partner will help you become more loving and caring. In sum: question your strategies always, your ability never.

The difference between evaluating your ability and your past actions is analogous to the difference between a healthy, sustainable marriage and a dysfunctional one. Healthy couples speak with openness, authenticity, and kindness about the *actions* the other commits that they like or don't like. At the same time, they avoid like the plague any assassinations of each other's *character*. Couples who do the opposite don't make it very far.

Which comment would you respond to more positively, and which would make you more defensive and angry: "It means a lot to me when you remember to take out the trash," or "You always forget to take out the trash. It's so self-centered of you."? Can you imagine someone constantly speaking to you with the voice behind this second comment? Do you feel grateful you don't have a negative person in your life squashing the motivation out of you with this voice?

Then don't become that person. When thoughts such as "I'm not a good person" or "If I were better-looking, he would have asked me out" or "If I were smarter, I would have done better in that class" attempt to enter your consciousness, note that the Caller ID says "Negative Thought That Won't Get You Anywhere" and turn your attention elsewhere instead of picking up the phone! The construction of self-faith is a deliberate, everyday process that begins with the thoughts you allow into your consciousness.

REBUILD YOUR INTERNAL VOICE

American Civil War president Abraham Lincoln perceptively observed, "It is difficult to make a man miserable while he feels worthy of himself." No one can force you to believe even one thing about yourself without your consent. Not a single person has the power to open up your brain, climb in, and determine how you perceive yourself.

Protect this inalienable right. Be careful about the voices you allow into your head because you just might believe them. Especially your own. Once you become aware of your internal voice, you can make the decision to replace it with a stronger, more supportive voice. You can reclaim the nurturing voice you used to have before you allowed others to corrupt it.

Have you ever noticed how small children have a searing honesty and tell it just like it is? To keep them under control—which, depending on how you look at it, can be called either discipline or the desire of adults to hold on to power and order their environment to their liking—their parents or other adults often crush any semblance of self-belief and self-actualization out of them.

Like the unhealthy partner upset about the trash, your parents or other authority figures may have gone straight for the throat and repeatedly attacked your character instead of your past actions—over and over again until the desired subservience took root in you. Instead of "Why don't you let your brother play with the fire engine?" they may have said, "Stop being so selfish and let your brother play with the fire engine." Rather than imparting a life lesson such as "It's not good to throw your food on the floor," they may have insensitively trespassed into your self-domain by saying, "Good girls don't throw their food on the floor." The conclusions of your innocent, emerging mind were "I'm selfish," or "I'm not a good girl."

These long-forgotten early episodes mark the genesis of both the downward spiral your self-esteem has very likely been traveling on for decades and the negative emotions such as guilt, remorse, self-doubt, and worry that may have become so common in your life. While this destructive virus may have already infected many of the best years of your life, you can prevent it from doing any more damage. Ask yourself one simple question: "If someone gives me a gift and I no longer want it, why do I have to keep it?"

It is within your power to return this gift and reclaim your belief in the inherent beauty you were born with. You can transform your internal voice and reinstill your self-love by saying, "I'm not going to spend my inheritance for one more day. I hereby make a commitment to take the leap from doubt to faith, and to becoming unwaveringly supportive of my ability to accomplish anything I set my mind to."

To get started, stop being your own greatest critic. Instead, become your greatest fan. Write down positive affirmations like the one above and repeat them to yourself every day until you finally get the point: you are a good person who is worthy of love, and your love begins with yourself.

LOVE YOURSELF NOT FOR WHAT YOU DO, BUT FOR WHO YOU ARE

Actress Lucille Ball shared these sage words with her fans: "I have an everyday religion that works for me. Love yourself first and everything else falls into line. You really have to love yourself to get anything done in this world." Do you love yourself first, or is that something you're planning to get to later? As the *I Love Lucy* star suggests, you can't skip this mandatory step if accomplishing anything of merit is high on your list of life priorities.

I'm not just stressing the importance of believing in yourself because it's the foundation of everything. There's another reason ... it's true! You are a unique, beautiful human being with a tremendous amount to contribute to this world. If you don't discover the greatness within you and then develop it with everything you have, you'll leave enormous potential on the table. It is your discovery of this uniqueness and your willingness to share it with others that will make everything you say and do sincere and compelling. Besides, if you don't believe in yourself, who will? It's not a task you can outsource. Like eating, sleeping, breathing, or any other natural human function required for your survival, self-love must come from, for, and by yourself.

I'm not asking you to have conditional self-faith, to say "I believe in myself as long as I'm happy with what I do." I'm urging you to take the leap to *unconditional* self-faith—to say, "I believe in myself *no matter what I do.*" You are a wonderful human *being* who deserves your love because of who you *are*, not a "human doing" who only deserves love if you *do* something well.

This doesn't mean what you do doesn't matter. Actually, it's the opposite. Self-belief doesn't obstruct self-improvement but encourages it. Why? First, because your self-opinion isn't linked to your actions, you can improve them in the same disinterested way you would repair a lawn mower, a flat tire, or anything else you do not identify with your pristine, inviolable Self. Second, your belief in yourself transmutes into a belief in others, leaving you with no choice but to work for their well-being. This belief compels you to say, "I have something special and unrivaled to contribute to this world. And my fellow citizens—especially those living in material or psychological poverty—need me to do exactly that. There is too much for me to do to spend my time languishing in self-doubt. I will find my purpose and not waste another day!"

Having faith in your Self is like having faith in God: you'll never *think* your way into it. Just *believe*. Like your faith in a higher power, your faith in a higher Self that will make sound decisions and guide you through whatever comes your way *is* its own proof. Illogical? Exactly.

THE LOWEST BAR FOR YOUR INTERNAL DIALOGUE

Earlier in this chapter I shared the common saying, "You have to love yourself to be able to love others." Here's another that's much less common: "You have to love others to be able to love yourself." This is the path I walked personally to discover self-love. It wasn't until I devoted myself to helping rural African communities obtain resources for their schools that I realized I had something of value to give to others. That same love, since it now had value, became worth giving to myself. One of love's most magical qualities is that once it's created, it can move in any direction.

Understanding how you love others takes on a whole new importance when you recognize it as one of the fastest routes to self-love. Let's make this concept concrete. Bring a person whom you love unconditionally into your mind. Visualize your child, brother or sister, mother or father, partner, or best friend. Now ask yourself two questions: "Does my love for this person depend on their performance or behavior?" and "Do I love them only when they act in ways I approve of?" Alternatively, do you love them always, no matter how they act? I suspect you do. Then know this to be true: to live a full and happy life, *the same must be true for your love for yourself.*

Other-love is the gateway to self-love. Why? Because *the unconditional love you give to the (other) person you care about the most in the world must be the lowest bar for the unconditional love you give to yourself.* Just as your love for her or him doesn't change based on what they *do,* neither should your love for yourself be contingent on what *you* do. At any rate, how can you be so tolerant and understanding toward another person—the basis of love—but not toward the person you'll spend more hours with than anyone else in your life: yourself?

You can't. If you throw your self-love out the window whenever you say something that you later regret, or invest in the market at the wrong time, or embarrass yourself in front of your colleagues, or in any other way don't do what with perfect hindsight you wish you had, you won't be able to maintain the internal capacity to love anyone else. You don't discard your love for your closest friends or family members when they embarrass you, or fail to acknowledge your feelings, or leave you waiting for them in public, or in any other way don't live up to your expectations. You may tell them how you feel about their *actions,* but you don't abandon your *love* for them. So why not apply this same unflinching loyalty to yourself, and leave your self-love intact when *you* don't live up to your expectations?

BE AN ALL-WEATHER FRIEND TO YOURSELF

A cartoon shows a man with low self-esteem opening his diary and writing, "Dear Diary. Sorry to bother you again …" We've all had our moments when our confidence is low and we feel like no one—starting with ourselves—truly wants to listen. Unfortunately, these moments define us. Your internal voice, like your faith, self-confidence, and strength, is not defined when times are good. It's defined when times are hard, when you feel doubt.

You don't know how strong a dam is unless there's water trying to push it over. Eighty to 90 percent of the time, you may feel good about yourself. Yet it's not these moments that test your self-faith—it's the remaining 10 to 20 percent. Make a commitment right here and now to love yourself completely—rain or shine, no conditions attached.

Author Alice Walker offers these prescient words in a recent book: "We are the ones we've been waiting for." The moment you fully accept the truth of the statements "No one else will save me" and "My happiness will never come from another person" is the moment you open your hand and the key to your prison cell materializes. In this moment, you become free. In this moment, you realize you must put a stop to being a fair-weather friend to yourself and become an all-weather friend. In this moment, you learn one of life's most difficult lessons: there is no other person who will ultimately protect you, so you better start doing your job.

Bring the image of a person with unconditional self-love into your mind. Does her self-opinion plummet when she doesn't achieve a desired goal? By no means. Does she act stable one day and then go off the deep end the next because something doesn't go her way? Not at all. Does she shrink into a corner when someone doesn't reciprocate her affection, or does she say, "It looks like he's not interested. At least I shared my authentic feelings. It's time to move on"? She maintains her poise and self-confidence even amid difficult circumstances because she does not identify her Self with her daily tally sheet of losses and victories.

While others spend every waking moment filtering through their daily happenings and saying, "This was good for me" or "That was bad for me," the person with self-faith transcends such obsessive, transactional thoughts. While others are busy keeping score, they've burned the scoreboard. They have replaced thoughts of "Good for me" and "Bad for me" with *Love for me*.

I know you can leave the years of self-doubt behind and take the leap to self-faith. This is the most important decision I'm asking you to make in this book. I promise it's worth your time and effort to become a leading patriot in the nation of self-faith. Here are some of the rules: first and foremost, protect your sovereignty. Provide passports and renew visas only for friends and family members who also believe in you. Whenever you're faced with military strikes, cultural imperialism, or political manipulation from other nations, defend your nation from harm. Finally, get down to the hard work of building your nation's culture, which, as you'll learn in the next chapter, is only possible when you stop worrying about what other cultures think of you.

Your self-faith will make your every moment on this earth livable and, most of the time, enjoyable. If inner peace is high on your list of desirable qualities, simply make a commitment to maintaining an unshakable belief in yourself. Let go of that faith for a moment and your natural state of contentment will dissipate. So regardless of what anyone has ever told you, of what you have ever told yourself, of whatever you have done that you wish you hadn't or didn't do but wish you had, make the decision today to convert to the new faith of believing in yourself. It's the necessary foundation you can't do without if you want to bring unlimited success and happiness into your life.

Chapter 6

Make Peace with Disapproval

Fans don't boo nobodies.
—*Reggie Jackson*

Some people have glowing memories of their junior high school years. Not me. Getting robbed on my way to school. An older kid forcing me to put my nose in raw egg on the ground. Spending months working up the nerve to ask a girl out and her responding with the same gesture she might have shown to a fly landing on her cafeteria lunch plate. Not my most glorious years.

I used to wear a pin with a picture of the rock group The Police on my shirt. One day another student in my gym class asked me, "Do you like The Police?"

"Yes, they're one of my favorite bands," I replied.

"I don't think they're very good," he countered.

"Some of their songs are OK," I muttered. My self-esteem was so low I couldn't even stand behind my own views.

Here's the irony of approval: *the less you seek it from others, the more you receive*. Conversely, the more you focus on winning the approval of others instead of just striving to be strong, centered, and directed, the less it naturally flows in your direction. People are drawn to (and give their approval to) those who are stable and authentic—people who don't seek reinforcement of their self-view from others.

TAKE BACK THE BALL

An inability to draw your approval from within will spill into every area of your life and pull you away from your purpose. I once worked with a man in his late thirties who fit the classic define-from-outside mentality. David was a senior partner in an architectural firm who worked sixty to eighty hours a week and had virtually no personal life. For David, working and interacting with many people was an escape from confronting intimacy with one person. Every time he started dating a woman he tried so hard to be what he thought she was looking for that he lost track of himself. David had serious commitment issues because he did not know how to be connected with another human being without losing his sense of Self.

When David wasn't dating anyone, his need for approval took other forms. "When a beautiful woman walks by me," David shared, "and I look at her and she doesn't look back, my self-esteem tanks. It's like she literally walked away with it by ignoring me."

I used a visual image to help David rid himself of his approval dependence. "I want you to visualize a glowing ball. Every time you pass a woman and desire her approval, imagine she is carrying the ball. Literally imagine this ball glowing in the hands of each person whose approval you need to feel good about yourself."

"There are a lot of people who have that ball." David said, grimacing.

"Each of those people can manipulate and control you when they have the ball. This ball is bouncing all around you, all the time. It dictates your every move because you need it to survive."

"So how do I stop them from controlling me?" David asked.

"To become a whole person, you must put the ball back where it belongs: within you."

Who are the people in your life who carry the ball? When your confidence at work hinges on your boss liking a report you've submitted, he has the ball. When you do not feel comfortable unless your father is on board with your career plans, the ball is in his possession. When you're upset because your viewers or readers or fans or students or teachers or coaches or employees or managers or business partners or clients don't rate you more highly, you are trying to make all the glowing balls that surround you shine favorably in your direction. Wouldn't your life be so much easier, happier, and more carefree if instead of trying to perform this impossible juggling act, you could just light up the ball inside you and make it glow?

The father of Andrea, a blind man from a small town in Tuscany, Italy, had the ball. Andrea's father wanted him to become a lawyer. So he did. After finishing law school and practicing law, Andrea said to his father, "My passion is singing. I've done law as you asked. Can I practice my passion now?" Perhaps you've heard of him—his last name is Bocelli. He has one of the most beautiful voices you'll ever hear.

Getting the ball back is not optional. Until it's once again located within you, you will desire a relationship but not be prepared for it. The other person will manipulate and control you—not because that's their intention, but because you instruct them to do so every day by giving them the ball. They have the very human desire to order their life by keeping their fears and insecurities in check. They will try to mold you accordingly to fit their mental image of what they need unless you show them you will not be molded. If you pass them the ball, the relationship will not be sustainable because you will grow to resent their control. Neither they nor you want that. It is in the best interest of both of you, then, to keep the ball out of play.

THE SEARCH FOR APPROVAL

Abraham Lincoln is highly regarded by many as the president with the most integrity in U.S. history. He was known to write angry letters and never send them, and to gently reprimand his generals without losing their loyalty during the Civil War. When "Honest Abe" was once asked his opinion of a book, he replied, "People who like this sort of thing will find this the sort of thing they like." Wake up to this stark reality: the people who like you like you because you're the sort of thing they like, and the people who don't like you don't like you because you're not the sort of thing they like. If you change yourself to fit their preferences, while you will have a shot—but no guarantee—at becoming the sort of thing they like, you'll unquestionably lose your status as the sort of thing *you* like.

Imagine you pass someone on the street selling a new potion to double your workload and achieve lesser results. Would you buy it? Of course not! But this is exactly what you're signing up for when you waste your valuable psychological and emotional resources seeking approval. When you seek approval, *you think about what others think about what you think*. That's a lot of thinking! Wouldn't simply focusing on your own thoughts be easier? Doing the hard work of understanding how you think is already a full-time job. If you want to streamline your mental workload rather than work double shifts, let others be entitled to their thoughts while you concentrate on your own.

I would be a hypocrite to tell you I don't enjoy it when others approve of what I do. It's OK to enjoy approval from others in the same way you enjoy an ice cream cone. But if you need to eat ice cream to feel comfortable or happy, you'll stop enjoying it the moment you become conscious of your dependence. Attending to a cone of mint chip or raspberry vanilla will become a functional task you need to carry out to feel whole—like brushing your teeth or reporting for work. Just like ice cream, approval only becomes a problem when you transform it from a *want* into a *need*.

Shakespeare once wrote: "He who commends me to mine own content, commends me to the thing I cannot get." Other people can give you money, records, fishing poles, iguanas, old roller skates, and new shoes—but they can't give you inner contentedness. If you can't get your approval from inside, neither will you get it from outside—this I promise you. And the more energy you futilely expend trying to sway the opinions of others, the less remains to define your own.

THE ONLY PATH TO LONG-TERM APPROVAL: YOUR OWN

Although his father wanted him to be a farmer, a seventeen-year-old from Michigan dropped out of school to follow his passion for mechanics. In his own words, his family had "all but given [him] up for lost." In 1899, his employer offered him a promotion on the condition he give up his private obsession with designing a gasoline engine that would inexpensively transport people. He refused, and quit his job.

Once he made some headway with his invention, he became the object of much derision for trying to "democratize" the automobile by producing one at a price the "common man" could afford. Thanks, Henry! The founder of the Ford Motor Company went on to become that rare person to mass-produce his own invention. By the time the Model T gave way to the Model A in 1927, the pioneer of modern assembly-line production had sold fifteen million worldwide.

Concentrate your mind on a situation where you may incur some disapproval, such as drawing attention to a dysfunctional process at the office, or defending a friend who is unpopular but whom you believe in, or taking up a new hobby you don't have any experience in such as playing the guitar or writing poetry. Then ask yourself, "Am I avoiding this situation because I'm afraid of being judged, or of my views not being accepted, or of losing the popularity I've worked so hard to attain?"

When you change the way you act to win someone's approval, you ironically incur more of their disapproval in the long run. Here's why: let's say the person whose approval you seek (e.g., your parent) tells you they think you should go left, yet deep in your gut you know you should go right. If you go left and fail because you should have gone right, make no mistake—*they'll blame you*. And you will fail if you go left because you won't be acting with the conviction necessary to sustain your interest and motivation.

Securing approval from within means not waiting to see what others think before sharing your opinion. It means making decisions about your career trajectory based on what you *feel* you *want* to do as opposed to what you *think* you *should* do. It means recognizing that when you say, "I should do this," it usually translates as, "Other people think I should do this."

The paradox of disapproval is that the more you make peace with it, the less it shows up on your doorstep. When you don't pay attention to disapproval and instead just focus on moving in the direction you instinctually feel is right, you become successful on your own terms—the only way to gain approval in the long run. This leads us to a counterintuitive point about approval: *To maximize the overall approval you will receive in your lifetime, you sometimes have to go against the opinions of the very same people whose approval you seek.* The fact is, most people have better things to do with their time than send disapproval messages to those who are confident and refuse to tune in to their frequency.

I know I'm asking you to rise to a daunting challenge that will cause you discomfort. Let's face it: receiving disapproval isn't a lot of fun. Julie Andrews didn't include disapproval on her list of favorite things as she sang and danced in the Austrian mountains in *The Sound of Music*. It's not at the top of my list of favorite things either. But what's more important: having fun or walking proudly toward compelling goals that will motivate you for a lifetime?

MAKE IT HAPPEN:

What does "going left" (what *you think others think* you should do) mean in your life? What constitutes "going right" (what *you feel you want* to do)? Does "going left" mean going to a top-name college that doesn't have a program that interests you, or going out with someone who is intellectually and physically impressive but who excites you almost as much as cold soup in winter?

In the table below, first write down what you feel compelled to do to please others under "Going Left." Then write what you *really* want to do under "Going Right." (Add additional sentences on a separate sheet of paper if you need more space.) Consider the directions these two conflicting feelings are pulling you in with respect to the various areas of your life.

"Going Left" (Approval) *What* you think others think *you should do*	**"Going Right" (Conviction)** *What* you feel you want *to do*
Career:	Career:
Intimate Relationship/ Dating:	Intimate Relationship/ Dating:
Family:	Family:
Friendships:	Friendships:
Hobbies/ Personal Time:	Hobbies/ Personal Time:

IF YOU DON'T ACCEPT IT, DISAPPROVAL STILL BELONGS TO THE OTHER PERSON

An unknown writer from Louisiana unsuccessfully looked for a publisher for his book for over eight years. Simon & Schuster commented that John Kennedy Toole's book "isn't really about anything." At age thirty-one, Toole gave up, and committed suicide. His mother spent another five years searching for a publisher with no luck. After she accosted him repeatedly in his office without an appointment, a literature professor at Loyola University in New Orleans, where the novel is set, finally took some interest in the manuscript and helped her publish it. Within a year of publication, *A Confederacy of Dunces* became the first book ever published by a university press to win the Pulitzer Prize. In my opinion, it still stands as the funniest book ever written.

Here is a new definition of disapproval: *an emotional transfer from a stronger human being to a weaker one.* Like any gift anyone wants to give you, disapproval only becomes yours if you accept it. If you bring it into your possession, you allow the strength of its supplier to overpower you and reduce your self-esteem. Yet all you have to do is say "Thanks but no thanks," and the disapproval still belongs to them!

Consider a situation where someone is offering you their gift of disapproval, such as when your boss says you need to work on your writing style, or your partner says they don't like what you're wearing, or your mother says your hair looks thinner. Now consider your internal strength and God-given right to accept or deny anything that's offered you.

This is not to say you shouldn't take other people's opinions to heart: they can provide a valuable source of feedback to help you determine how to improve your writing, or dress to impress, or do anything even better—and it can always be done better—the next time around. But the moment it goes beyond constructive feedback and trespasses into the realm of disapproval—and it's *you* who allow it to cross this frontier and call into question your goals, integrity, and self-respect—it paralyzes you and ceases to be an asset to your growth. Most of the time, the criticism you receive says much more about the need of the person supplying it to be critical than it does about you. Keep in mind: their habitual patterns that make them critical toward you also make them very self-critical.

In his wonderful novel about self-discovery, *Demian*, German author Hermann Hesse writes, "If you hate a person, you hate something in him that is part of yourself. What isn't part of ourselves doesn't disturb us." Think about it: Do you see "For Rent" signs when you walk around your neighborhood? Only if you're looking for an apartment. Do you notice how many Volkswagens are on the road? Yes, if you're in the market to buy one.

A few years ago, I contracted a roofer who showed me a page of sample shingles and asked me to pick the color I wanted for my roof. The next day, I walked around my neighborhood and was surprised to discover the shingles on my neighbors' roofs were all different! I had never even noticed them before. Do you even know what color the shingles are on your own roof?

You only see in the world what's already inside you. The same is true for every other person you know, and this is why fretting over disapproval is not worth your time. Where every single person you associate with stands on how you should live your life depends on where they sit. When you don't get the job, or your call isn't returned, or you get stood up on a date, it means the other person has projected their cumulative life baggage onto you and you haven't passed their subjectively designed test. You remind them too much of their older brother who stole all the attention, or their ex-girlfriend who was too needy or not needy enough, or their teacher who never called on them, or the kid down the street who always made them the butt of their jokes. Approval is not a reflection of you, but of how others project themselves onto you.

WHY ARE THEY GIVING YOU THEIR APPROVAL?

In the ancient Sanskrit text the Kama Sutra, if a man gives a prostitute less or more money than usual, it means he probably won't return. If he pays less, he may be dissatisfied with the services provided. If he pays more, he may either feel guilty that he won't be coming back or pity the prostitute's life situation. Not that I want you to compare yourself to a fourth-century Indian prostitute, but try asking yourself *why* someone is giving you more or less than usual before taking it personally.

Up until now we've been presuming that others act as if they like or don't like you without any ulterior motives. Not always the case. There are two kinds of approval or disapproval: *genuine* and *manipulative*. Genuine approval roughly translates as: "You performed an action the way I would have if I were you" or "Your actions are aligned with my Vision for how you should act." Genuine disapproval means: "You performed an action differently than I would have if I were you" or "Your actions are *not* aligned with my Vision for how you should act." If someone genuinely disapproves of you, there's a mismatch between your actions and their values. So what! Diversity is what makes life interesting. If we all thought the same way, there would be no reason to go outside!

Each of us has our own definition of success. Winning someone's approval simply means your actions fit with how *they* define success—based on what *they* value. Yet what they value may be completely unrelated to who you are or want to become! The first African-American to win the Best Actor Oscar (but not the first to deserve it), Denzel Washington, incisively remarked: "My mother used to tell me man gives the award, God gives the reward. I don't need another plaque." Instead of trying to win the award, question why you're in the contest in the first place.

Although it can steer you away from your goals, at least genuine approval or disapproval is genuine. It's the other person's true opinion, agree with it or not. When others direct *manipulative* approval or disapproval toward you, on the other hand, it has nothing whatsoever to do with whether they agree or disagree with how you're acting. Far from it. They are handing out approval, withholding approval, or expressing disapproval for only one reason: to control your future behavior.

You receive manipulative approval or disapproval every day without even noticing it. If your boss tells you that you're doing a good job, he may either fear you're considering moving to another firm or believe it's an effective way to motivate you to work harder. If a friend tells you that you're looking overweight, it may not be because she believes it to be true, but because she feels threatened by how confident you've been acting lately. She may prefer you to be weaker to ensure you won't go anywhere regardless of how she treats you. If your mother takes issue with how you're going about your search for a new apartment, it may have nothing to do with the apartment and everything to do with the anxiety she feels about losing her influence in your life now that you've moved to a new city.

Look beyond why someone is lauding or criticizing your actions to their inner motivations and you will realize that—just like every other human being on this planet, including yourself—they have a unique history that influences their agenda. This can be a particularly difficult task, especially when they are your own parents. You may feel more comfortable placing them beyond scrutiny. If you shoot holes in your security blanket, after all, it will no longer keep you warm.

DISAPPROVAL IS THE PRICE YOU PAY FOR LIVING

I had become redundant. After six months of teaching five classes per day, my course load dropped to two classes. There were enough trained Kenyan teachers, and I couldn't figure out why the Peace Corps had placed me in this rural high school three hours from Mombasa. I decided to look for other ways to be useful. A local educator, Barnabas Mwakisha, took me to visit some of the local primary schools and my life was changed forever. I had never seen children endure such severe hardship to struggle for their education. They sat on the ground with welts in their legs from insects because there were no desks. The only textbook in most classes was the copy the teacher had bought with their own savings. Two classes of sixty students each shared the same small classroom divided by a bamboo partition. Each teacher frequently shouted at their counterpart, "You're teaching too loud. My students can't hear me."

I left my school to launch a matching-funds project where Kenyan families raised 50 percent of the resources for a school development project that they designed themselves for the benefit of their children, money that was matched with donations I raised from American families. Some communities contributed their hard-earned resources for textbooks, other communities selected desks, others a new classroom.

This new project model—other development projects in the region were almost entirely funded by foreign aid organizations with zero or very little contribution from the community—took off like wildfire because each rural school community took ownership over *its* project. Parents contributed their own limited resources and held community auctions where they sold vegetables and livestock from their farms to raise the local contribution. Instead of being treated like passive recipients, the parents became participants in the development of their own schools. The project also appealed to donors—both because of the local sustainability model and because their funds doubled after being matched by community-raised funds.

Instead of support, I received resentment from the other Peace Corps teachers. The headmasters of their schools, who had consistently ignored their requests for school materials, saw the results of our efforts and wanted to enroll their schools in the project. Some of the Peace Corps volunteers made comments such as, "He's trying to be a super-volunteer," and "He thinks he's Mr. Kenya." One Sunday I was walking in the hills with Juma, a friend from the Luhya tribe, and I told him how it hurt to see some of the people from my own culture directing so much anger toward me. Juma shared some words I have never forgotten: "When I was growing up, my father once told me *An upright person is always surrounded by critics.* You are doing what you believe in, Bwana Tony, that is the most important thing."

Mwakisha and I went on to complete the matching-funds education project in fifty-eight rural schools over the next two years, raising sixty thousand dollars from Kenyan families and sixty thousand dollars from American families. I stayed in touch with Mwakisha while in graduate school, and within three weeks of graduation I returned to Kenya. We launched a nonprofit organization together dedicated to providing rural schools with basic educational resources using the cost-sharing partnership model. Over the next eight years I raised over twelve million dollars and expanded the model to include business and job skills training for low-income youth in Oakland, California, Washington, D.C., Kenya, Tanzania, Guatemala, and Indonesia.

Did I please everyone along the way? Of course not. Neither will you if your goal is not to placate, but to create. Making peace with disapproval is the litmus test of your self-reliance. Not self-reliance in the sense of "I will do whatever I please, no matter how it affects others." Self-reliance meaning "I will live by my conscience and values, not to win the approval of others. When others disagree with my actions, I will take their opinions into account when there is something to learn from them. I do not wish to harm others or disturb them. Yet there are times when to live by my values others will be disturbed, and I will pay that price when necessary."

PUSH THE SEAM OF SOCIETY AND SOCIETY WILL PUSH BACK

Cassius Clay disturbed many people when he became a conscientious objector and refused to honor his draft notice to fight in Vietnam. They were disturbed even more when he joined the Nation of Islam and changed his name to Muhammad Ali. How did he handle all their disapproval? The greatest prizefighter of all time wasn't only strong in the ring:

> I am America. I am the part you won't recognize. But get used to me. Black, confident, cocky; my name, not yours; my religion, not yours; my goals, my own; get used to me.

Can you also "float like a butterfly, sting like a bee" and boldly stand up for what you believe in regardless of how others perceive you?

If you want to live a complete life, expect to disturb others who do not agree with your goals or the strategies you practice to achieve them. Your parents will be disturbed when you go against their wishes in choosing your career. Your teachers will be disturbed when you disagree with their views. People who hold on tightly to their power will be disturbed when you take up causes that diminish unfair treatment of workers, immigrants, people of color, or women. They will consider your agenda a threat to their well-being. Are you willing to disturb them?

Any new idea you come up with by definition hasn't been thought of before. If it has, it's not your idea. To be unique, therefore, you have to threaten the established order. Do you expect to accomplish this without receiving any disapproval? Do you expect everyone around you to say, "Hey, you're changing what I've held to be true all my life. That's great! You are so smart! Thank you for showing me how wrong I've been all these years!"

Although his brother owned an art gallery in Amsterdam and displayed his work, Vincent van Gogh did not sell one painting during his entire life. Yet he has added inexpressible beauty to the lives of millions of people. Most people who think ahead of their time will be misunderstood, laughed at, and ridiculed. Yet they will be remembered while most are forgotten. They will live on not in awards or speeches, but when their once-dismissed ideas are regarded as truth and become the springboard for society's evolution. All progress in our society, in fact, depends on those who innovate by questioning the status quo. They push the seam of society because society in its current state does not contain what their values guide them to create. And they are not deterred when society pushes back.

Guglielmo Marconi is testimony to Emerson's prescient words, "Genius always finds itself a century too early." The Italian inventor was taken to a mental hospital for believing he could "send messages through the air." After he was discharged, he invented the radio. To get an idea of how innovative Marconi's invention was at the end of the nineteenth century, consider how Einstein helped people to understand it: "You see, wire telegraph is a kind of very, very long cat. You pull his tail in New York and his head is meowing in Los Angeles ... Radio operates exactly the same way: you send signals here, they receive them there. The only difference is that there is no cat."

Are you willing to believe in something and stick with it even if others laugh at you or you don't get immediate results? If you are unwilling to risk others taking issue with what you say or do, save yourself some time and take self-fulfillment and making a breakthrough off your list of potential results you will experience in this lifetime. If, on the other hand, your goal is to live a happy, purposeful, angst-free life, my advice to you is simple: focus on the actions you take, not on how others take your actions.

THE VENOMOUS EFFECTS OF APPROVAL

When he was fourteen years old, Paul Hewson's mother died of a brain hemorrhage at his grandfather's funeral. Paul spent much of his teenage years feeling rebellious and confused, with an overwhelming feeling of regret that he had never expressed his true feelings to his mother. According to Paul, "My mother's death just threw petrol on the fire … I felt hopeless. I thought about suicide."

Paul channeled his grief into playing the piano. Meanwhile, his father repeatedly told him it was not worth having dreams because he would never achieve them. Then one day Paul returned home and the piano was gone. His father had sold it. In Paul's words:

> If you were a kid like me, that is like somebody taking away your oxygen tank. You can't breathe. … I think the seeds of ambition were sown, paradoxically by this repression of the spirit. … I was going to have my revenge on the world. Everyone was going to have to listen to me!

He wanted others to listen so badly that he took up singing—loudly. So loudly, in fact, that one of his teenage friends claimed he was singing for the deaf. His friend nicknamed him after a hearing aid shop they passed regularly in Dublin called "Bona vox" ("Good voice"). Over two decades later, the songwriter and lead singer of the world's most successful music group (U2 has won twenty-two Grammy Awards, more than any other group in history) is still making sure his voice is heard. In Bono's words:

> You don't become a rock star unless you've got something missing somewhere, that is obvious to me. If you were of sound mind

or a more complete person, you could feel normal without 70,000 people a night screaming their love for you.

When the approval fades and they cease to be the flavor of the month, many celebrities have little remaining. Then come the drugs, the infighting, the self-destruction—anything to avoid the vacant sense of a Self they never took the time to construct. While some celebrities—like Bono, who used his rock-star status to launch a one-man campaign for debt relief to alleviate poverty in developing countries—show us how high we can rise if we believe we can, others provide our most intensified living examples of the hollow shells we can become due to the venomous effects of approval.

The problem is that your *appreciation* of approval comes from the same place within that causes *depreciation*—of your Self—when you don't get it. When you seek approval you give control of your life to others, who can then manipulate you based on giving or withholding it. Your parents or other authority figures may believe they know how you should live your life. When you win their approval, you can note that—unless their praise hinges solely on your living according to *your* values—this victory means you have been successful in pursuing *their* ambitions and approaching your life the way they would if they were you. They're not.

Ask yourself this one question: "Do I *want* to be liked by everyone?" If your answer is yes, your end goal translates as: "I want my actions and opinions to be aligned with the values of everyone I know." That's tantamount to answering the question, "What music do you like?" with "Whatever is currently in the Top Forty," or responding to the question, "What is your favorite football team?" by exclaiming, "Whichever team wins the Super Bowl." Opinions are like friends: choose a few and your life has meaning. Choose them all and you end up with none.

DISAPPROVAL AT THE FRONT LINE

Who in our society do you think incurs the most disapproval? Who constantly wins or loses, succeeds or fails, and is commended or ridiculed in the media every day? Two groups of people who can teach us a thing or two about handling disapproval are politicians and athletes. Politicians win or lose elections that determine their entire careers. Athletes win or lose games and competitions every single day.

Even if a politician is elected in a "landslide victory," they're lucky if 60 percent of the population voted for them. They then have to govern knowing that 40 percent of their constituents did not approve of them, and in fact would have preferred someone else! Bill Clinton voiced this dynamic—which I call the "underbelly of leadership"—when he said, "I feel like a fire hydrant surrounded by a pack of dogs."

How do they do it? The top players stay focused. They know that even if they're doing well by any objective standard, some of the fans just won't like them. To use the civil rights mantra, they keep their eyes on the prize.

Roger Maris broke Babe Ruth's home run record in 1961. Throughout the season, hordes of Yankee fans shouted "Get off the field, you bum!" every time Maris did his home run trot around the bases. They were rooting for Mickey Mantle to break the record. Mantle was in his tenth season with the Yankees, and they didn't feel Maris deserved the home run crown because he was only in his second season and wasn't a New Yorker. If you were a major leaguer, to what extent would you listen to the fans express what in reality is their internal dissatisfaction with their own lives rather than anything to do with you?

When you attempt to control your environment by seeking 100 percent approval from everyone around you, your need for approval ironically ends up controlling you. When you deny the natural existence of some disapproval in your life rather than recognizing that sporadic disapproval "keeps you honest," you scatter your energy and prevent yourself from enjoying the (much more frequent) moments of approval you experience every day. Full approval from everyone is impossible, so you might as well just give up that idea right now—it's never going to happen!

Those who fear losing their reputations are usually the ones who lose it. The eight-season National League base-stealing leader Lou Brock wisely remarked, "Show me a guy who's afraid to look bad, and I'll show you a guy you can beat every time." Make a pact with yourself to give up trying to prove anything to anyone, and to stop making adjustments so nothing you say or do creates disharmony with the people around you. You will be pleasantly surprised with how this simple act of letting go will make you feel centered rather than diffuse, and relaxed rather than preoccupied about how others react to you.

STAY IN THE GAME

Receiving disapproval is the price you pay for being fully alive. A once unknown actress shares her struggle:

> I got fired off *Beverly Hills 90210.* It was in its last stages, when no one was watching it, and I thought, "If I'm not even good enough for this, I'm never going to make it." So I was coming off this one-hour show, and I was testing for another one-hour show with this very well-known producer who said, "I would hire you, but you're just too 'half-hour.'" But you have to trust fate, because four months later I got [the lead role in] *Boys Don't Cry.*

Not only did she get the lead role, but Hilary Swank won the best-actress Oscar for her captivating portrayal of a lesbian woman living in a homophobic community in the Midwest.

When you seek approval, you allow the motivations of others—rather than your own—to be your guide. In the sage words of former Los Angeles Dodgers manager Tommy Lasorda: "If you start worrying about the people in the stands, before too long you're up in the stands with them." Reflect for a moment on your most important life goals. Who is sitting in the bleachers at your stadium? Who is reclining in a comfortable seat and giving you their unsolicited two cents on your career choices, or the kind of people you date, or the way you raise your children? How will you spend your time—working on your game or trying to gain their approval?

Your most important decision is not whether or not you will play the game, but which game you will play. Suppose you could choose between playing either Game A or Game B every Saturday for the rest of your life. Game A is more difficult, but you really enjoy playing it. You build up your skills at Game A and win it two or three out of every four Saturdays. Game B is easy yet also boring. You play it perfectly and never lose. Yet playing it does not fulfill you because it's the same thing every week and you know what to expect. Which game would you choose to play for the rest of your life? A more stimulating game which you lose sometimes, or an unchallenging game you always win?

If you chose Game A, then you have selected a life of being your true Self and weathering the occasional disapproval that is an inextricable part of being fully alive. Even if you didn't win 50 to 75 percent of the time, I suspect you would still opt for Game A because it makes you feel like you're unabashedly going for what you really want in your life. Game B entails sitting at home, playing it safe, having limited, sterile interactions with others, and generally not making waves in anything you do. You win each week if the goal is not to receive any disapproval, but what kind of trophy are you carrying home?

If you opted for Game A, make a commitment to no longer complain about the sporadic disapproval that is as integral to your life as clouds are to the sky. Get used to your father saying it's unfeasible for you to become an actor, or your mother giving you that look when you say you're going to see so-and-so, or your boss telling you the report wasn't quite what he expected. Make your peace with disapproval and—like a world-class athlete—you will sustain your participation without burning yourself out mentally.

THE POVERTY MOST LIKELY TO DESTROY YOUR LIFE IS PSYCHOLOGICAL

While athletes, CEOs, and politicians who have become thick-skinned from constantly being "in the game" have taught me a lot about how to make peace with disapproval, my greatest personal source of inspiration for how to stay poised amid personal attacks doesn't come from any of the above. The rawest front line of disapproval is experienced every day by people who undergo much more devastating circumstances than winning or losing a game or a bid for power. Poverty is a hostile virus that breeds tremendous negativity and self-criticism among those it afflicts. When people despise themselves for their own perceived inferiority, they project the only voice they know—their internal voice—onto the only people willing to listen: those around them living under similar conditions.

"Some of our teachers don't even care about teaching us," Latisha Brown shared with twelve other youth during a group session when she was only fifteen years old. Latisha was a high school student in inner-city Oakland I used to teach, or rather who taught me.

"Tell me about it!" chimed in another young woman. "Most of my teachers don't care about nothin' but their paycheck."

"It's hard to work with them," Latisha continued. "Last week one of my teachers even told me, "Latisha, I don't like you.'"

"What did you do?" another student asked. "How can you work with someone who doesn't even like you?"

"I told him, 'Your job is not to like me. Your job is to teach me.'"

Observing the unbelievable composure of some of my students in the face of tremendous adversity keeps me teaching leadership to youth. Watching young people like Latisha and many other youth I've mentored in Oakland, Roxbury (Massachusetts), and Washington, D.C. maintain their poise and confidence while living in neighborhoods rife with drug abuse, prostitution, gang violence, and family breakdown is like witnessing firsthand the irrepressible beauty and resilience of the human spirit.

It shouldn't be this way. I can attest from recent leadership conferences I've provided to youth from low-income neighborhoods in Washington, D.C.—which, ironically, has a poverty rate higher than any state in the country—that all the worst things about poverty sensationalized in popular movies are still a reality in our nation's capital: kids gunned down for drugs, their shoes hung over phone lines as trophies by their murderers; mothers prostituting their sons to men to get money for crack; children with nowhere to go home to, unable to even find a change of clothes; homeless men who choose to live on the streets rather than stay with a family member and jeopardize their chances of receiving their next welfare check.

Yet as in a prison camp, even in extreme poverty some retain their hope and dignity. Young people like Latisha have taught me that the poverty most likely to destroy your life is psychological. When you are paralyzed by what your family will think about your choices, or willing to let an innovative idea die because it might not be accepted, or reluctant to share your genuine feelings because others might laugh at you, or willing to compromise who you are to keep your so-called friends by your side, you are living in the worst possible type of poverty: the kind that takes control of your mind.

THE ONLY PERFECTION IS WITHIN YOU

You don't have to live this way. Instead of suffering for even one more moment, design your exit strategy from poverty. Shift your mental paradigm and take the leap into a spiritually affluent life that is rich, vital, and authentic. Start by viewing approval and disapproval as equally tangential to your life goals. View both as unsolicited commentaries from people in the stands that have the potential to prevent you from ever getting on base. The next time anyone says something critical to you or about you, filter it through your value system, learn from any part you consider relevant to your growth, and discard the rest.

I realize this is no easy task. I'm in effect asking you to shift the locus of control in your life—the glowing ball—to inside yourself. This is a daunting life challenge many people never rise to. If you're willing to do the difficult work of reframing criticism and praise and seeing them both for what they truly are—external perceptions tangential to your life goals—the long-term payoffs will be enormous. You will finally be able to take your eyes off the sidelines, construct your self-value from within, and move squarely downfield toward becoming a self-realized person.

Let go of your need for approval and you will see confidence and inner strength replacing a manic, nervous attention to what others say and do. You will free up immense amounts of emotional energy as you shift from being other-directed to self-directed. Take this giant personal step now. Make a pact with yourself to recognize disapproval as an essential part of your life and to stop feeling rejected, anxious, undermined, or "imperfect" when you receive it. Commit yourself to the simple goal of making peace with disapproval and you will remove one of the most significant roadblocks to your happiness and inner peace.

Think of your life as a balancing act of two alternating functions: choosing how to live and living with what you choose. You shuffle back and forth between these two tasks—each of which requires a different skill. To choose how to live, you develop your Vision for your life, which we covered in Part One. To live with what you choose, you must—must!—make peace with disapproval. Otherwise you will abandon the path toward your Vision to obtain the drug of approval you so crave—and lose your direction. Remember, no one else has to live with what you choose—and hence has anything to lose by taking shots at you for choosing it—but you do.

Your journey into self-faith and inner strength in the last two chapters is good preparation for the final chapter of Part Two, *Discover Your Passion*. This next chapter is one of the most essential in this book. Without passion there is nothing. Until you go through this process of self-discovery and determine what deeply motivates you—which, as you will see, is cloaked in the suffering you've experienced in your life—you will be unable to create a viable Vision that emanates from your innermost depths and inspires you for a lifetime.

This next chapter can be likened to a "final questioning." In no uncertain terms, it insists that you reconsider, at the deepest level, what you truly value. You may find it difficult to read because it puts you in touch with some memories you prefer to avoid. Yet I include it because I believe you need to go through this process if you want to commit the *right* actions—actions that spring from your most deeply rooted motivations. After this next chapter, we will cover *how* to commit these actions in *Part Three: The Skills*.

CHAPTER 7

DISCOVER YOUR PASSION

A man can be short and dumpy and getting bald
but if he has fire, women will like him.
—*ACTRESS MAE WEST*

"Will you help me?" my brother asked. "I really want to get into business school this year. I hate my job and need a change."

It was music to my ears. My brother rarely asked me—or anyone else in our family for that matter—for help with anything. He had not been accepted to business school the year before, so I knew it would be a challenge. I asked to see his essays from the previous year.

"I can tell you why you didn't get in last year," I said a few days later as we started the late-night phone calls that would go on every night for three weeks until he finished his applications. "I hate to break this to you, but they don't care as much as you think they do about what you've done. These admissions officers receive thousands of applications, and every applicant has had great internships, done impressive volunteer work, been in this or that club, had this or that job. All those facts become meaningless to them.

"While it's true they want to see that you've accomplished something in your life, what they care about most is not *what* you've done, but *why* you've done it. They care how you *felt* during those critical points in your life when you had to make tough decisions, and how those decisions *shaped* you as a person."

ACHIEVEMENTS GO, PASSION STAYS

Almost every admissions officer or employer I've ever worked with has told me that the Number One quality they look for in an applicant is passion. Essays (often called "Statements of Purpose," a clear reference to the applicant's inner motivations), letters of recommendation, and interviews have come to play a more prominent role in college admissions over the last century because they provide a much clearer window into an applicant's passion than do grades or standardized test scores.

Why do interviewers care so much about passion? Because while your achievements fade into the past, your passion stays with you. Imagine that the events that have taken place in your life are interspersed along the banks of a river as it winds its way downstream. Now visualize your passion for something greater than yourself as the river. Your passion, like a flowing stream, has guided your life decisions and winded through all your past accomplishments. Admission officers and job interviewers know that this same stream will lead you toward everything you will accomplish in their company or university and beyond. It's the Number One indicator of how far you will go and how your achievements will reflect on them. They also know that while it's possible to train someone with passion to have specific skills, the converse is not true.

SOUL OPENS ANY DOOR

What are *you* passionate about? What is the thread that weaves your story together and makes it meaningful and inspiring? Soul diva Aretha Franklin said, "If a song's about something I've experienced or that could've happened to me it's good. But if it's alien to me, I couldn't lend anything to it. Because that's what soul is all about." Do you take contracts, pursue career opportunities, and build relationships that tap into your passion, or do you just belt out any old song that comes along? If you don't sing your own songs, people will stop listening.

Have a heart-to-heart conversation with yourself and identify the stream of passion that has carried you to where you are today. Visualize the inner motivation that's guided you past both the rocky cliffs that tested your resolve and the warm meadows where you tasted the fruits of your efforts.

Current research in the field of narrative therapy indicates that narrating your life story in your own words enhances your comfort with the past, your sense of personal responsibility, and your inner resolve for self-initiated change. Once my brother recognized that his passion for being a creative entrepreneur and launching educational companies to help children study better was the thread that wove his past experiences together, he wrote application essays that were not just impressive, but *moving*. He was accepted the second time around. Why did this strategy work for him, and why will it work for you? Simple: there is a tremendous shortage of genuine passion in the world. Like any commodity in short supply and high demand, passion is highly marketable and holds tremendous leverage.

So don't waste any more time. Discover your passion and share it with the world. Tell your story and others will be unable to resist you.

When you find your true voice, all kinds of resources you never imagined will come your way. The alternative? Neglect your inner calling and you will not live, but exist. Others will observe you going through the motions, will instinctively know you won't add much value to their lives, and will treat you accordingly.

Speak with passion and your words will strike like thunderbolts to the core of the existence of other human beings. You will inspire them out of their slumber to believe they, too, can feel alive again. This is why every successful fundraiser or salesperson I know speaks from and to the heart, with passion as the bridge that connects them with others. Speak with reason and appeal to people's minds and they may agree with you. But they won't give you money. To open doors and answer the question posed by hip-hop lyricist Rakim—"How can I move the crowd?"—you've got to have soul.

PAIN CHANGES YOUR PARADIGM

Fyodor's father, a retired military surgeon and violent alcoholic, served as a doctor at a hospital in one of the poorest neighborhoods in Moscow. After returning home from work each day, his father took a nap and ordered Fyodor to remain absolutely silent, stand at his bedside, and swat flies from around his head. Against his parents' orders, Fyodor spent many hours during the day visiting with the hospital's patients and listening to their tales of suffering.

Both Fyodor's parents died before he turned twenty. At the age of twenty-eight, Fyodor was sentenced to hard labor at a prison camp in Siberia for belonging to a liberal intellectual group. Here's how he described this experience: "In summer, intolerable closeness; in winter, unendurable cold. All the floors were rotten. Filth on the floors an inch thick ... we were packed like herrings in a barrel." In this suffocating environment, he had the first of many epileptic seizures.

After Fyodor became one of the world's greatest existentialist writers, he declared, "There is only one thing that I dread: not to be worthy of my sufferings." Meditate on Dostoevsky's words for a moment. They suggest a transformation in how you can relate to the pain you've experienced in your life. Consider the question he raises: Are you *worthy* of your suffering? In other words, have you *done something* with your pain? If you were abused as a child, or had a difficult breakup that sent you reeling, or were hit by a car and seriously injured, or are living with cancer, have you let your pain get the best of you or have you channeled it into something positive?

The English romantic poet Percy Bysshe Shelley wrote, "Our sweetest songs are those that tell of saddest thought." Do you sweep your saddest thoughts under the carpet and hope they'll go away, or do you try to understand what they've shown up to tell you? If you are pursuing a Vision you deeply identify with, there is meaning in your suffering just as there is meaning in your happiness. Both are merely the travel companions on your journey. At any moment, you can make the decision to no longer be shackled by your pain. Instead, you can become worthy of it.

ADVERSITY IS THE PRECURSOR OF CHANGE

The problem with fighting or ignoring the pain within you is that it's within you. The enemy is not "out there," but is looking back at you in the mirror. Fortunately, you are more intelligent with your physical pain. If you cut yourself, you clean the wound. You know if you ignore it, it won't heal. Why don't you apply this same self-nurturing to your emotional wounds? Swabbing the cut on your leg while glossing over your deeper emotional scars is like painting the outside of your house for all to see while leaving the inside in utter disarray.

When pain is collectively experienced by a group of people, it generates a joint passion to pursue a common agenda. A person from

Oklahoma is more likely to identify himself as a "Southerner" than someone from Massachusetts is a "Northerner." Why? Because the South lost the Civil War, and this painful history yields solidarity. This is the same reason an American with darker skin is more likely to call herself "African-American" or "black" than an American with lighter skin will "European-American" or "white."

It's also why our vocabulary contains the word feminist, but not "masculinist." If men earned 70 percent of what women earned, had been barred from voting for centuries, and were consistently underrepresented in political office, in the boardroom, and in the professional schools leading to the highest-paying professions (e.g., engineering, computer science, business) the word "masculinist" would make its way into our lexicon with surprising velocity. In whichever form it takes, group discrimination is a sure-fire way to provide that group with something concrete to rally around and feel passionate about.

The same is true for the individual. Almost every significant change you've ever made in your life has most likely followed a period of intense suffering. Think about it. Something or someone hurt you. You didn't want to experience that pain again. To protect yourself, you changed.

Recall the last time you were deeply hurt in a relationship. The breakup so devastating your emotional pain manifested in physical ways: you couldn't hold down food or sleep, you woke up early in the morning unable to get the other person off your mind, you felt as if a truck had just run you over and then backed up again to check what happened. In the aftermath of this breakup, you probably retreated from relationships. You needed time to reflect on what you were truly looking for. You had the very human desire to avoid feeling that pain again. In short, pain changed your paradigm.

Now remember the last time you were going out with someone you didn't feel very strongly about. "Oh well," you thought after the breakup. "I guess it didn't work out." A few weeks later, you were dating again.

You couldn't be bothered to analyze how you approach relationships. No pain, no change.

The same is true in your career. If you get fired or receive a negative performance review from a job you deeply care about, you first feel devastated, and then begin to think profoundly about how you can improve your work. Yet if you were fired from a job you did not care much about, you would brush it off and quickly find another job. Business as usual yields Vision as usual.

I'm not suggesting you become a stoic or go through undue pain so you can make changes in your life: that would be unnecessary and masochistic. But some suffering is necessary to become a whole person and find the right path—because it puts a fire in your belly to change what caused the suffering in the first place!

Become living testimony to the words of the English romantic poet Lord Byron: "Adversity is the first path to truth." Instead of belittling the adversity you've experienced, own it. Embrace your pain in its entirety as an inextricable part of who you are, as a key ingredient in your search for truth, and as a critical element in the inimitable composition that makes you a complete human being. In so doing, you will convert it into your fuel for self-change.

THE PREDICTION FOR TODAY'S FIGHT

The mohawked actor Mr. T made his mark on the nation in *Rocky III* when he was asked by a television reporter, "What is your prediction for tonight's fight?" Mr. T glared into the camera with steely, menacing eyes and calmly replied: "Pain."

As the commencement speaker at a recent high school graduation, I surprised many students when I started my speech by saying: "Instead of your usual cheery graduation speech promising you the world, I'm going to tell you there's only one thing I can guarantee you will experience from this day forward: Pain." Although I didn't try in vain to duplicate Mr. T's intimidating glare, the jaws of more than a few parents still dropped. I then continued, "The single factor that will most determine your future success is what you do with it." Since suffering will play a vital role in your life whether you like it or not, you might as well embrace it.

This is a revolutionary concept. *It means you can choose to benefit from every single event that transpires in your life, no matter how negative, difficult, or unhealthy it appears at the time.* A life-threatening illness can give you the resolve you need to start taking care of your health and to go for what you really want in your life. The death of a loved one can motivate you to stop working your life away and spend more time caring for those who are still around. A spate of hostile insults directed toward you can ignite your desire to teach others how to get their points across without abandoning compassion.

The next time someone betrays your trust, cheats on you behind your back, treats you like yesterday's meatloaf, or takes you to the cleaners financially or emotionally, remember the sage words of the fifth-century Roman theologian Saint Augustine: "God judged it better to bring good out of evil than to suffer no evil to exist." You have the choice every day of your life to either give in to your suffering or to bring good out of it. Stagnation or positive action—which will you choose?

Before you make your decision, consider these words: *You only fear what you feel powerless against.* If you have zero power to do something with your pain then you are squarely under its control. If you lost someone important to you, you have no power to bring them back. Yet you do have the power to learn from what they experienced in their life and apply this learning to the way you live from this day forward.

Rather than allowing your suffering to debilitate you for even one more precious moment of your limited time on this earth, welcome it as yet another tool to help you embrace your complete life experience. This mental reengineering will provide you with an inner strength unlike anything you've ever known before. You will access unprecedented power to truly experience the only remaining moment available to you for the rest of your life—the present moment—and take the necessary risks to live the life you desire.

Stop for a moment and take a look within. What consistently causes you distress in your life? Which thoughts of what you want but don't have keep floating back into your mind to torment you like a long, slow, aching pain? A relationship that didn't work out? A parent who doesn't believe in you? An important career goal you just can't seem to achieve? A coworker who is always putting you down or upstaging you?

Sit with the source of your suffering for awhile. Clear your mind, take a deep breath, relax, and see it for what it truly is. Ask yourself, "What can I learn from this pain?" and "What can I do differently so I will not continue to experience it?" If you refuse to learn from and then transform your pain, it will become a chronic theme that plays throughout your life like an irritating song you hear over and over again on the radio and can't get out of your mind. Instead, make the decision to embrace your suffering and learn what it has shown up to teach you.

RETURN TO THE SOURCE

It's no coincidence the word "passion" is derived from the Latin verb *patire*, which means "to suffer." What has motivated you more in your life—your desire not to suffer (or see others suffer) or your desire for happiness? Consider the life trajectories of extraordinary leaders like Malcolm X, Nelson Mandela, Martin Luther King Jr., and Mahatma Gandhi. What do you think woke them up each morning? A desire for happiness? To walk in the sunshine, enjoy the day, have a delicious dinner, and go on relaxing vacations? Alternatively, was it a relentless drive to prevent the further suffering of their families and communities from the racial oppression they themselves had experienced?

Passion from suffering is the hallmark of Christianity: the "passion of Christ" refers to his suffering and crucifixion. The same is true for almost everyone else. Just about every individual I've ever helped to understand their inner motivations derives their passion from the tragedy they've experienced in their lives. A former client in her late forties exemplifies the pain-to-passion connection. Deidre spent a large part of her childhood racked with the suffering she and her mother experienced while taking care of her father as he withered away from an incurable cancer.

Deidre is now a doctor in a major hospital. She has dedicated her career to cancer research and the advancement of the medical field so fewer families will suffer as hers did. In every possible way, passion is the bridge that takes you from pain to change.

My own story reflects this same dynamic. My childhood was fraught with divorce and physical abuse from a stepfather. I often ran away and slept in parks because I didn't feel safe at home. I felt like a liability to my mother's marriage. My lack of self-esteem extended into every area of my life: other students at my high school routinely made fun of me because I didn't have the internal strength to repel them. I blamed my parents for my low self-esteem and a pervasive feeling of "not fitting in" socially. I felt like a victim.

Then I went to England for my junior year of college. I traveled throughout Europe and to Morocco where, for the first time, I witnessed extreme poverty face to face. I realized that, far from being a victim, I was actually very fortunate to be able to travel and live abroad. For the first time in my life, I discovered a good friend within myself. During that year in Europe, far from family and friends at home, I decided to take responsibility for my life. From that day on nothing has ever been the same. I returned to America a few months later and it wasn't the same. I came home to see my family and they weren't the same. After a while, I realized it was I who was no longer the same. I continued to interact with many of the people I had known throughout my life, yet felt I understood them for the first time.

I felt a renewed self-confidence and a tremendous appreciation for what life had to offer now that I was no longer living in a place of fear. While my mother removed this source of negativity from our family by divorcing my stepfather, I would never forget the feeling of being powerless in my own home—of having a stranger come into my house, sleep with my mother, and beat me up. To this day, those memories provide a profound inner fuel that permeates every ounce of my being.

No vocation has made any sense to me since then except to help those who feel powerless to access the power they deserve in their lives. For many years I dedicated myself to working only with the most economically marginalized—in Africa, Asia, Latin America, and U.S. inner cities—because I considered them the most worthy of my efforts. If I was going to dedicate my life to helping people reach their potential, I felt I should only work where the needs were the most severe.

Then something happened.

TRANSFORM YOUR RELATIONSHIP WITH YOUR SUFFERING

It was a cold winter day about five years ago. I was sitting in a café in Bethesda, Maryland, writing the first draft of this book. A woman in her mid-twenties with permed brown hair entered and sat at a nearby table. She started talking to a friend on her cell phone about a guy she was seeing, and I couldn't help overhearing the conversation: "He's never sure if he wants to get together … I finally saw him but he said his ex-girlfriend was coming to town and he would be busy because he had to see her … after dinner he wouldn't even walk me home and I had to walk on a dark street by myself …"

After she put her phone back in her pocket, I watched her walk out of the café with her shoulders hunched over and a look of quiet resignation on her face. I felt deeply the lack of self-esteem she was feeling. A tremendous desire to help her reach her potential and access the happiness and strength she deserved in her life welled up within me. Right then and there, at that moment, I knew the purpose of my writing. The words came into my mind with lightning clarity: "I'm writing this book for her."

In that moment, I realized that just about every person on this planet feels the way I did all those years—as if there is something wrong with them, as if they're not good enough. I knew then that my purpose was not to help only the most economically disadvantaged, but anyone who was suffering in one way or another in their life and wanted to make a positive change to reduce that suffering.

My passion, in short, is to help people access the power that's rightfully theirs. This book is about Vision-Alignment because you will only feel powerful and reach your potential if *your life is aligned with your Vision of what you know it can be.* Most of us put our hands over our eyes and then cry about the darkness. My goal is to help people remove their hands and see the same issues that have been plaguing them for years, but in a different light. This is what wakes me up in the morning.

That's my story. What's yours? Can you recall some defining moments in your life when you felt profoundly hurt, and to this day feel a stifling discomfort with what you experienced? You may have grown up with a father who was never around or who left your mother for another woman; your passion may be to become the father he never was so your children never experience the suffering you went through. You may have had parents who were so full of themselves they left you feeling empty; your passion may be to make your children and friends feel like there is something in them.

It is 100 percent possible to create a new defining moment in your life. In this watershed moment, you can commit yourself to helping others avoid the suffering you experienced for many years. Yet this is only possible if you first acknowledge that suffering. Embrace your pain, capture the lesson it has shown up to provide, and you will transform your life.

DON'T LET SOMEONE ELSE'S PASSION SPOIL YOUR OWN

There's an old saying: "Don't let someone else's pain spoil your own." Neither should you allow someone else's passion to spoil your own. One person's passion is another's drudgery. Instead of running from whatever you've been through, slow down enough to sit with it and try to understand it. Then transform it into your passion for what you want to change in your family, your school, your company, or the world.

Make the decision right here and now to stop shunning a natural emotion that, like every other emotion you feel, has shown up to teach you something about your distinctly human experience. Keep these thoughts in mind, especially when you feel hurt by a comment your partner makes, you get the raw end of a deal, or you are rebuked by a coworker: "I will not avoid my suffering any more than I will avoid my happiness. Instead, I will own it, and thank it for providing me with the inner fuel to make positive changes in my life."

Every time you feel sad or depressed, and are holding back tears, do not cry for your pain but for your essential humanness. Sit with your pain long enough to understand it, but not so long that it consumes you. If your pain goes undetected, it will take the form of ulcers, episodic illnesses, drowsiness (what you experience when you don't want to be awake), and nausea. Make the effort to understand your pain and it will no longer intimidate or control you. Instead, it will feel like an old friend whom you don't always love to see, but whom you respect and know how to handle.

Like that old friend, process your pain in doses. Don't sit with your pain in the sense of, "I will focus every waking moment on this pain at the exclusion of everything else in my life until it goes away." Sit with your pain meaning, "I will not just take a superficial view of my pain, but will try to deeply understand it. At the same time, I will recognize when I have absorbed enough and am in danger of losing my center. At those times I will let my pain go, and will return to it when I'm ready to continue processing it."

THE QUESTION THAT DETERMINES YOUR FUTURE

It's compelling that the word passion literally contains the word "pain" within it. Imagine pain so extreme it would be almost unbearable. What if your six-year-old son was abducted from a Florida department store and brutally murdered? What would you do?

If you were John Walsh, you would start the television show *America's Most Wanted*. You would put over eight hundred fugitives behind bars. You would lobby the federal government to sign into law various Missing Children's Acts, increased penalties for sex offenders, and a national Amber Alert system to recover abducted children. In Walsh's words, "I'd like to be remembered as the father of a murdered child who fought back. As someone who tried to make a difference in honoring his son's name."

Walsh channeled his pain into a passion to make the streets safe for other people's children. Beneficial for society? Tremendously. Brought immense meaning into his life? Without a doubt. This is the power of passion.

Your future success also hinges on how you answer one critical question: *What will I do with my pain?* You are certainly free to mope around the house, wallow in your room, and let your mind digress into the barren wasteland of "No one understands me" and "Why me?" thoughts. After the death of his son, Walsh most likely went through such a period before he discovered his life's calling. Alternatively, you can take a page from Walsh's book. You can sit with your pain long enough to understand it, and then design strategies to diminish the chances of it recurring in your life and in the lives of others.

Pick a situation and ask yourself if you're working with your pain or if your pain is working on you. If your father is always critical of you, you have every right to feel hurt and languish in self-pity. Yet you also have the right to ponder what he experienced in his life that's made him so critical. Once you accept that you will not change him, you will be ready to convert the suffering you've incurred because of his critical nature into a burning motivation to help those who *do* want to change to become less judgmental and more accepting of others.

THE ROOTS OF COM-PASSION

A question I am often asked is, "If I haven't suffered a lot in my life, does it mean I can't have any passion?" I respond that the good news is your passion doesn't have to come from *your own* suffering. I've observed in many of my clients that the flip side of an easy, sheltered childhood can be a lack of passion to change anything in the world. (If you're content with the cards the world has dealt you, after all, why change the deck?) I've also had the privilege of working with many others who have learned the life-changing lesson that they are connected to every other human being they've ever encountered by a universal life force, and that this synergy can give rise to their passion.

When someone else suffers, you suffer too. If this weren't the case, you would never cry during a movie. The same is true with joy. Watch someone smile, and you will smile. When a friend laughs, you laugh. The passion created inside you when you observe others suffering comes from compassion—*com,* "with" and *passion,* "to suffer." Compassion doesn't mean "to suffer with," which would bring you down and render you unable to sustain your caring for another person, but "to be *with* someone in their *suffer*ing."

There is so much suffering in the world already that there is no good reason to add any more of your own to the mix in the hopes of finding your passion. Instead, spend enough time with someone who is suffering to understand at least some of what they are experiencing. You will become emotionally moved, which will impel you to work toward preventing their future suffering or the suffering of others from the same affliction.

You've already experienced this feeling of compassion many times. Recall when you watched a family member or friend experience devastating pain after they were emotionally hurt by another human being. Think back to when you visited people living in poverty and made the profound realization that they aren't any different from you. Remember a time when you passed someone on the street, looked into their eyes, and saw their suffering. Recall those moments when you questioned why you are so fortunate and felt compelled to make the lives of others better in some concrete way.

You may have had one of these experiences and then forgotten about it and gone on with your life. Bring it back into your mind and your long-dormant passion will return. You experience moments when the future rushes in and you see what your life can become—if only you pay attention. Reflect on the illuminating words of former British prime minister Winston Churchill: "Men occasionally stumble over the truth, but most of them pick themselves up and hurry off as if nothing ever happened."

Can you recall the times in your life when you stumbled over the truth—when you realized what your true inner calling is, or the kind of person you want to spend your life with, or what family truly means—even if only for a brief moment? Most of the time you let these moments pass you by because your ego doesn't allow your soul to fully absorb what's holding its attention. Your ego diverts you back to your worries about what you have to do tomorrow, or your insecure need to regain your traction on the hamster wheel to nowhere you've been sprinting on in your job, or your impulsive desire to follow up with so many people so you can feel as if you know everyone—while in truth you know no one.

Due to your constant preoccupations, you turn a blind eye to that faintly perceptible feeling inside instead of letting it grow. Here's my simple advice: go back to those moments in your life when you actually *felt something*. Remember those feelings, give them room to freely evolve, and learn what they came into your heart to teach you. This is your passion.

FREEDOM IS NOT FREE

I hope you've accepted by now that the issue is not the pain you've been through. The issue is how you *relate* to the pain you've been through. Befriend your pain, or the pain you've seen others experience, and you will receive a tremendous gift: a sense of purpose. Never again will you count the minutes until you go home on the clock at work or in class. Gone will be the days when you felt lost and confused about your life's mission. You will wave good-bye to all the negative vices and self-recriminations that stem from an inner aimlessness.

Best of all, the day you confront your pain and convert it into your passion will be the last day you have to work. You will never again have a job. You will no longer even have to ponder, "What will I do in my career?" Instead, you will have a *calling*. Your greater purpose will evolve out of a deeply rooted inner passion you won't be able to shake even if you try, and it will drive you to achieve spectacular results.

Why is it so important to discover your passion? Because you have something unique and unrivaled to contribute. You can discover it and integrate it into your life's purpose by asking yourself, "What have I been through, or seen others go through, that I could dedicate myself to preventing?" and "What about the world agitates me and makes me feel uncomfortable?" Make your resolve concrete by asking yourself, "What would wake me up in the morning and make me want to go through the doors of my office, my school, my hospital, or my stadium and *do something* with my life?"

Make this metamorphosis happen in every area of your life—starting today. If you feel your ex-husband betrayed you by leaving you with two children to raise so he could chase after a younger woman, don't subordinate your pain by going on a dating spree. Instead, process whatever pain you can handle and ask yourself the hard questions about why your marriage didn't work. Consider the qualities you were looking for when you met your ex-husband. Then envision the qualities you will look for now to find a man whom you are more compatible with—and who will stand by you when the going gets tough. The choice is yours: you are certainly free to play the victim role and complain about your pain. Alternatively, you can feel it, heal it, and transform it into your passion.

I visited the Korean War Memorial in Washington, D.C. earlier this year and was struck by an inscription that read: *Freedom is not free.* To develop your own Vision for your life and relentlessly pursue it is the only freedom I know of. Like anything of import, it's not free. The cost is to drill down to the core of your suffering—because confronting the pain that lingers inside you is precisely what will liberate you from it. You will then be able to discover your passion for what you want to change in the world.

"But why go through all this pain to confront even more pain that's better forgotten?" you may be thinking. "I'd rather focus on what makes me happy." I realize what I'm asking you to do isn't easy. Let's face it: "Confront My Suffering" probably isn't the first thing you want to put on your "To Do" List. Yet it's worth your time to fight the human tendency to avoid thinking about the pain you've experienced. Why? Because once you integrate these periodic self-dialogues into your schedule alongside "Meet Mary for Tennis," your life's mission—like a mountain lake after the sediment has sifted to the bottom—will start to become clear. Where you once saw an abundance of time and a scarcity of opportunities, you will see the opposite. Most importantly—for you and the rest of us you share this planet with—you will find a sense of meaning in the brief amount of time you have left on this earth, which will guide you toward thoughtful, compelling action.

MAKE IT HAPPEN:

1. You entered this world and you're going to leave it. What will be *different* about the world when you check out of it that will be attributable to your actions? In other words, what will be the *impact* of your life?

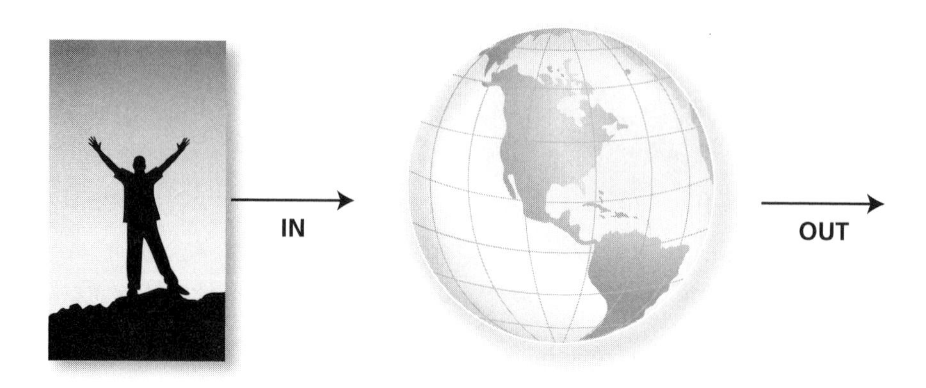

2. Write a paragraph about what makes you uncomfortable about your community and/or the world. Put into words what makes you feel like saying, "This is *not* as it should be—and I'm going to do something about it!"
3. Revisit the thoughts you've had while reading this chapter about what truly drives you and what you want to dedicate yourself to changing in the world. Integrate this profound inner learning into your Vision Statement. For your Vision Statement to be sustainable and motivate you for years to come, it *must* reflect what you are most deeply passionate about.

Up to this point, you have been focused on choosing how to live (*Part One: The Direction*) and building your inner strength so you can live with what you choose (*Part Two: The Foundation*). The third and final step for achieving Vision-Alignment is to learn *The Skills*—the daily actions and strategies for engaging with others that will keep you moving toward your Vision every day, every moment.

You envisioned the destination in Part One. You built your inner strength to endure the journey in Part Two. Now let's turn to the techniques: the sharp axe you can use to cut back the brush on your path.

You have probably heard the popular expression, "The devil is in the details." You may not have heard these words from a Catholic bishop: *God is in the details.* While developing your Vision was a critical step, it's your nuanced ability to effectively take actions that move you toward it—and avoid actions that don't—that will determine your ability to create a life that's consistent with what you've envisioned.

In these next three chapters, you will learn the skills to make your dream a reality. Without these skills, you will have nothing but lofty ideas to take with you to the grave, and you will not leave a legacy. These skills will enable you to transform your Vision into what you actually experience every day of your life. In short, this is where the rubber meets the road. Take a deep breath, strap yourself in, and let's put the pedal to the metal.

Part Three:

The Skills

It is no use walking anywhere to preach
unless our walking is our preaching.
—St. Francis of Assisi

It was my first college literature course. My class at Berkeley had just read a story about an old man lying on his deathbed ruminating about his life. This man thought he had deceived the world his entire life because no one else knew about the evil thoughts he often had. He thought he had fooled others into believing he was good by being kind to them and suppressing his true, darker Self. I listened for over an hour to other students discussing how unfortunate it was he couldn't have been a better person.

Then I had an epiphany I've never forgotten since. I raised my hand and exclaimed, "He was a good person!"

"What do you mean?" another student asked, squinting at me.

"If he was kind to other people his whole life, he was a good person." I replied. "What does it matter what he thought? He was a good person because that's how he treated others. He just never realized it."

I feel even more strongly today that the old man in that story was a good human being. His thoughts shaped his perception of who he was, and nothing more. And I would argue that his perception was erroneous. His thoughts had very little *impact* on the world. His impact, or the difference he made in other people's lives, was determined by his actions.

The only ideas that will make any difference to anyone else in the world are those you act upon. The rest you will take with you unrealized to the grave. The Austrian founder of psychoanalysis, Sigmund Freud, astutely remarked, "He does not believe who does not live according to his belief." Even the man who spawned the largest stop-and-reflect-on-your-childhood movement in human history knew actions are the only way to make thoughts matter.

People react to you based on your actions. The thoughts you do not translate into actions are exactly that—thoughts—and nothing more. A thought only becomes real when you act on it. Your actions are the only means at your disposal to manifest your thoughts in the physical world. This critical decision—determining which thoughts to empower into action—is where your power lies.

The strategies in these next three chapters are about how to transform your Vision into concrete, everyday actions. They are some of the most challenging in this book; herein is where many people lose their way. Most people have dreams. Yet many are unable to develop effective strategies to bring them to fruition. If you can become adept at translating your thoughts and feelings into effective action, your potential to create a life filled with success and happiness will be limitless.

LEAD WITH ACTIONS, NOT WORDS

Your words mean very little unless they are backed by concrete actions. Many people spend their lives telling others who they are. Their words rarely have the intended effect. Why? Their private versions of themselves are usually inaccurate. They're almost always either too inflated or too modest. People don't tell you who they are. They either tell you who they wish they were or share a lesser version of themselves to keep your (and their) expectations low and easy to manage.

People form their opinions about you based on only one thing—how you act. They read you like a book. The pages? Your actions. Not grand, sweeping actions that will shape your relationships forever. It's not that easy, unfortunately. Your friends, family members, and romantic interests have already been burned enough times by empty promises and high-flying declarations with lots of air but no weight. For this reason, Emerson's words, "What you do speaks so loud that I cannot hear what you say," guide the way they interact with you.

Your everyday actions create your relationships. How you treat your children when they're cranky. How you respond to criticism. How you deal with little things that don't go your way. How you speak on the telephone to a service rep who doesn't understand what you want or can't give it to you.

The expression "The road to hell is paved with good intentions" has weathered the years for a reason. It means nothing to your children that you "intended" to pick them up after school. Your father does not place any value on your excuse that you "intended" to call him on his birthday. Your boss couldn't care less that you "intended" to deliver the report on time. The police officer will not appreciate as much as you'd like him to that you "intended" to pay for the CD before you walked out of the music store. People read you, relate to you, trust you (or don't trust you), and react to you based on only one thing: your actions.

When you see the word "in-ten-tion," think "in-ten minutes," "in-ten hours," "in-ten years"—the road to hell is paved with good intentions because in-ten-tions don't get immediate at-ten-tion. Intentions don't cause change; actions do. You are what you give your attention to *now*, not what you intend for later. We don't have racial integration because Martin Luther King Jr. had the in-ten-tion to march from Selma to Montgomery. We share the same sinks and buses because MLK put his immediate at-ten-tion to working toward change in the present—not in ten days, ten years, or whenever. Someday never comes. The only moment in which you can commit an action is in the present. Over 99 percent of the rest of the tens of thousands of thoughts that pass through your mind every day are just conjecture about the future that will never happen.

Enough on *why* action is important. In some ways it's a no-brainer: we all *know* we want to transform our dreams into reality by acting on them. Yet why do so many of us fall so far short of *doing* it? The next four chapters are dedicated to concrete, easily practicable strategies to help you determine *which* actions to commit and *when* and *how* to commit them. I hope you will find them use-full.

So let's begin!

CHAPTER **8**

THE SOURCE OF YOUR MOTIVATION

Whatever you can do or dream you can, begin it!
Boldness has genius, power and magic in it.
—*GOETHE*

"I feel like I never get to some of the most important things in my life," Kristin said. "I've been thinking about volunteering with the elderly for over five years. I set it as a personal goal each year, and sometimes even write in my weekly planner to get more information on volunteer programs. Yet I can never get myself to actually do it." The CEO of a graphic design firm in her late thirties, Kristin believed in *theory* she should volunteer, but with her sixty-plus hours per week work schedule, somehow it never happened.

I encouraged Kristin to just go and spend an hour in an elderly home and see what it's like. She made a few calls and scheduled a visit for the following Saturday. She found the home somewhat unorganized and unsure what to do with her. After an hour of not feeling particularly useful, she planned another visit for the following Thursday evening. When she arrived, she was greeted by an eighty-year-old woman named Serena with whom she immediately bonded. She found Serena and the other people she met so kind and appreciative of her taking the time to visit them.

"Listening to these isolated individuals talk about their health issues and feelings of loneliness was like splashing cold water on my face," Kristin said. "It made me feel many of my concerns about my company and my family are so trivial."

Kristin's new image of herself as responsible and caring about her community made her feel stronger and more purposeful. Up to this point in her life, she *thought* volunteering was a good idea. Until she went out and *did* it—even just a little bit—she couldn't *feel* what it's like to be a volunteer. She experienced firsthand the feeling of being generous, and liked this new image of herself. By experiencing being giving, she became giving. Because of what she experienced during those first few visits, which became stronger over time, Kristin volunteered weekly at the elderly home for two years. She then started a community outreach program in her company, which she has expanded over the last eight years to include over a hundred and fifty employees.

FROM "NICE TO DO" TO "NEED TO DO"

What important goal do you keep putting off that leaves you feeling your life is incomplete? To learn how to play the piano? To further your education? To speak another language? To buy a bicycle and start riding on the weekends? You may feel overwhelmed by this goal and ignore it, hoping it will leave you alone. It won't. To help you take action, I want you to understand the difference between what I call "theoretical motivation" and "experiential motivation." Theoretical motivation is motivation that's driven by the intellect. Your mind *thinks* you *should* do this or that, and you hope that by thinking about it enough you will actually do it.

Experiential motivation, or motivation derived from experience, is different—it's driven by the heart. Your heart *feels* you *want* to do something, and so you naturally move toward it. You start by doing something small, and from this active learning and the feelings it creates, you find the energy and passion within to do more.

The difference between theoretical and experiential motivation is similar to the difference between theory and practice. Theoretical motivation is an attempt to motivate yourself by thinking about and *analyzing* a situation. It rarely works. You *deconstruct* and tear something apart to better understand it, and in the process create reasons why it can't be done.

Experiential motivation is a much more powerful motivator. You *construct* and strengthen your self-confidence as you *experience* the invigorating feeling of actually achieving something. The feelings of strength and inner reassurance you gain from doing a small amount actually increase your capacity to do the rest!

While you may *think* you should take yoga classes, or enroll in a photography course, or act on a hunch and test your idea, it's usually not until you start doing it that you actually *feel* like doing it. You might *think* to yourself, "I should learn Italian. I bet it would be really useful and would round out my life." Go to Italy and you will *feel* like learning it. You may *think*, "I should write more cards to my family. I wouldn't be where I am without them. I need to slow down and show them how much I appreciate their being in my life." Pick up the pen and write your first card or two. Your love for the people who have stood by you through thick and thin will fill you and make you *feel* like writing more cards. This really works! Actions generate more actions!

Actions give ideas a sense of urgency. It may be high on your priority list to make phone calls to promote your big event. Lift up the handset and start dialing. Have a few interesting, unexpected conversations about what's going on in the lives of your clients and in your life. Gradually steer the conversation back to the event, feel their enthusiasm, and you will *feel* like making more calls. Here's the essence of this chapter and the power of tapping into your feelings as a motivator: *Experiential motivation transforms a long-term goal into something you actually feel like doing right now.*

Experience motivates because it speaks to the heart. When Kristin went to the elderly home, she *experienced* a connection with others. That connection filled her with feelings of empathy for real people (as opposed to the amorphous image of "elderly people" she previously had in her mind) and transformed volunteering from "nice to do" to "need to do." That same connection also enabled Kristin to connect with her higher Self—the one within all of us that believes strongly in giving to others. Her heart, once moved, led her to compelling action.

GET STARTED

Action and inaction have one thing in common: they're both self-generating. Each propels you down its own path. Take Kent, a former client in his mid-thirties. Cleaning his apartment was on Kent's "To Do" List every week (theoretical motivation). Yet he was so busy with his job he never seemed to get to it. Inaction in this area of his life generated nothing but more inaction. In Kent's words: "My life is cluttered in every way, starting with the physical space I live in. I just can't ever get myself to clean it up." I encouraged Kent to turn on some of his favorite music that evening and clean his bedroom for ten minutes (experiential motivation). Kent reported back in our next session:

> I have to say it wasn't as bad as I thought. Actually, cleaning my apartment was kind of meditational and relaxing compared to sitting at my computer all week typing up documents. You're not going to believe this, but within two hours I'd cleaned my whole place! I'm going to keep it clean from now on because I've

> noticed I can now concentrate better in other areas of my life. It also gave me some time to listen to some old Sinatra records I'd been meaning to play. I now associate cleaning my apartment with something I enjoy doing. I guess I just needed to get off my butt and get started!

Concentrate your mind on an important project—a task you've been meaning to get to that somehow never happens. Whether it's creating a garden in your backyard, or encouraging your children to study, or motivating people in your company to pursue a new initiative, breaking a large task into smaller, easier tasks and just getting up and doing one is the best way I know to jump-start forward movement.

Winston Churchill put it this way: "The chain of destiny can only be grasped one link at a time." The Nazis weren't defeated because Churchill hemmed and hawed and did a lengthy cost-benefit analysis of the situation in Europe, but because he stood up for the values he believed in and took action. So here's the secret: *Do something!* Do anything that moves you in the direction of your Vision. Instead of thinking about it for a moment longer, grab the first link on the chain and get started! It really is that simple!

Yes, I know this is easier to say than do. You may be used to sitting around and watching the world go by. You may spend year after year waiting for a promotion, or to be "discovered," or for the person of your dreams to stumble into your life, or for that dream job to drop into your lap. Once you become accustomed to spending your days stumbling around in the terrain of your mind—an appealing endeavor because your thoughts are under your control, do not bring rejection, and do not require you to actively confront deeply entrenched fears—developing a propensity for action is no easy task.

BE NOW WHAT YOU WILL BECOME

Here's one of life's great ironies: you become not what you *think* you will become, but what you *do* while you're having those thoughts! Your life happens while you're thinking about your life! Plan to buy a house while going to Vegas every month to gamble and you become a renter who gambles. Talk about traveling to distant lands while working your days away and you become an office drone who daydreams.

Psychologist William James put it this way: "Begin to be now what you will be hereafter." If you want to become strong, take strong actions! If you want to become empathetic, act empathetically—starting right now! Reading books on empathetic communication and studying how empathetic people act will give you plenty of theory to hide behind, but are unlikely to make you more empathetic. The same applies to any significant change you want to make in your life. Whatever you wish you hadn't done in the past … don't do it now! Act differently!

Activity in the present pushes adversity into the past. We've all messed up many times in our lives—it's an inescapable clause in the human contract. Accept your fallibility now instead of fighting, denying, or feeling guilt about it, which will only keep you stuck in the past. And why would you allow yourself to become paralyzed? There are two primary reasons. First, to sit and stew about what might go wrong requires much less of your inner resources—such as personal initiative and courage—than to actually go out and accomplish something.

Second, taking action can destroy the hope that is your psychological lifeline. As you learned in *Chapter 3—The Timeless Power of Vision*, hope is a powerful opiate. While thinking provides a never-ending supply of potential next steps, taking action removes options from the table—and hence leaves you with less to hope for. As Goethe once wrote, "Thought expands, but paralyzes; action animates, but narrows."

Your capacity to take bold action may just hinge, then, on your willingness to relinquish the mental security of knowing there are still untapped possibilities. "Exercise these possibilities and what's left for me to do?" may be the driving concern of your subconscious mind. This primal fear of feeling useless ironically prevents you from being useful. It also doesn't acknowledge that taking action creates new options and opens doors to even greater opportunities not previously available.

"But," you might say, "if I'm not cautious and don't think something through, I may make a crucial mistake." While this is certainly true, brace yourself for another truth: if you *are* cautious and *do* think something through, you may make a crucial mistake. Here's the real question: at what point will you shift gears from thought to action? Consider when you will reach a comfort level with your thoughts that enables you to act, and whether the bar you've set is practical or merely a means you've subconsciously designed to remain safely inactive.

To take care of the future, take care of the present by taking action that's consistent with your Vision. The choice is always yours: be occupied or preoccupied. The prefix "pre" means *before*. To be "pre-occupied" is to spend your time *before being occupied* worrying about what might happen if you were occupied—which keeps you from ever being occupied! Convenient cop-out if I've ever heard one!

Instead of living in fear a moment longer about receiving a bad performance review, or your partner breaking up with you, or your investment portfolio plummeting, or any other negative outcome that *might* happen, spend your waking hours taking Vision-guided action. The outcome? You will both decrease the chances of whatever you're worried about actually taking place and continue moving forward toward your goals.

DO TO UNDERSTAND

Confucius was one of the earliest proponents of experiential motivation. The Chinese philosopher once wrote, "I hear and I forget. I see and I remember. I do and I understand." I take Confucius' words of wisdom to heart when designing leadership development programs. Many of the participants in my conferences learn more about leadership in our "leadership laboratory"—where they are placed in real-life leadership scenarios—than from any set of theories. Their preconceived notions of how a leader should act—which they learned from observing their parents and former teachers, coaches, and bosses—play out. During this "mental rewiring" process, each person refines their Vision for how they want to lead.

You don't become a leader, an astronaut, a ballerina, or anything else by just talking about it. To develop a deeply rooted understanding of your vocation that will stay with you when you really need it—that is, when you're under pressure or the next crisis hits—you have to practice acting out your role.

You can apply this to every area of your life. Consider dating. Whatever he tells you he is usually is either how he wishes he were or how he perceives himself, but not how he truly is. In our microwave society, many people have come to believe you can just add water, have a few dinners and—*poof!*—you understand another person. The only true indicator of how someone will act in the future is how they act in the present—especially when they have to handle adversity—which is only revealed over time.

Have you ever heard the saying, "Watch how your date treats the server. It's how he will be treating you in six months"? Whether it's a romantic interest, a new friend, or a potential business partner, there are no shortcuts to getting to know someone. A farmer can't throw seeds on the ground and expect a good harvest. Neither is there an express lane to understanding another person. The only tried-and-true method is to patiently observe their daily actions over time.

EXPERIENCE GENERATES COMMITMENT

You can leverage the power of experiential motivation no matter what your line of work. Here's a lesson from a friend who works in commercial real estate. In Sam's words:

> When I meet with a client, it's my job to identify their "requirements" for an office. I just listen to them, even if I know there's no way they'll find what they're looking for. Their "requirements" are almost always way out of the league of what they can afford. However, if I tell them they want a Rolls at Pontiac prices, they won't listen, and they'll probably resent me. So I take them on their first tour of properties and show them their "requirements" and how much they cost. I let their own experience—not my advice—teach them. They inevitably come back and say, "Well, we talked about it and we don't necessarily need to be in a classic building" or "It's not an absolute must to have a corner office" and so on.

If Sam were to tell his clients they're wasting their time, they would only feel he's trying to take away what they've *thought* they can get for months or even years. They only become more flexible once they *experience* what their "requirements" truly cost.

Action generates feelings and feelings generate commitment. When you open up to others about your book idea, or the new company you want to launch, or your desire to travel to Southeast Asia, your relationships evolve to make room for your dreams.

"Not my relationships," you may be thinking. "The people in my life get in my way." The people in your life *are* the way. Without them, you're taking a long walk on a short pier. The people in your life either become your greatest resources or transmit a blocking energy that informs you that you need to bring new characters onto your stage if you want to move toward your calling.

The indelible experience of a single connection with another human being will do more than volumes of books and all the theories in the world to provide your deepest wisdom, passion, and conviction in life. This is why finding mentors is so important. If you want to have an intimate relationship that's healthy, meaningful, and sustainable, observe someone who has an intimate relationship that's healthy, meaningful, and sustainable and ask them how they do it. If you want to develop empathetic listening skills, observe someone with empathetic listening skills and ask them how they do it. And so on. You have to do more than think about something you want to do well after reading this or any other book. You have to feel what it's like to be in the shoes of someone who does it well. And you have to start doing it.

PARTYING IN THE THIRD MILLENNIUM

Imagine being stuck at a party for half an hour on the living room couch next to someone you don't find very interesting. Doesn't sound too enticing, does it? Society has been working in your favor over the last few decades to help you avoid this social trap. Have you ever noticed that most guests at parties these days prefer to stand and congregate in the kitchen or a large room without chairs? It's because there's no commitment involved: they can mingle freely with whomever is around as opposed to getting stuck in a seated conversation with someone who excites them almost as much as a shot of cod oil.

Why has society evolved this way? Developments in technology have multiplied exponentially both the amount of information we receive every day and our ability to customize its content. We are constantly in information-overload mode and have very little patience for any medium—including drawn-out chance encounters—that forces us to listen and receive information we don't consider relevant to our lives.

Conversations evolve more naturally when you're standing in that large room. Some sticks rub together and create a fire; others have no mutual traction and create nothing. When a conversational flame heats up, you become more engaged. When you don't feel stimulated, you turn in another direction. You don't sit down with someone for half an hour and think, "I hope this conversation becomes interesting." You simply start conversations with enough people until you find someone with whom you *feel* engaged, at which point you become animated and remain engaged. This is experiential motivation at work. Doing, not thinking, illuminates the path ahead.

Thought not balanced by action can steer you in the wrong direction. Recall a time when you spent weeks *thinking* about an important relationship issue—yet it wasn't until the words came out of your mouth that you realized they didn't accurately represent the way you *feel*. Sharing your thoughts with others (an action) can give you the "reality check" you need.

Taking action is the only way to break your routine and catapult yourself in a new direction. Like all other human beings, you develop habitual patterns you're comfortable with and continually act them out. You churn through the same static set of information repeatedly to analyze whatever comes across the plate, yielding the same set of thoughts and actions over and over again into oblivion. As Yankees catcher Yogi Berra succinctly observed, "If you keep doin' what you been doin', you'll keep gettin' what you been gettin.'" You think you're experiencing each day, but in reality you're only projecting your past experience repeatedly onto the present. You're not living 365 days each year, but one day 365 times.

While thoughts about moving forward yield thoughts about moving forward, moving forward yields forward movement. The pressure you feel when you take the first step forces you to figure out how to take the next step, and so on. This is why lifting ten-pound weights for years will not necessarily enable you to lift a twenty-pound weight. The only way to lift a twenty-pound weight is ... to lift a twenty-pound weight! It may strain your muscles the first time, but you'll gradually get used to it.

Apply this way of thinking—and acting!—to every area of your life. If you're stuck in a dead end job, interviewing for a new job—even one you're unsure about—will help you understand how you truly feel about your current job in much less time than sticking with your current nine-to-six routine. The twenty-pound weight may be a new job, or the same job and a new perspective. Either way, action will generate change and move you forward—in an unexpected direction perhaps, but forward.

Similarly, the only way to learn public speaking is to practice public speaking. Neither do you learn how to speak a new language just by studying it. Learning the intellectual framework (e.g., the grammar and vocabulary) is important, but you don't truly learn how to speak Spanish, Vietnamese, or Arabic until you put yourself into situations where you have to break out and start speaking them. Whether you want to learn a language, travel the world, make a career change, or become a better parent, consider your options, make a bold choice, and then take action. This is the only path to becoming successful and realizing your potential.

BATTING PRACTICE

Imagine you have to go through ten interviews with senior managers at a major company to land your dream job. Each manager asks you different questions and shares their perceptions of the company. If you fare well, they ask you to return in a few days to meet the next manager—all the way up to the CEO. How would you approach this series of interviews? Would you ask identical questions and act the same in all ten interviews, or would your behavior in each interview depend on what you had learned about the company in your prior interviews?

This is a rhetorical question with an obvious answer. Most likely, you are willing to accept that if there are ten steps between you and a major goal, the only way to know how to take the tenth step is to take the first nine steps and then use your best judgment. If you work back from there, you will realize you won't know how to take the ninth step until you take the first eight, and so on. While this sounds simplistic, it illuminates the main point of this chapter and the reason experiential motivation is the most effective means of achieving any goal: *you won't know how to take steps two through ten until you take step one.*

This metaphor has startling implications. It illustrates why sitting around and pondering how to reach a goal—whether it's to find a new job, or to earn another degree, or to meet the right person—is an attempt to make a decision with incomplete information. The more practical and effective way to achieve your goal is to get off your rear cushion and take your first step. There's no other way to get the information you need to proceed to step two.

"OK, but how do I get started?" you may be thinking. I am often asked this question by people in sales, business development, or fund-raising. They share their dilemmas by saying, "Sometimes I just don't feel like being 'on,'" or "It's hard to get myself motivated to talk someone into a deal when I'm tired and didn't sleep well the night before." I advise them to start their day by calling or meeting with a few less-important clients and then work up from there.

"Look at your first few calls or meetings as 'batting practice,'" I suggest. "Trust your instincts. You'll know when you're in your groove and it's time to pitch to more important clients."

Pick a situation and ask yourself if your mind is taking you on a long ride to nowhere or action is fueling your heart and generating more action. If you're tired of sharing the highlights of your week with your cat and want to meet someone new, stop letting your mind play the leading role. When you stand against the wall for hours and convince yourself each person you see is too arrogant, or bossy, or unattractive, in truth you're just finding reasons not to step up to the plate and start a conversation.

You become a modern-day apparition of the potbellied man sitting on the couch with beer in hand screaming at the television. Because you're unwilling to put yourself on the line and approach someone, you never work up the courage or verbal flow to talk to anyone. Don't prohibit the sublime beauty that could enter your life through a new friendship or intimate relationship for a moment longer. Instead, let experiential motivation work its magic. Imagine there is an invisible hand pushing you in the direction of someone who looks interesting and just walk up to them and say something. More often than not, the imaginary obstacles you erected in your mind will vanish right before your eyes.

THE TYRANNY OF PERFECTION

A client once told me he has to exercise every day or he won't do it at all. More CEOs than I can count have shared their plans with me to make a lot of money and then give most of it away after they retire. I tell them all their goals are unlikely to happen. This is the tyranny of perfection. Waiting for any complete state before choosing to act is like waiting for snow in Miami. You never start because you always feel there's more that must first be in place. You create a bar that's too high and then spend your life staring up at it.

If you were asked the question "Why are you so far behind in writing your thesis, or creating a new plan to improve your company, or completing a long-term project?" you might say, "I still have more information to obtain" or "I need to do more research" or "I still have to get it approved by so-and-so." In other words, you would focus on what you don't yet have instead of the specific actions you can take *now* to move closer to your goal. Alternatively, you may say to yourself, "I'm not ready yet. I have to be patient." If you don't feel ready, *do something to make yourself ready.*

Any teacher can tell you there's no more effective way for a student to truly understand something than to experience it. The students to whom I taught business at Castlemont High School—located in one of the lowest-income neighborhoods in Oakland, California—launched the most successful student-run business at any airport in the country (a coffee concession at the Oakland airport that has grossed over $40,000 a month in sales and provided college scholarships to other students from Castlemont High for over ten years) not because of their ability to study business or my ability to lecture them about it. They were successful because in the first week of the program—with the help of a small amount of start-up capital—they launched a one-day business!

One group of students designed a business selling bag lunches to other students; others sold umbrellas on a rainy day; another group sold flowers on Valentine's Day. They gave themselves titles such as "director of marketing" and "chief financial officer." They learned how to run a business by experiencing the motivation that only comes from doing, from unleashing their creativity, from having fun in the process, and from picking up a small win that built their confidence to pursue something even greater.

What has been looming large on your conscience that you know could be life-changing if you could just get to it? Even if all you can do right now is something small—it doesn't matter. Do it anyway. In the words of the ancient Greek historian Plutarch, "Many things which cannot be overcome when they are together, yield themselves up when taken little by little." Consider something you've desired for a long time—whether it's to act in a play, or to reconnect with your father, or to move an initiative in a new direction—and make a vow to take a small action in the next week to generate forward motion toward your goal.

THE OTHER WAY AROUND: ACTION REFINING VISION

Robin arrived at her apartment in Boston at ten one evening in a good mood after a relaxing dinner with a friend. The operations director of a major fashion company in her early thirties, Robin led a busy life and usually returned home late. Seeing the light flashing on her answering machine, she walked over and pressed the button. She stood there motionless as she listened to the message. It was from her mother. A close family friend, William, had called. He was in a hospital in Vermont with a terminal illness, and was most likely going to die within the next day or two. He had become reclusive and had not even shared his illness with close friends. Neither Robin nor her mother had spoken with him in over six months.

William told her mother he wanted to speak with Robin. She had been like a daughter to him when she was a little girl. Within minutes, she realized she had to call William at the hospital. She called her mother to ask for advice, but she was already asleep and didn't answer the phone. She walked into the bathroom, looked in the mirror, and broke into tears. Through blurred eyes, she asked her reflection, "How will I say goodbye to him?"

William was a reminder of the first half of her life when she actually shared love and caring with others and was at peace with her emotions. She knew the woman looking back at her in the mirror had lost herself to the big city, and William would carry away the last vestiges of that little girl's innocence when he passed. After a few minutes, she splashed cold water on her face, collected herself, and dialed the hospital. William was soon on the line. When she heard his voice—quiet, weary, reflective, and lonely—she knew it was the last time she would ever speak with him.

Recall a time when you made a significant life change. Did you think through the new course of action for months or years, or did it come about after an unforeseen event changed the way you view your life? If you finally decided to take a risk and become vulnerable in a relationship, was it attributable to months of self-analysis or did this emotional breakthrough follow your meeting someone who made you feel both safe and inspired enough to love again?

If you made a career change, what pushed you over the edge to let go of the familiar and leap into the unknown? Was it months of self-introspection, or a break in a key office relationship, or both? While your thoughts "set the stage" for a significant life change, a strong move by one of the actors is often necessary for it to come to fruition.

DO IT AND THEN SEE IT

Dimitri, an investment banker in his early forties, arrived early as usual at his office on the fiftieth floor of the South Tower of the World Trade Center on the morning of September 11, 2001. Just before nine, a plane hit the North Tower. He immediately headed for the exit and began running down the stairs. Two security guards confronted him and ordered him to return to his office and stay calm. After sitting at his desk for a few minutes, he walked back into the hallway, snuck into an elevator with a few friends, descended three floors, returned to the stairwell and exited the building.

The decisions you make at times that demand rapid and effective action help clarify what you truly value. Robin had to decide within minutes how to convey her parting words of love to a dear friend. Dimitri had very little time to decide whether to follow his instincts or subordinate them to authority. How would you have acted in Robin or Dimitri's shoes? I can assure you both Robin and Dimitri reviewed and questioned their life priorities many times over after recovering from these eventful moments that called forth everything inside them.

The premise of Part One of this book is that you can bring your life into alignment by developing a Vision for how you want to live and then letting this Vision guide your actions. Crisis situations like those Robin and Dimitri confronted illustrate the opposite, and the premise of Part Three: you can also bring your life into alignment by taking actions that cause you to question and then refine your Vision. Part One was about how you can use the visualization techniques commonly practiced by athletes to *See it and then do it*. Part Three proposes the converse: by following your natural instincts you can *Do it and then see it*.

In which area of your life do *you* need to bite the bullet and take action? What is the writing on the wall you've been refusing to read? Pick a situation and ask yourself if you're in motion or paralyzed. If you've met someone you like, are you getting to know them or convincing yourself that—like all the others—they don't score well on all forty-three of the preferences you've meticulously outlined in your "Compatibility List"? Get to know them more and number thirty-eight may diminish in importance. If you're experiencing moments of revelation about a new web site you want to develop, are you making a blueprint or telling yourself you don't have time because it doesn't fit with your career plans? Spend a few hours writing a first draft and your plans may change.

ACTION GENERATES FEELINGS

Johann Wolfgang von Goethe was living in Weimar in 1806 with his girlfriend, Christiane, and their son. Napoleon's army invaded the town and occupied their home, bursting into their bedroom with bayonets drawn. While the German philosopher stood petrified, Christiane took charge of the situation. She barricaded the kitchen and cellar and quarreled with the marauding soldiers until they retreated. The next day, Goethe married Christiane.

While thinking can help you crystallize your Vision, so can acting. Without action, your thoughts can go on tangents that distance you further and further from reality. Being in the line of fire with Christiane and observing her courage provided Goethe with the wake-up call he needed to clarify his feelings toward her.

While your mind generates thoughts about what you want to do with your life, your actions generate *feelings*. As we learned in *Chapter 4—The Confluence of Heart and Mind*, to be sustainable your Vision must be a composite of your thoughts and feelings. To confirm whether you want to become a singer, dancer, or podiatrist, you have to do more than study those vocations. You have to belt out a few tunes, get jiggy with some new moves, or put your hands around a few feet and experience how it makes you feel.

Practice taking bold action instead of thinking your days away and you will feel energetic rather than lethargic, and confident rather than timid as you witness yourself unabashedly living your potential. I know it's not easy to take this leap and sidestep the inertia that prevents you from moving forward in your life. Yet it's more difficult to live with the deflated self-image you entrench when you allow yourself to become immobilized.

The greatest benefit you reap when you take action is you come to see yourself as a person who takes action. You replace the self-image of someone who sits around and never gets anything done with that of someone who acts authentically, boldly embraces change, and does what it takes to transform their dreams into reality.

Let's conclude with the simple secret of this chapter: *Your whole life is batting practice.* Your life *is* the rehearsal. Your preparation for the big day *is* the big day. With this in mind, recognize when you are overthinking. Counter your paralyzing "Why not" thoughts with a much more compelling "Why"—and move forward in your life. Go work out once this week. Give away some of your money to a worthy cause. Write the first page or two of that screenplay. Just do a bit, whatever you can, and experience how it *feels*. Then do some more.

MAKE IT HAPPEN:

1. Give a name to whatever it is in your career or a personal relationship that has you feeling unsure about what to do next and paralyzed in a state of inaction.
2. Write down a time frame for action, such as one day or one week.
3. Take time during this period to reflect deeply on the following questions:
   - "What does my higher Self guide me to do?"
   - "What does love guide me to do?"
   - "What does truth guide me to do?"
   - "What does God guide me to do?"
   - "What does my Vision guide me to do?"
4. Choose an action and schedule it during the time frame you selected.

CHAPTER 9

DEVELOP YOUR CAPACITY FOR RISK

Just ten years ago this beautiful September morning, yon bright sun beheld me a slave—a poor degraded chattel— trembling at the sound of your voice, lamenting that I was a man, and wishing myself a brute. The hopes which I had treasured up for weeks of a safe and successful escape from your grasp, were powerfully confronted at this last hour by dark clouds of doubt and fear, making my person shake and my bosom to heave with the heavy contest between hope and fear. I have no words to describe to you the deep agony of soul which I experienced on that never-to-be-forgotten morning—for I left by daylight. I was making a leap in the dark. The probabilities, so far as I could by reason determine them, were stoutly against the undertaking. ... I was like one going to war without weapons—ten chances of defeat to one of victory. ... [Yet] I embraced the golden opportunity, took the morning tide at the flood, and a free man, young, active, and strong is the result.

—FREDERICK DOUGLASS, FROM A LETTER WRITTEN TO HIS FORMER OWNER, CAPTAIN THOMAS AULD, ON SEPTEMBER 8, 1948, THE TENTH ANNIVERSARY OF HIS ESCAPE TO FREEDOM

Do you continue down certain life paths—a job, a daily routine, a pattern of communicating (or not communicating) in a relationship—because they feel secure, even though you know they're no longer working? One of the most difficult skills to learn and successfully integrate into your life is how to take risks. Just like any other human being, you have a natural tendency to stick with what you know, with your habitual patterns, with what feels safe—rather than stepping out of your comfort zone.

THE RELATIONSHIP BETWEEN RISK AND RETURN

Without taking risks, you will be unable to keep your actions aligned with your evolving Vision. By definition, your Vision—unless it paints a picture of a future that is exactly the same as the present—requires you to commit actions that will propel you into uncharted territory. You may prefer the safety and ease of sticking with your habitual patterns to putting yourself on the line and allowing the possibility of failure.

It's easier to say, "I'm too fat" than to go to the gym and lose weight. It's easier to say, "I'm too ugly" than to ask someone out on a date and face possible rejection. It takes less effort to say, "I'm too old" than to follow your passion and become an artist. Which "I'm too" excuses do you conveniently use to avoid taking risks?

You may also underestimate others to avoid risk. It requires much less courage to say, "There aren't many quality people out there" and stay at home than to risk finding the love of your life and stretch yourself in a relationship. It's easier to say, "He'll never understand" than to attempt to improve a relationship by broaching a difficult issue with a friend, parent, or coworker.

Risk is the way station of success. Without taking risks, creating anything in your life—a family, a new approach to your work, a new pattern of relationship communication—would be impossible. To create is to bring something into existence that wasn't there before. If you want to create, you must become a self-initiated pioneer and step into new lands where old rules no longer apply. Risk is the necessary traveling companion on your journey.

The relationship between risk and return in self-development follows the same principles as in investing: *When you have a low capacity for risk you are guaranteed a low return. When you have a high capacity for risk you are not guaranteed a high return—yet it is the only way to achieve a high return.* In other words, if you want to be successful in any area of your life—whether it's your career, an intimate relationship, or even just how you spend your free time—you must develop a high capacity for risk.

BEFRIEND YOUR FEAR

I've spent over fifteen years helping people confront their fears and take the necessary risks to move toward a higher level of self-realization. It's my experience that the path toward personal fulfillment begins with a willingness to have a genuine, potentially disturbing, no-holds-barred conversation with yourself. You must become aware—no matter how hard it is to accept—of where you currently are in your life. A former client in his late thirties is a classic example of how risk taking begins with self-awareness.

Eric was single and working for a technology company he didn't believe in. He was bored in his job and spent his weekends watching movies at home. Eric was consumed by his fears of both failing at his dream of starting his own business and being rejected by women who wouldn't accept him for who he is. In his own words, Eric didn't know how to break out of the "self-imposed prison" he was living in.

"My father always told me I'd never amount to anything," Eric said, fixing his eyes on the wall behind me as if searching for an answer there. "In elementary school other kids easily detected and took advantage of my lack of self-confidence. I reinforced the belief my dad had given me with everyone around me. I think I subconsciously vowed never to give my dad any reason to reject me again. So now I live in this place where I don't take risks so I never have to face rejection."

Eric was allowing his fear to control him instead of simply acknowledging he was afraid. To help Eric move past his fears, I used a strategy for befriending emotions inspired by the teachings of Thich Nhat Hanh. This gentle Vietnamese monk has lived in exile in France for over thirty years, was nominated for the Nobel Peace Prize by Martin Luther King Jr., and has developed a disarmingly effective philosophy for cultivating inner peace and living consciously called "mindfulness."

"Stop running from your fear, Eric." I said. "Instead, imagine yourself welcoming it into the guest room of your house. Try to picture your fear actually showing up at your front door. What does it look like? Go ahead and say hello to it. Walk up to it and say, 'How are you doing, fear? I see you've stopped by to visit me today.' See if you can become friends with your fear."

Through a gradual process of accepting his complete range of emotions instead of pretending the more difficult ones didn't exist, Eric was eventually able to identify and confront his fears. A year after our first meeting, he left his job to start his own data retrieval company. After a few dating mishaps and brief relationships, he is now engaged to a woman he has been seeing for the last two years.

Many people believe that to achieve anything in life you first have to get rid of your fear. That's ridiculous! You may be waiting forever for that. Just like your pain, jealousy, insecurity, joy, or any other natural human emotion, *your fear will never completely go away.* Instead of trying to push it away, make the life-altering decision to develop a healthy relationship with your fear.

KEEP YOUR ADVERSARIES CLOSE

Best-actress nominee Annette Bening was asked by an interviewer before the 2005 Academy Awards, "Does the fear of failure ever go away?" Bening responded: "It's not a question of getting rid of the fear. It's a question of tolerating it. You just say, 'Yeah, my heart is pounding, OK.' You learn to live with it."

Can you also learn to accept your fear and move forward anyway? To transform your relationship with fear, simply say to it, "I know you're there, and I accept you as I accept any other emotion I naturally feel. But I will never allow you to control me again."

A Machiavellian strategy is to keep your adversaries close. By keeping an eye on them you can prevent them from becoming too unruly. Apply this same strategy to your relationship with fear. Keep it under close supervision so you can anticipate the direction it's going to push you in next.

Note that I use the word "adversary" instead of "enemy" to describe fear. If you allow any part of yourself to become an enemy—even the emotion with the most formidable power to pull you away from loving others and realizing your dreams—you will drag yourself onto the battlefield and become injured in the process. Choose instead to regard even your most difficult emotions as "worthy adversaries" whom you do not detest, yet keep a close watch on so you don't fall into the traps they lay for you.

Make peace with your fear and you will discover its source. You will then be able to counter its gravitational pull by allowing your Vision of making a career change, or developing a healthy intimate relationship, or traveling to a distant land—not the fear you associate with the risk involved—to act as your guide.

RISK IS THE CONVERSE OF ITSELF

At the age of nineteen months she suffered from a disease that left her blind and deaf. Rising to the challenge posed to her by Anne Sullivan, a gifted teacher, she learned how to use Braille to read and communicate in five languages. In 1904, she graduated magna cum laude from one of the top universities in the country, Radcliffe College—becoming the first deaf and blind student to graduate from a U.S. college. She went on to author several books and travel the world campaigning for the rights of the disabled. Helen Keller sagely remarked, "Avoiding danger is no safer in the long run than outright exposure. Life is either a daring adventure or nothing." Since you are never completely safe anyway, why not go for it and choose the daring adventure?

The world is filled with leaders and followers. You either follow someone else's path or cut your own. Leaders develop a Vision, a sense of purpose, and then singularly pursue it. They embrace risk as an intrinsic part of creating and adding value to the world. In the words of former U.S. president Theodore Roosevelt:

> Far better it is to dare mighty things, to win glorious triumphs, even though checkered by failure … than to rank with those poor spirits who neither enjoy much nor suffer much, because they live in a grey twilight that knows not victory nor defeat.

Roosevelt's words shed light on one of the basic tenets of risk: *Risk is the converse of itself.* In other words, not to risk is a risk—and in the long run a much greater one. In *Chapter 2—The Timeless Power of Vision*, you read some of Viktor Frankl's observations on the effects of a loss of purpose on prisoners in a Nazi concentration camp. When pursuing your Vision requires you to take a risk, you risk something much more significant—losing your sense of purpose and inner fulfillment—by not taking it.

You are ultimately accountable, after all, to yourself. When you look back on your life, you will know like the back of your hand whether you lived fully and aggressively pursued your Vision or hid in a corner and let life pass you by. How are you living now? Are you residing in the "grey twilight" Roosevelt describes? What are you afraid of that impedes you from taking the necessary risks to achieve your most important life goals? I strongly advise you to confront it now, because later on you will hold yourself accountable not just for what you did in your life, but for what you didn't do.

BABY STEPS

"OK, I know I *should* risk," you may be thinking, "but *how* do I get myself to do it?" To find some answers, let's go back to when you were a child and first had to confront risk. Visualize yourself back in your mother's arms in the doorway of a large square room. You feel cozy, comfortable, and secure. You don't have a care in the world. You feel loved. Your mother sets you down on the floor in front of her. You start to cry. You want to return to her arms. Gradually you accept that you're lying on the floor. You look around. You're curious about this room and wonder what's on the other side.

You stand up and flex your recently acquired walking skills. You take a few steps away from your mother. Suddenly you feel a jolt of pain! Fear sweeps over you. You think, "I'm all alone!" You run back to your mother and cling to her leg. After about five minutes, you look into that huge, daunting room again. Once your eyes adjust and take it in, it doesn't look as scary anymore. You venture out again. This time you walk a few steps farther. Again, fear hits you like a lead brick. You think, "What will I do without my mother?! Who will protect me?!" You run back and clutch her leg again. After hours of this out-and-back process, you eventually make it to the other side of the room. You breathe a sigh of relief, and say to yourself, "It's not as bad as I thought!" and "There are even some new toys over here!"

Congratulations—you just remembered taking your first risk! It's hard to believe you've come so far—and you've still got a long way to go on your journey. An ancient Ashanti proverb from Ghana reminds us: "No one tests the depth of a river with both feet." The way you took your first risk is the same way I want you to approach risk now: with baby steps.

Test the river with one small foot, prepare to take another step, and soon you will be ready to take the plunge. To test the river, first concentrate your mind on one of the entries in your Vision Statement, such as "To speak more authentically with others." Take a small action to move out of your box. (Your "box" is your habitual patterns, which have encompassed you like a cocoon over the years as a surrogate for the security of your mother's arms.) Bring up a slightly sensitive issue with someone you feel comfortable talking with, practice your communication skills, and then initiate a more challenging conversation with a family member, coworker, or friend.

Alternatively, if one of your Vision Statement entries is "To become more independent and capable of traveling alone," take the baby step of traveling alone in the countryside or a nearby town for a day. Then travel to a more distant city or national park for a long weekend. Soon you'll be ready to travel the world!

CLOSE THE DOOR

My dream was to become a professional baseball player. Even as I write this I remember the aching, yearning feeling that kept me up at night staring at the ceiling, envisioning myself playing in the big leagues.

When I arrived at Berkeley for my freshman year of college, I tried out for the baseball team and didn't make it. I was ashamed to be one of the slowest runners among the over fifty guys trying out. I gave up on baseball and focused on other things popular among students at Berkeley, like trying to forge a unique social and political identity and protesting for causes such as more campus diversity and the anti-apartheid movement in South Africa. I took a strong interest in international development and spent many late nights pondering how I could make a difference in the world.

Yet as my senior year approached, I knew deep inside that playing baseball was still my dream. I trained all summer like never before. This time I was the third-fastest person to finish the mile. My hitting and fielding had also greatly improved. Yet when I went to look at the new team roster, my name wasn't on it. I was crushed. I went out onto the field afterwards and sat on the grass, knowing it would be my last time there. I felt like I no longer had a home.

I wasn't going to give up. I joined a local semiprofessional team and had a good season. After graduating I traveled to Mexico to play in the winter leagues, thinking it would be a good way to break into the minor leagues in the U.S. the following year. Each Mexican team was allowed two U.S. players, and I was competing with minor leaguers who were much better than I was. I tried out for five teams. They cut me one after the other. I didn't call home once during that month because I was too ashamed to speak to anyone. My father was so worried he put out a search for me with the State Department.

After the last team cut me I continued south to Guatemala, where I lived for six months in a rural town on Lake Atitlán and started a teacher-training program. I had a lot of time to stare at the pristine water, to gaze out into the surrounding mountains, and to think. I was proud of myself. I knew I had confronted my fears and given it all I had. I also knew I had to let my dream of becoming a pro baseball player go. As this childhood dream finally faded, in its wake came other dreams—dreams that have taken me to where I am today.

I don't live with feelings of what I "coulda, shoulda, woulda" been. This facet of risk taking is often overlooked: risking and *not* achieving the goal you desire is more strengthening than not trying at all, because you can finally close the door on the original goal and move on with your life. Your expanded self-image—you see yourself as someone strong enough to confront their fears and take the more challenging path in life—carries you forward toward other goals.

Have a candid dialogue with yourself about your capacity for risk. Ask yourself: "In which areas of my life have I historically been unable to take risks?" Give a name to the lifelong dream you can't shake no matter how hard you try. If inner peace is something you desire, you must pursue this dream.

Why do this? Because how will you ever feel that your life is complete if you skirt its very purpose out of fear of what *might* (but probably won't) happen? What kind of life is that? It's an existence, not a *life*. Whatever you accomplish will always be second best to what *really* drives you. And why wouldn't you go for what you really want? You may be paralyzed by an all-encompassing fear that if you prove to yourself that you're incapable of realizing your dream, you will no longer have anything left to hope for. The truth is that if your first dream is unfeasible, as it was in my case, you will dis-cover other dreams that will also fill you with hope, longing, and motivation.

RAISE THE BAR

Going for what you *really* want, while a good principle to live by, in practice is scary as hell. One simple thought returns to your mind over and over again: "But what if I risk and fail?" The truth is you never fail. You learn. You grow. If that's failure, I'll take it any day over its alternative: stagnation.

Besides, courage is contagious. Acting boldly and going for what you truly want in your life will attract untold people and material resources toward you. As Virgil, the poet who authored the Roman Empire's national epic *The Aeneid*, once wrote, "Fortune favors the daring." Success doesn't smile on the bold only for large, cosmic reasons. There's also a very logical explanation. Taking small risks builds your self-esteem, which enables you to take larger risks.

Even a small risk expands your self-trust, as long as you're taking the risk to move in the direction of your Vision. This happens not because of the risk itself, but because the risk enables you to experience the wonderful feeling of *alignment*—of observing yourself taking an action, no matter how small, that's consistent with what you value. Feeling that alignment and the courage it took to make it happen will build your self-esteem and become the cornerstone of your success.

The converse is also true: low self-esteem diminishes your capacity to take risks because you're unable to handle failure. When you're already down it's hard to accept that you might take another fall. When you're unwilling to risk, your self-image reflects your awareness that you're living in a place of fear, weakness, and anxiety. Shakespeare put it this way: "Cowards die many times before their deaths. The valiant never taste of death but once."

The best way to extricate yourself from this downward cycle in which low self-esteem reinforces risk aversion and vice versa is to forget about the concept of risk for a moment and just take a small step in the direction of your Vision. Pick one concrete goal and do something—no matter how small—to move toward it. Achieve a small win and build up from there. The internal dynamics that cause this strategy for risk taking to help you become successful are similar to those of experiential motivation: by doing (risking) a little, you feel good about yourself and are able to do (risk) more.

The following diagram outlines how taking small risks increases your capacity to take larger risks and will propel you on your road to success.

DEVELOPING YOUR RISK CAPACITY

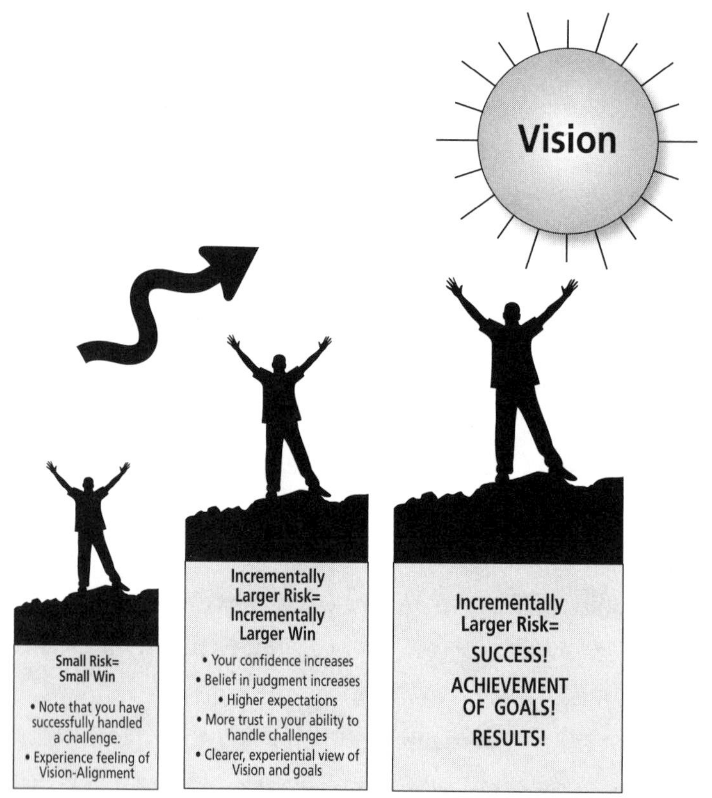

Every time you take a successful risk, you raise the bar on yourself. You expand your expectations of what you can accomplish. You occupy a new mental space where you're no longer content with a limited and mediocre existence.

KNOW WHEN TO SWING

Do you remember the character in *Huckleberry Finn* who, whenever anyone had a new idea, listlessly said, "It'll never work ..."? To build your capacity for risk, replace the nay-saying from the character in your internal theater who always tells you "It'll never work ..." with more positive characters who say, "Go after what you really want. Whether you achieve it or not, integrate this process of courageous initiative and compelling action into the fabric of your being and apply it to every area of your life."

Let me be clear about what I'm asking you to do here: I want you to hold yourself to a higher standard. I want you to tap into your deepest inner reserve and expend a higher level of effort. Are you willing to do this, and accept more responsibility for your life? To give up your need for short-term comfort and stop sleeping in the back seat? Until you sit up straight and take the wheel, other people, your own past, or the status quo will continue to drive your life in the direction they've determined for you.

You learned in the last chapter to think of doing something—anything—that's aligned with one of your larger goals as "batting practice." Taking risks is also batting practice. Whether you hit the ball or not, each swing moves you toward your goal because it prepares you to step up to the plate with more confidence in the future.

Note that the path of risk taking in the above diagram is not a straight line toward your goals, but a series of steps in various directions. At times you will feel like a step has taken you off course and you're losing your way. Yet as long as you maintain your focus on your desired destination while evaluating each risk, each step will provide the information, skills, experience, and self-confidence you need to keep moving toward it.

How does this work in practice? When you ask someone out, you increase your skills and confidence in asking someone out. When you interview for a job, you become better prepared to interview for a job. When you bring up a difficult issue in a calm, loving, nonthreatening way, you become more experienced in bringing up difficult issues in a calm, loving, nonthreatening way. Just as the only way to learn how to hit a baseball is to hit a baseball, the only way to learn how to take risks is to take risks.

The baseball analogy goes even further. A good batter *knows* when to swing. He knows when to keep the bat on his shoulder, when to swing hard, and when to unleash his full strength and swing *really* hard. It's all in the timing. So is risk. You don't go for it until you go for it. You don't ask for the promotion, or pop the question, or make an offer on the house until the feeling deep in your stomach tells you it's the right time, and not a moment sooner—nor too many moments later.

Trust your instincts. Move across the room, but not too fast or too soon. Keep sight of your mother, the shore. Wait for the right climate, the right wind conditions, and then sail out of sight. In the dazzling words of Kahlil Gibran: *Alone and without his nest shall the eagle fly across the sun.* At some point, unless you want to spend your life pursuing the dreams of your parents, your boss, or whomever else wields influence in your life, you must leave your nest, fly across the sun, and become your own person.

THE SPACE BETWEEN PASSION AND REASON

Risk taking, like any other art, is a balance of opposing forces. In the case of risk, these forces are passion and reason. At the center—as any great painter or sculptor will tell you—is awareness. Be aware of both your passion to take a bold step forward—whether it's to earn another degree, or share a long-held secret, or pursue a new client—and your reasoned ability to determine the right time to move. If your passion is not grounded by reason you will take great risks too fast that will fall flat and discourage you from taking further risks. When you feel like sharing your ideas for how the company should change during your first week on the job, listen to the voice of reason urging you to first observe for awhile and gain a better understanding of the organizational culture.

But don't wait too long. Reason without passion is (literally) too grounded and will keep your ship at the dock. Jawaharlal Nehru, the man who fought for India's independence and became its first prime minister, said: "The policy of being too cautious is the greatest risk of all." In which area of your life are *you* being too cautious? Are you tired of using the same overworn excuses to dissuade yourself from taking bold action, such as "I'm planning to take a trip to Europe once I save up enough money" or "I'm going to tell her how I feel one day, but I don't think she's ready for it now" or "I'll learn how to play the guitar once I have a little more time in my schedule"?

There is never a shortage of *reasons* to justify delaying your plans for another day. You are probably very adept at convincing yourself these reasons are legitimate, even when you know deep in your soul they've been skillfully manufactured by your fear. To become successful in your calling, or to meet the right person, or to build a healthy family, you must learn how to say "Enough already!" to your mental deliberations and trust the inner wisdom that emanates from your faith in a stronger, more realized you. To clear away the brush and find your path, focus your mind on an important goal, believe in your ability to get there, and then simply pay attention. Your internal compass will guide you toward the bold action you need to take.

Yogi Berra was once asked, "What do you think about when you're hitting?" He responded, "How can you think and hit at the same time?" If you want to think before taking a risk, let this old saying float into your mind: *While a ship may look magnificent in its harbor, that's not what ships are for.* If you want the ship to be capable of moving through the rough waters ahead, passion is the essential fuel you have to bring on board. Make a pact with yourself not to allow the reasons *why not* to control you for a moment longer. Instead, fill your tank with the passion that tells you *why*, cast off the bowlines, and start on your journey.

While passion is the fuel that enables you to leave the pier, take risks, and continue moving your ship forward, reason is the rudder that helps you take the *right* risks and move in the right direction. In the same way you learned how to detect the confluence of your heart and mind in Chapter 3, discover the intersection of your passion and reason. Hold the tension these opposing forces create within you, operate from that sacred space, and start building your risk-taking portfolio.

THE CLEAN-SINGLE STRATEGY

Did you know that when Babe Ruth hit his famous sixty home runs in 1927, he also broke the major league record for strikeouts? This dynamic hasn't changed at all over the years: the home run kings are still the *whiff* kings. Many avid baseball fans tip their hats to Sammy Sosa for being the only major league player to ever hit over sixty home runs in three different seasons. Most are unaware he's also one of only three players in the history of major league baseball to ever strike out more than 170 times in three different seasons! If your strategy is to swing for the fences, at least acknowledge that you're going to strike out more often. Most of the time, the clean single—a safer, more calculated risk—is a better option. It builds your self-esteem and gives you the capacity to keep hitting single after single, all the way to where you want to go.

Visualize a risk you instinctively feel you need to take to move toward an important life goal. You may need to start a new project in a field you don't have a track record in, or take a language immersion course in another country, or open up about what you truly need in an important relationship. Now imagine you are transformed into one of two people based on the risk's outcome. If the risk bears fruit, you become Person A. If it doesn't, you turn into Person B.

First, envision yourself as Person A. See, feel, smell your success. Literally picture yourself after you have successfully taken the risk and come out the better for it on the other side. Ask yourself, "So how does it feel? How do you look at the risk now? Why did you allow your fear of taking it to hold you back for so long? Will you do anything differently now that what you set out to accomplish has become your reality?"

That was the fun part. Now take a deep breath, and visualize yourself as Person B. Have an honest conversation with yourself about how you are handling not getting what you want. Visualize Person B standing on the other side of the risk, look them in the eye, and ask, "How does it feel to have faced down your fear? Do you feel stronger or weaker for having taken the risk? Was it worth the psychological, emotional, and financial resources you expended? Although you didn't get the result you wanted, did you learn important life lessons you never would have gained otherwise? Will these lessons help you take smarter risks in the future?"

Now for the most important question: What do you *feel* for Person B as you watch them, standing there alone after taking a difficult risk with only their renewed inner courage and self-determination to keep them company?

HAVE PASSION, WILL TRAVEL

I assume you would rather be Person A—the successful risk taker—than the person you are now. But now for the central question of this chapter: Would you rather be the person you are now or Person B? Would you rather know you acted with courage and faced a temporary setback, or that you shrank away from life? That you strived for your higher purpose or sat on the bench paralyzed by fear and did nothing?

Taking risks requires you to internalize the central lesson of *Chapter 7—Discover Your Passion*: you can convert your pain from a liability into an asset by transforming it into your passion to make positive changes in your life. If you allow your pain to drag you down instead of appreciating it for what it is—the writing on the wall that guides you toward positive growth—taking risks becomes impossible.

A prerequisite for taking risks, then, is a healthy tolerance for pain. Why? Because if you are set on avoiding difficulty, you will be unwilling to risk incurring even more of what has already made you feel miserable. What risk would be worth that price? When you get hurt in a relationship, you'll convince yourself you need to be alone for a few years to work on yourself, when in truth you want to avoid getting hurt again. When your idea for a new project is bypassed in a staff meeting, you'll start keeping your creativity to yourself because you don't want to feel frustrated and powerless. When a friend shuns you for taking a stand on an important issue, you'll stop being authentic in the relationship rather than risk further rejection.

Until you see your challenging moments as the genesis of learning and positive change—whether in an intimate relationship, a friendship, or your career—your desire to avoid difficult feelings will render you unable to take the necessary risks to achieve your most important goals.

RISK FOR A CAUSE

Risk ceases to be a choice when your conscience demands it. Former Israeli prime minister Golda Meir once said, "I can honestly say that I was never affected by the question of the success of an undertaking. If I felt it was the right thing to do, I was for it regardless of [its] success." Meir's words illuminate the main point of this chapter: *The secret to taking risks is to be so driven by a higher purpose that the risks inherent to achieving it shift to the periphery of your mind.*

Put more simply, don't choose risks by thinking about them. Discover what you were placed on this earth to do and then let the risks choose you. Ask yourself this question: "What do I stand for that's greater than myself?" Whether it's being authentic in your relationships, or providing health care to people in developing countries where doctors are scarce, or practicing law with strong ethics, your convictions will command you to do what you believe to be right independent of the outcome. You will come to realize that to risk and not get what you want is a far more salutary long-term option than to neither risk nor live by your values.

Visualize yourself again as the successful and unsuccessful risk-takers: Person A and Person B. Assess both your desire to be Person A and your willingness to be Person B. In reality, most risks do not have binary outcomes, and most of the time you end up somewhere in between these two self-images.

Balance your ambition to move toward something greater in your life with your need to hang on to some reserves—psychological, financial, emotional—that you are not willing to risk and can fall back on. Practice taking risks and you'll realize that whether you become Person A today or Person B tomorrow is unimportant—because regardless of which one you are at any given moment, your propensity toward bold action makes you feel courageous, strong, and *completely alive.*

Your enhanced self-image will translate into every area of your life. You will start pursuing the clients who have the most need for your core services rather than the low-hanging fruit who offer easy contracts but steer you off course. You'll start asking out the people you really *want* to ask out, not the ones you approach just because they'll accept your invitation. While you may get more personal and professional rejections by stepping it up to a new level, you'll eventually be going out with someone you're more excited about and working with people who push you to work with your full passion and potential.

Take bold risks and you will stop killing time and start living it. You will put an end to stifling your true feelings in an important relationship out of fear of the other person not reciprocating. Instead, you will initiate the genuine conversations that are the stepping stones to either becoming closer or growing apart. The key word here is *growing*. You may not always get the answer you want when you take a risk. Yet regardless of the result it yields, the risk will *bring what you need into your life* by finally providing you with the necessary information to move forward toward the life you desire.

EVOLUTION OR REVOLUTION?

That dubious, perplexed look nearly tops the list of what I don't look forward to in my work. Fortunately, I don't see it very often; yet when I do, making peace with it is part of my calling. It's easy to decipher when someone at one of my conferences doubts whether they can take a strategy I'm sharing and apply it to their life. Either the squinting of their eyes or the skeptical curvature of their upper lip that says "I don't think this will work for me" always gives it away. A woman in her mid forties sitting in the third row had that look written all over her. After remaining silent throughout the workshop, Monica approached me afterward. She told me she had two children and very little savings and wanted to quit her job as a receptionist to pursue her dream of becoming a real estate agent.

"I just don't know how I can do that while staying true to my children," Monica said with a resigned tone.

I helped Monica envision herself as both Person A and Person B on the other side of the risk—first Person A landing a new job as a real estate agent and then Person B living in unemployment with two children in tow. I suggested that—given her children—she may want to find a real estate job before leaving her current position, or at the least take some real estate courses and put away enough savings to weather the transition. In short, I encouraged Monica to hit some clean singles instead of swinging for the fences.

"I need to go for this new job now," Monica shot back. "I've been putting it off for eight years. In my line of work you never really save much of anything. I'm always going to feel I should continue in my job for a few more years. It's now or never."

I meditated on Monica's dilemma over lunch, and approached her later in the day. "Trust what your instincts are telling you," I shared. "Every situation is different, and there are no magic formulas. There are times when you feel you need to swing for the fences. You feel like you have to swing extra hard because you haven't been taking risks for such a long time. If you've walked way off the path you want to be on, sometimes you have to run with every bit of strength and agility you have to get back on it. Yet the best way to live is to hit clean singles regularly so you don't get that far off your path in the first place."

Monica looked frustrated, as if I had just made her decision even more complicated. "So what is the answer then?" she asked. "What should I do?"

"There is no answer I can give you, Monica. The answer is located in only one place: within you."

Monica left our discussion with the same resigned look. Two years later, she sent me the following letter:

> Well, I did leave my job a few weeks after the conference. I realized I couldn't go another day being someone who wasn't me. I

was living a slow death and had to get out. Then I struck out a few times. I couldn't get a job as a real estate agent, so I had to ask my parents for money and rely on them for six months, which was humbling and not what I wanted for my kids. We had some challenging family issues, but we worked through them.

The good news is I finally got into a training program and am now on my way to becoming a real estate agent! I came in at the right time. Property values have been skyrocketing and they need more quality people to sell houses. The woman who is training me is her own boss and spends her days driving around and meeting interesting people. That's going to be me one day! I may not have chosen the easiest route, and I realize I have to be more mindful of my finances in the future because of my kids, but I have to say I don't regret it for one moment. I've got something now no one can take away from me: I'm proud of what I'm doing, and where I'm going. Thank you.

RISK FORWARD

Let your mind focus for a moment on a critical risk you know, deep in your heart, you need to take. Concentrate your mental energy on a monumental life change that has you swinging like a pendulum between avoidance and attraction—a new direction that calls you with a voice louder than your fear. Consider the salsa lessons you've considered signing up for, or the counseling you've known for some time that your marriage needs, or the business opportunity that would tap into the creativity that has lain dormant within you for too long. Then ask yourself: "What will I choose—to hit a clean single or swing for the fences?" Keep in mind that it's easier to take a home run swing if you have a Plan B—as Monica did because she could count on her family to bail her out in the interim—because you know you'll get to step up to the plate a few more times.

Most importantly, stop overthinking how you're going to do it and just start doing it! Plumb the depths of your consciousness to your innermost dream—whether it's to become a professional dancer, or take a sabbatical and live in Sevilla, or sail around the Caribbean, or act in a theater troupe, or actually be yourself and express what you genuinely feel to others—and start taking baby steps toward it. Singularly focus your thoughts on your dream. Act like it's *going* to happen—so you better start preparing for it!

If your dream is to live in Sevilla, take a Spanish class once or twice per week. Go to the bookstore and read travel guides on Spain. Search the internet for housing options. Set a date for your departure. Begin acting like someone going to Sevilla, and soon you will be someone going to Sevilla.

I know you can learn how to swing at the right time and transform your dreams into reality. It's my experience that the most effective risk takers start by taking small risks they instinctually feel are manageable and then build up from there. So start hitting some clean singles—and keep hitting them! You will surprise yourself with your capacity to take bold risks and move with continuous, assured steps toward your goals.

Practice taking risks and a renewed strength will surge within you as courage and self-confidence replace fear in your life. The alternative? You will not become either Person A or Person B. Instead, you will become Person C: a shell of a person existing in the misty "grey twilight" where courage and strength do not reside.

Taking risks is not optional if you want to bring success and happiness into your life. Why? Because whether you become Person A one day or Person B the next, your willingness to embrace both mental images will fuse them into a new, stronger version of yourself that no longer leaves your potential on the table, but lives it every day.

MAKE IT HAPPEN:

1. Give a name to one of your deepest, most intense dreams, which—given your unique skills, experience, and passion—you could attain if you *really* went for it.
2. Think of a risk that's small and manageable—yet something you've never done before—that you could take to shorten the space between your dream and your daily reality.
3. Take that risk sometime in the next week.
4. At the end of the week, reflect on how you approached the risk and what you learned from it.
5. Prepare to hit your next clean single.

CHAPTER 10

DESIGN AN ACTION PLAN

A goal is a dream with a deadline.
—*HARVEY MACKAY*

A *New Yorker* cartoon shows two goldfish talking in a small goldfish bowl. The larger goldfish says to the smaller one, "You can be anything you want to be—no limits." Many of us limit others—especially our children—by sharing our expectations of what they can or should do. One father put his son into a small tank with his expectation that he should become a doctor. At the age of nineteen, his son was selling $50,000 in computer upgrades and components each month from his dorm room. When the father authoritatively said, "Get your priorities straight. What do you want to do with your life?" the son replied—to his father's dismay—"I want to compete with IBM!"

Two years later, the young entrepreneur's company had already reached $60 million in sales. Encouraged by his success, the twenty-one-year old established a goal for his company of *$1 billion* in annual sales within six years. Sound audacious? Michael Dell more than doubled it!

Ever since the 1960s, academics like David McClelland of Harvard and David Kolb of MIT have proven that entrepreneurs who set goals and then develop a plan to achieve those goals are likeliest to succeed. In Chapter 4 you began the process of developing your Vision Statement, which we defined as an *unattainable* description of your *timeless* core values. In this chapter, you will learn how to design an Action Plan filled with *attainable*, concrete, *time-sensitive* goals that are aligned with your Vision Statement and push you to achieve tremendous results. Let's look at a few examples of the differences between a Vision Statement and an Action Plan so you get the idea. As I mentioned earlier, one of the entries in my own Vision Statement is:

- To create and communicate ideas for personal and social change

At no point in the future will I have fully achieved this Vision Statement entry. There will always be more ideas for me to create and more individuals, organizations, and companies with whom to communicate them. Two corresponding goals in my Action Plan, based on a one-year period, are:

- To complete the writing of *Full Alignment*
- To develop and facilitate at least six one-week leadership conferences for a minimum of a thousand executives, including at least one conference in a developing country

Both of these goals are fully attainable, which should be the case for all Action Plan goals. While you will hopefully still find your Vision Statement entries relevant in another few years, Action Plan goals have deadlines and change from year to year. You can think of an entry in your Vision Statement like buying a house: you don't want to commit to it unless it's what you want for at least three to five years, and hopefully much longer. Your Action Plan, on the other hand, is more like signing a lease on an apartment—you hope you will feel comfortable with it for at least a year.

A time frame for an Action Plan that works well for most people is one year. Feel free, however, to choose the time period that works best for you. I recommend a year because it's far enough away to help you envision what you want to achieve in the future, yet close enough to impel you to take action *now.*

DEVELOP SMART ACTION PLAN GOALS

Your Action Plan goals should be SMART:

- **S**pecific
- **M**easurable
- **A**ligned (with your Vision Statement)
- **R**ealistic
- **T**ime-based

Why SMART goals? Social scientist Edwin Locke demonstrated that specific, measurable goals are most likely to be achieved. Think about it: If your goals are not *specific,* how will you pinpoint them so you know when you've attained them? Similarly, if they're not *measurable,* you'll have insufficient information to determine if you've reached them. And if your Action Plan goals are not *aligned* with your Vision Statement, they're the wrong goals—regardless of how talented you are at attaining them!

Current research shows that to be effective, goals must be self-imposed, build on one's strengths rather than weaknesses, and, according to psychologist Daniel Goleman, "fit into the structure and rhythm of your life." Any goal that does not fit smoothly into your life, work, and learning style you will discard quickly. This means if your goals are not *realistic* (by taking into account your strengths, preferences, and life rhythm) they won't motivate you because you'll soon realize they're beyond your reach. Even worse, your self-esteem will suffer when you fall short of achieving them. Finally, if they're not *time-based* with a concrete deadline, you'll always put them off. When your dream has a deadline, you realize you have to get started if you want to make it happen!

Suppose an entry in your Vision Statement is:

- To be kind, thoughtful, and giving to all my family members

You could develop three aligned SMART Action Plan goals such as:

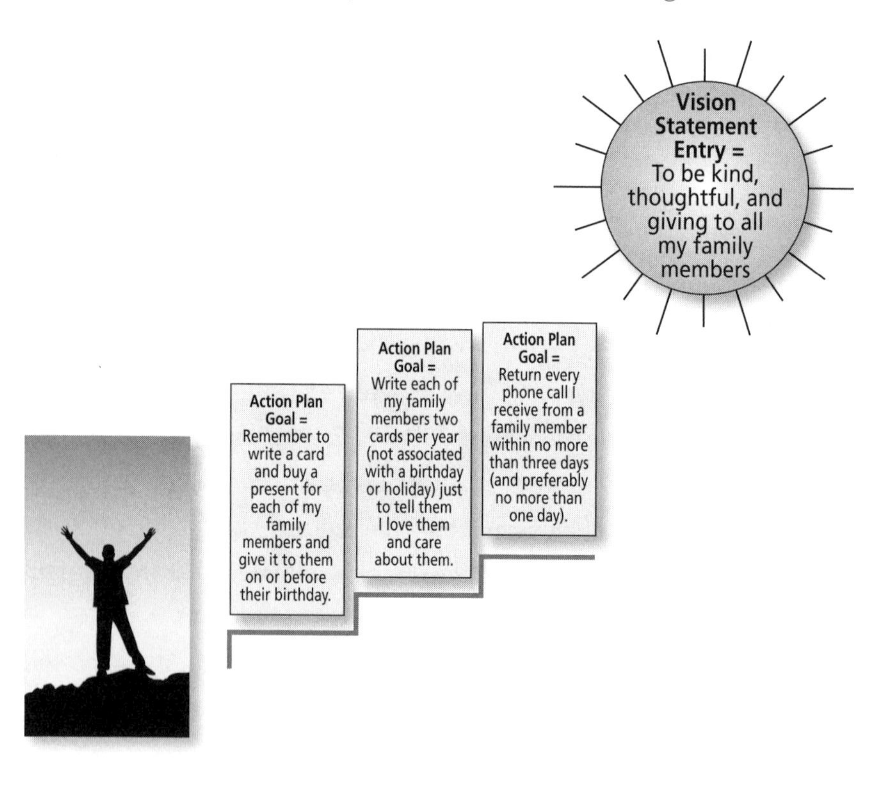

WHY SET GOALS?

In Sanskrit, *prajna paramita* means "perfection of wisdom." According to the Mahayana Buddhist scriptures of this ancient tradition, "The highest, most awakened mind ... cannot be attained or grasped, but it can be realized. It is realized through the practice of all good actions." This is a precursor—from over two thousand years ago—of the need for clear alignment between your higher Vision (reflected in your Vision Statement) and your everyday actions (outlined in your Action Plan). Why is this alignment so critical? Because when it exists, you can infer that you are realizing your Vision Statement when you achieve the goals in your Action Plan.

You *achieve* an Action Plan goal when you *deliver* on a commitment you've made to yourself. This is the "practice of good actions." It's not as clear when you *realize* your Vision, or your "awakened mind." You only know intuitively based on an internal *feeling* of whether your actions are congruent with your Vision.

While your Vision Statement reflects your *core values*, your Action Plan sets parameters on your *behavior.* Your Vision Statement is the closest description you have in words of who you *are.* Your Action Plan, on the other hand, conveys what you will *do* with your time.

"Now hold on one cotton-picking minute," you may be thinking. "If I plan everything out to the umpteenth detail—with these so-called rules on how I can and cannot act—I won't leave any room to be spontaneous and enjoy my life!" It's true that creating SMART goals limits your behavior. Yet any goal you come up with—whether it's to write cards to your family members, or to stay home and study, or to watch less TV and exercise more—by definition is an attempt to rein in your actions so you can move your life in a specific direction.

To set a goal is to push yourself to take repeated, focused action consistent with an underlying value. You may enjoy jogging, or painting, or using new software after you've begun performing the action—yet you may have trouble getting yourself to begin (see *Chapter 8—The Source of Your Motivation*). Setting a goal impels you to step out of the starting gate more often with the hope that you'll reach the point where you actually enjoy doing something enough to integrate it into your life.

Alternatively, you may wish to create something that doesn't currently exist in your life—such as earning a degree, or keeping your body in good physical condition, or learning rock climbing. Writing down a concrete goal helps you stay focused on what you want to create. This skill—maintaining your focus on a specific objective—has never been more critical in the history of humankind. With the advent of email, cell phones, and crackberries, never before have we had so many options—and distractions—at our fingertips.

In its essence, setting goals is a practice to help you base your everyday decisions not on how you feel in the moment, but on your larger life Vision. You will learn more about how to overcome the dissonance between your long-term goals and short-term desires in the next and final chapter.

MAKE IT HAPPEN:

Pick out two or three entries from your Vision Statement. For each entry, write down a few corresponding SMART Action Plan goals for the next year (or another time period you select). Use the same format as the "stair" diagram above.

GET READY FOR YOUR BIG DAY

Setting goals places your dreams firmly within your grasp. The magnitude of your Vision Statement can be overwhelming—so overwhelming, in fact, that you'll never get started. When you set a goal, you shrink your Vision down to a manageable size. Does your goal still seem too overwhelming? Downsize it again. Reflect on these words from "The Whole of the Moon," a song by The Waterboys:

> *I wandered out in the world for years ... while you just stayed in your room.*
> *I saw the crescent, you saw the whole of the moon.*

Your Vision Statement is like the moon in its entirety and your Action Plan is the crescent you can see—a small slice you can get your hands around and more easily manage. You create your Action Plan by dividing your most important goals into even smaller goals. The smaller you make them, the SMARTer they become. Consider an important life goal, such as becoming a physical therapist, or living abroad, or learning how to play an instrument. To break this larger goal into smaller, SMARTer goals, ask yourself, "What *tools* do I need to become capable of achieving this goal?"

Think of your life goal like your big day. Imagine yourself on stage in a Tony Award–winning performance, or in the finals at a dance competition, or running with a football tucked under your arm at the Super Bowl. Now envision all the training you will have to do in the theater, in the dance studio, or at the gym to reach your goal.

Here's why your Action Plan is your real, tangible pathway to success: *You don't achieve success by aiming for success. You achieve success by doing what you're passionate about to the best of your ability.* The glory doesn't come from focusing on the glory, but on the training. Whether your goal is to become a psychologist, or to write a novel, or to start a new organization, describe the training in as much detail as you possibly can. When will you train? How? How often? With what partner? With what mentor? With what intensity? Which milestones or interim goals will reflect your progress?

Shakespeare inimitably wrote: "And many strokes, though with a little axe, Hew down and fell the hardest-timbered oak." No matter how large your goal, what strokes will you take to bring it to the ground? If your larger goal is to become an excellent doctor, convert these strokes—the training milestones between you and the surgeon's room—into SMART goals:

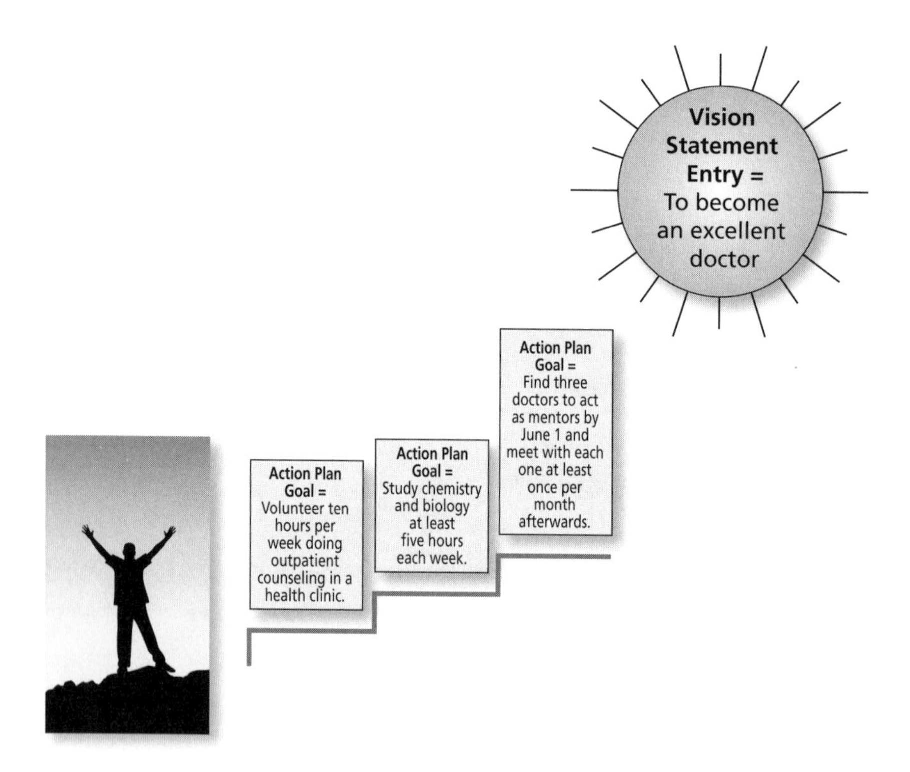

You can also set SMART personal goals. If you want to meet the right person and create a healthy family, you could add the following goals to your Action Plan:

FIND THE CRACKS IN THE ARMOR

Over fifteen years of coaching people on goal setting have taught me the right questions to ask when people create goals that are not SMART. I often refer to this process as "finding cracks in the armor."

Take Jim, a financial analyst in his late forties. Here's how I found cracks n his armor:

> *Jim:* One of my Action Plan goals is to study for the CPA accounting exams this year. *(Not SMART)*

> *Me:* So if you study one day all year will you have achieved your goal?
>
> *Jim:* Of course not. I'm going to study two weeknights and on Saturdays.
>
> *Me:* So if you study for fifteen minutes three times a week you will have achieved your goal?
>
> *Jim:* No. I'm going to study a minimum of ten hours per week until I take the exam on June 14. *(SMART)*

While my questions may seem petty, this focus on the minutiae is exactly what transforms an idea into a concrete, practicable, SMART goal. Here's how I put Janice, a medical researcher, through the mill:

> *Janice:* My Action Plan goal is to get into shape and start running again. *(Not SMART)*
>
> *Me:* So if you run once all year will you have achieved your goal?
>
> *Janice:* Of course not. I'm going to run almost every day.
>
> *Me:* So if you run for ten minutes every other day will you have achieved your goal?
>
> *Janice:* No. I'm going to run a minimum of forty-five minutes every other day.
>
> *Me:* So how many times per week will you have to run for forty-five minutes to achieve your goal?
>
> *Janice:* Four.
>
> *Me:* So what is your goal then?
>
> *Janice:* My Action Plan goal is to run for at least forty-five minutes a minimum of four times per week. *(SMART)*

Do you notice something similar about Jim and Janice's goals? They describe what Jim and Janice will *do,* not what they will *get*. Herein lies the power of the Action Plan—it's firmly within your control.

This goal-setting process is contrary to popular convention. I'm sure you've heard many people proudly declare: "My goal is to come in first place in the cross-country race," or "My goal is to get a B+ or higher on my exam." Most of the goals I'm encouraging you to set are not a statement of *desired results*, but a description of the *process* you will put into place to bring about those results.

Envision someone you consider successful. Speculate about their path to success. To become a world-class athlete, or to write a best seller, or to create a surprisingly useful new product, which question do you think they asked themselves more often: "Can I do this?" or "*How* can I do this?"

Instead of making grand proclamations of *what* you're setting out to achieve, or getting stuck in the do-I-have-what-it-takes self-defeating mental quagmire, focus your energy on *how* you will get there. Goals like "Run a minimum of forty-five minutes at least four times per week" and "Study a minimum of ten hours per week for the CPA exam" are certainly not as sexy as "Produce a Grammy-award winning CD," or "Become salesperson of the year in my company." Yet these are the real, tangible day-to-day activities that—through repetition and a commitment to continuously improving how you execute them—will get you across home plate.

"This is too small-time for me," you may be thinking. "I'm going to identify my larger goal and just focus on achieving it." Yes, I know setting smaller goals rooted in your daily actions requires you to slow down and look at the details instead of the big picture. But this process is more likely to bridge the distance to your larger goal. Why? Two reasons. First, as you learned in the last two chapters, focusing on small, tangible, distinct actions is a means of getting out of the dugout, hitting some clean singles, and gaining momentum toward your larger goal. The alternative is to stand paralyzed, like a deer caught in the headlights, in awe of a larger goal that is so daunting you doubt your ability to achieve it.

Second, if you define your goal by the result, then if you get a B- on the exam or don't cross the finish line first, you will feel like you didn't achieve your goal. Your perception of your own failure will decrease your self-esteem and actually render you less likely to achieve other goals.

Yet you should never feel like a failure when you've dedicated your full effort to a goal that's aligned with your deeper values. The sense of accomplishment in ascending any mountain is in the ascent, not in the view from the top. If you don't feel you did your best on the way up, the view loses its magnificence.

MAKE IT HAPPEN:

Revisit the two or three Action Plan goals you wrote down in the previous exercise. For each goal, search for cracks in the armor. Have a similar dialogue to the one above with yourself (or even better, try this exercise with a friend) to determine if your goal is SMART.

HOW YOUR GOALS EVOLVE

Shelley, the founder of Independence House, a homeless organization in Chicago, approached me after one of my strategic planning workshops.

"I just don't know what to do, Tony," Shelley said, clearly flustered. "Our shelter is losing its relevance in the community. I never thought I'd say this, but we have too many competitors now. It may be time for us to shut our doors."

Fifteen years earlier, Shelley and a few good friends had petitioned the city and cobbled together enough resources to purchase an abandoned building and convert it into a homeless shelter. Shelley and her friends started Independence House with a clear mission statement:

- To help homeless people live proud, self-reliant, fulfilling lives

Since this mission paints a desired picture of the future and is ultimately timeless and unattainable, I encouraged Shelley to integrate it into her personal Vision Statement. A matching goal in Shelley's one-year Action Plan for 2002 was:

- To provide shelter to over three thousand homeless people in Chicago

The year 2002 ended and Shelley achieved her goal. She set an even higher goal in her 2003 Action Plan to provide shelter to over 3,600 homeless people. In February 2003, however, three new shelters sprouted up in the same neighborhood as Independence House. When I met Shelley in June, Independence House had already lost over half its clients.

"There's no way we're going to achieve our goal." Shelley told me. "The organization is in crisis, and no one has the faintest clue how to proceed. We're all throwing our hands up in the air."

"Don't worry," I assured Shelley. "I don't think your work is over yet."

"But it is if no homeless people are coming to our shelter," she retorted.

"Let me ask you a question. Given the changes that have taken place in your community, how have the needs of the homeless people you serve evolved?"

"Well, they certainly have enough places to sleep now," Shelley laughed, lightening up for the first time. "Actually, it's really wonderful. This is what we were working toward all along. I guess we're all just anxious because we're not sure what to do next."

"What don't homeless people in Chicago have that they still need?" I asked.

Without skipping a beat, Shelley replied, "They need legal services. They can't afford to defend themselves when they are attacked, or unjustly evicted, or denied city services. They also need to know how to access programs that help them buy their own homes with very little start-up capital, because when they rent they only have a place to live for as long as they're employed."

Shelley was now speaking with passion.

"Let's go back to your Vision Statement," I said. I asked Shelley to reread the following entry:

- To help homeless people live proud, self-reliant, fulfilling lives

"Consider the transformed needs of homeless people in your community. Can you think of some new strategies to help you better realize your Vision Statement now?"

Shelley developed these three goals and put them into a new Action Plan for June 2003–June 2004:

- Sell the shelter by December 2003
- Hire two lawyers and provide legal services to over three hundred homeless people in Chicago by June 2004
- Hire a director of training and outreach and provide home ownership workshops to over a thousand homeless people in Chicago by June 2004

PRESERVE THE CORE AND STIMULATE PROGRESS

Like Shelley and Independence House, you will frequently change what you *do*—which your Action Plan highlights—to accommodate the needs of others or adapt to a changing environment. You will change who you *are*—which your Vision Statement describes—with much less frequency. Because they are durable and consistently relevant, your core values and

Vision (as outlined in your Vision Statement) are your refuge, your eye in the storm, the place you can always go to replenish your energy and feel strong, centered, and complete.

Here is the most critical skill for personal leadership: *to continuously design and commit the most effective new actions to realize your enduring Vision.* This leads us to the essential learning of this chapter and the power behind the Vision Statement/Action Plan combination: *The more comfortable you become with your core values (as reflected in your Vision Statement) the more you can innovate and change everything else each year (in your Action Plan).*

While your Vision Statement is the glue that holds you together and makes you a cohesive, grounded person, your Action Plan provides you with the resilience to adapt frequently to a rapidly changing environment. In short, when your self-definition and life values are changeless, you access unlimited power to change everything else. According to Collins and Porras:

> The fundamental distinguishing characteristic of the most enduring and successful corporations is that they preserve a cherished core ideology [Vision Statement] while simultaneously stimulating progress and change in everything that is not part of their core ideology [Action Plan].

Are you buying into this, or are you thinking, "Setting goals seems like just another way to add responsibilities and stress to my life"? The irony is that setting clear goals—while appearing to ratchet up the pressure to achieve them—actually makes you feel more relaxed and spontaneous. Why? Because you feel secure rather than confused about your life's direction. While it's true that you limit your behavior when you design a Vision Statement and Action Plan, it's also true that you reduce your "existential angst" about your life's greater purpose. You feel more complete, like you've "done your homework," and this feeling of alignment enables you to take more focused, innovative, and meaningful steps forward in your life.

MAKE IT HAPPEN:

At the end of the day, write down as many of the actions you took today as you can remember in the first column of the table below. Once you are finished, write down in the adjoining column the Action Plan goal that generated your action. Then, in the third column, note the Vision Statement entry that generated the Action Plan goal. If you like the action but it did not emanate from your Action Plan or Vision Statement, consider amending your Vision Statement and/or Action Plan to include entries that will yield similar actions in the future.

Action	Action Plan Goal	Vision Statement Entry

If you wish you hadn't taken the action, highlight it in red or circle it as a reminder that you don't want to repeat it. Try doing this exercise at the end of each day. This strategy will help you answer the question, "Did I live in line with my Vision today?" If you finish a day with no red marks, give yourself a reward. Do something kind (and aligned) for yourself to reinforce that you are living on purpose!

THE POWER OF POSITIVE THINKING

To set a goal is to take a bold stand. It's expressing your willingness to do whatever it takes to bring your desired future into existence. Most people spend their lives designing elaborate excuses to avoid this heightened level of self-effort. When you refuse to put your goals down on paper, your actions translate as either "I'm content to just go with the flow and see what happens" or "I'm not serious enough about my goals to hold myself accountable to them."

Without even realizing it, you may be stumbling around in a vault of negativity, continuously musing about what you *don't* want. When you create a Vision Statement and Action Plan, you replace these thoughts, which focus on the negative—how you've been hurt, what intimidates you, the times you or others let you down—with positive thoughts that describe what you *do* want in your life.

You may hold permanent residence in the mental labyrinth of trying to figure out why your ex-es didn't measure up, of focusing on what you *no longer want* in your life. As a result, you attract energy associated with your negative memories—angst, frustration, lost hopes—toward you. You see new potential partners in this light, and wait vigilantly for them to do the slightest thing that resonates with the negativity you're expecting. The lens you cover your eyes with determines what you see, shapes your perception, and becomes what you experience. If you instead visualize what you *do want* in a life partner (in your Vision Statement) and how you will meet and attract that person (in your Action Plan) you will do exactly the same thing: draw the energy you focus your mind on in your direction.

You choose the type of play you spend your life in—a comedy, a drama, a romance, or a suspenseful thriller. When you select the theater, you send energy to the world that attracts the characters you need to complete the story onto your stage.

This really works! Try it! Envision what you *really want* in your life—whether it's to find the ideal job, or to transform a friendship, or to develop hobbies that nurture you. Write it down in your Vision Statement and Action Plan, and review them regularly to keep the picture fresh in your mind. You will send energy to the world—and to the Actionary within you, who will make daily decisions based on this positive image—that will bring what you desire into your life.

This is not New Age read-this-book-and-uplift-your-day mumbo-jumbo. It's the practical, tangible combination of *intention* (in your Vision Statement) and *commitment* (in your Action Plan) that attracts what you want into your life and enables you to achieve your most profound life goals.

STAY ON YOUR OWN CUTTING EDGE

In a recent *New Yorker* cartoon, two cats are sitting in front of a sofa with claw marks all over it. The cat who has been shredding away at the sofa turns to the other cat and says, "I have a couple of other projects I'm excited about." It is human (but perhaps not feline) nature to always need a "stretch task" that both challenges you and provides a sense of opportunity and adventure. Otherwise, you show up for the same job, the same hobbies, the same vacations, and feel like a robot as you methodically repeat yesterday all the way to your coffin. Any physical trainer will tell you if you do the same exercises day after day your muscles will not experience growth.

The Vision Statement/Action Plan combination is the best rut-breaking strategy I'm aware of. I've literally used this strategy to help thousands of individuals rediscover their motivation and find a new sofa to shred. Take David, a young man in his early thirties whom I've mentored ever since he participated in a life skills program I taught in an inner-city high school in Oakland, California, when he was sixteen. After David graduated from our program and started college, I encouraged him to create his own Vision Statement. Here's an entry from it:

- To put my full effort into my education and continuously learn and grow *(timeless, unattainable)*

During David's senior year of college two of his Action Plan goals were:

- Finish college in June 2000
- Make the honor roll in fall 1999 and spring 2000 *(both goals are SMART)*

After David graduated with honors, he started working as a medical assistant. Two years later, we met for lunch in downtown Oakland.

"I'm doing a lot of menial work and not feeling very motivated," he said with a resigned look. "I'm bored and in a rut."

I encouraged David to return to his Vision Statement to remember his core values. Then he could identify some new goals that would provide a challenge again. David returned home, found his Vision Statement and reread the following entry:

- To put my full effort into my education and continuously learn and grow

David called me excitedly three days later. "I've realized why I'm bored: I've stopped paying attention to my Vision Statement. I know I've graduated from college, but I don't ever want to graduate from learning." David created four new Action Plan goals, which he read to me over the phone:

- Take an extension course in art history starting in September

- Read at least one educational book per month
- Take at least one salsa class per month until I can dance salsa well
- Make a decision about applying to medical school and becoming a doctor by June 2003

GOALS PROVIDE MEANING

Without compelling goals there's nothing to wake you up in the morning. Two-time Olympic gold medal–winning runner Sebastian Coe astutely observed: "Athletes always have to believe that there is something [more] they can do in the coming season. It's when they can't visualize themselves running any more quickly that they give up." What will be your monumental accomplishment in the coming season? Do you have some projects you're excited about, or are you short on motivation and long on routine? Identify a significant challenge or "stretch task" that will provide a call to action and return to purpose. It may be exactly what you need right now.

Pushing yourself to complete and renew these "stretch tasks" (in your Action Plan) is the only way to stay on your own cutting edge and continuously achieve spectacular results in your life. Why? First, your ceaseless effort to find a balance between your timeless Vision Statement and time-sensitive Action Plan yields "creative tension." This tension keeps you focused and moving forward toward compelling goals that inspire you to reach your potential.

Second, you need a new season in life. When you were younger it was all set up for you—next semester, football season, summer camp, school clubs, new courses, school trips, the prom, a study year abroad—there was always something around the corner to look forward to. Now it's up to you to either create your own program and determine new milestones for your life or fall prey to office-drone syndrome. If you succumb to this national epidemic, one season will start to blend into the next and before you know it you won't know why but you just won't care anymore.

Just as David has, you can also "preserve the core" of what you stand for while "stimulating progress" toward the future you envision. Your Vision Statement and Action Plan, in concert, enable you to preserve both *change amidst order* (by creating and pursuing new "stretch tasks" in your Action Plan) and *order amidst change* (by reverting to your Vision Statement periodically to reconnect with your deeper values). It's precisely this balance of change (when your life feels too antiseptic and routine) and order (when you are feeling diffuse and need to find your center) that fuels your motivation and fills your life with meaning.

YOUR MAJOR GOALS

Jennifer, a small business owner from Atlanta in her late twenties, designs her own clothing line called R-Bella. I helped Jennifer identify her two most important Major Goals for her Action Plan (which she wrote in March 2006):

- To develop R-Bella into one of the top five clothing lines in Atlanta in sales by July 2012 (when I turn thirty-five), enabling me to start a foundation for women's economic empowerment programs
- To get married and start a family by July 2011 (when I turn thirty-four)

In direct contradiction to the Action Plan goals set by Jim and Janice earlier in this chapter, Jennifer's Major Goals are a description of *desired results*. I realize this contradicts the reasons I've encouraged you to create process-oriented goals up to this point. I recommend that you include (only) a few bold, ambitious, results-oriented Major Goals in your Action Plan. Why? Because setting a few goals that are potentially attainable yet require your highest level of effort will enliven your sense of purpose and motivation to rise to a difficult challenge. You can then outline how you will expend this effort week by week in your other Action Plan goals.

Note that Jennifer's Major Goals also break the mold of the one-year Action Plan time frame. I recommend setting one or two Major Goals in your Action Plan that span up to five or ten years—for three reasons. First, they force you to summarize what will become your greatest long-term accomplishments. Second, they paint a more concrete picture of your desired future than the less tangible entries in your Vision Statement. Third, they act as a bridge between your Action Plan and Vision Statement that enhances their alignment.

After she identified her two most important Major Goals, Jennifer began to make day-to-day decisions based on whether they would move her toward these goals and her ideal future. She based her hiring and promotion decisions less on whether the person would become a good friend and more on whether they shared her values and were capable of enabling R-Bella to reach its sales targets. Her decision to go on a second date became less influenced by appearance and more by the long-term potential of the man she was sitting across the table from earlier in the week.

Many people are reluctant to establish aggressive goals because they don't want to fail. There is no such thing as failure, only learning. After Sony's Beta format lost the long battle for VCR market share to VHS in the 1970s, Sony reverted to a Vision Statement entry it had declared after World War II:

- The elevation of the Japanese national culture and status

The company reviewed once again its Major Goal of:

- Becoming the company most known for changing the worldwide image of Japanese products as being of poor quality

Since producing Beta format was in its old Action Plan, not its Vision Statement, Sony got rid of it and adapted to VHS—and then later to DVD. Over thirty years later, Sony is now a market share leader in more electronic products—including stereos, televisions, DVD players, and computers—than just about any other company in the world.

I recommend keeping your Major Goals to no more than two or three, writing them down in bold, and putting them at the top of your Action Plan. Jennifer makes decisions and keeps her level of motivation high by looking daily at the piece of paper she hangs above her desk with the heading "Major Goals for R-Bella."

Emerson once wrote, "Death comes to all, but great achievements build a monument which shall endure until the sun grows cold." Commit yourself to achieving a few Major Goals that will build a monument, a legacy, a tribute to your life.

Meditate. Go for a walk. Change the scenery. Do whatever you have to do, or stop doing (see *Chapter 1— Dream* to refresh your mind and get some ideas) to enter a space where you can create your Major Goals. I know you can set goals that are ambitious yet attainable and create the inner momentum that precedes self-change. Practice this strategy and you will feel motivated rather than listless, and directed rather than confused about what you want to accomplish in your life. Designing an Action Plan is not optional if you want to consider your life a success. Why? Because you'll never bring what you desire into your life if you don't name it first. Give this strategy a try. Your capacity to create something spectacular in your limited time on this planet will expand exponentially as a direct result of this simple act.

MAKE IT HAPPEN:

If your life could be anything you want, what would that be? Would it be the life you're living now? If not, how would it be different? What *could you do* that's bold, powerful, and aligned with your deeper values to create an unprecedented breakthrough in your life? What ambitious and far-reaching goals can you set over the next five to ten years to create the life you have imagined? Put a few of these Major Goals into your Action Plan. Are there any Vision Statement entries you'd like to add or amend based on these new goals?

CHAPTER 11

DISCIPLINE: CULTIVATE THE ACTIONARY WITHIN

No man is free who is not master of himself.
—EPICTETUS

Your success in your personal and professional life is built on the quality of your relationships. Your relationships hinge on one factor more than any other: your ability to deliver on your commitments. When you keep your word, you forge bridges of trust. Other people learn they can count on you. When you don't make good on your word, the bridges you've painstakingly constructed erode and eventually collapse.

The key question you have to answer to live a successful life, then, is "How can I make commitments I can keep and keep the commitments I make?" Here's the first clue to help you find the answer: *The foundation for making and keeping commitments to others is making and keeping commitments to your Self.* You can't earn the trust and respect of others until you first earn it from yourself. This skill—delivering what you promise to your Self—is at the core of discipline. It's the only way to become the kind of person first you, and then others, can count on.

THE ORIGINS OF DISCIPLINE

Discipline is derived from the word *disciple*, or "follower." In our modern society—which places such a high value on individualism—this word has taken on some very negative connotations. When you think of a "disciple," what image comes to your mind? Do you think of a follower of another person's Vision or principles? Does the word evoke images of people blindly following the decrees of megalomaniacal leaders all the way to their own demise, such as the more than nine hundred Americans who followed the orders of Jim Jones and drank cyanide in Guyana, or those who followed David Koresh in Waco, Texas?

How about the word "discipline" itself? Does this word dredge up negative memories of teachers, parents, or coaches who were constantly "disciplining" you when you were growing up? You may have been conditioned to think of discipline as something imposed on you from the outside. Like anything else that obstructs your freedom, you most likely perceive discipline as something you want to rebel against.

When you were a child, you may have had a teacher who didn't care about you or have your best interests at heart. Your acts of rebellion may have actually been acts of conformity—to your higher Vision for what you knew was possible for your life. Your survive-and-thrive instincts may have told you to disrupt a damaging power relationship and pursue your own agenda.

Alternatively, you may have been a "rebel without a cause." You may have intuitively realized that you needed to destroy a power relationship that wasn't working without considering what you wanted to replace it with, like a revolutionary who hasn't yet learned how to govern.

To reconstruct your relationship with discipline, ask yourself this question: What if the teacher, head honcho, or boss-man were your higher Self? Would you still want to rebel against discipline if the person imposing it were none other than the you that you know you can be?

BOARD YOUR OWN SHIP

Why is it important to understand your early encounters with discipline? Because you have rightfully taken issue with the *form* it has taken in your life. Yet when you blindly rebel against it you deny yourself the considerable benefits of its *function*. Your rite of passage to growing up just may be to stop equating rebellion with progress. It may be to realize that your rebellious instinct when others try to control you *and* your willingness *not* to rebel against your higher values are *both* acts of Vision-Alignment.

Here's the secret ingredient for becoming a fully formed human being: *Replace the discipline others used to get you to do what* they *wanted you to do with your own discipline to get yourself to do what* you *want you to do.* To achieve self-discipline, you have to get with the program—*your program!* You have to walk the path you yourself laid.

Take this leap of the imagination. Feel the presence of two powerful forces within you. You are the Visionary and also the "Actionary." The Visionary develops a Vision for what you want to accomplish in your life and how you will act toward others. The Actionary takes these lofty ideals, this higher "code of ethics," and transforms them into your daily actions. While the Visionary chooses how you want to live, the Actionary lives by what you choose.

You are both the director writing your life scripts and the actor reading from them. You are the one making the decisions and the one acting them out. You are the one who makes commitments and the one called upon to deliver. Part One of this book was about how to develop the Visionary within you. Part Three is about how to develop the Actionary. In every single moment of your life in which you become the Actionary and make your Vision happen—especially the moments that test your resolve because you would rather be doing something else—you exercise discipline.

In an earlier chapter, we discussed how "to lead" comes from "to guide" or "to travel." You are the only one fit to guide your journey, to be the Visionary or leader of your Self. You are the captain of your ship as it sets out to sea. Yet you are also the passenger on the dock searching for the right ship to board. Here's the key question this chapter urges you to answer: *Will you choose your Self as your captain or will you board another ship?*

No one else fully shares your Vision for what you want to achieve in your life. Everyone else has another agenda. Some care about you immensely and truly desire for your happiness. Nonetheless, their own agenda. They have a unique Vision for how they—and you—should go about this thing called life. Without discipline you are unable to follow your leader within, the designer of your own agenda. Instead, you give up on it and follow the agendas of others. You board another ship.

DISCIPLINE IS CHOOSING YOUR VISION OVER YOUR MOOD

"But why wouldn't I follow my Vision?" you may be thinking. "It doesn't make sense to do anything else, so what's the point of this chapter?" During the moments when you *feel* like living your higher ideals, you don't need to read this or any other book. Your feelings will naturally guide you toward your purpose. This chapter is about what to do when you *don't* feel like following your Vision.

A former client in his mid forties provides a window into the all-too-familiar struggle with self-discipline. A partner in a Virginia law firm, Fred was significantly overweight and declared being in good physical condition as one of his most important goals. He made a commitment to run or do some form of cardio exercise at least four times per week, and to not eat desserts until he had lost forty pounds. The following

Thursday, Fred finished work and didn't feel like going to the gym. Instead, he felt like stopping at Ben & Jerry's for an ice cream cone.

Recall a moment in the last month when you felt an intense emotion pulling you away from your Vision—such as anxiety about a parent's visit, or insecurity about how someone you just started dating feels about you, or fear of an impending conversation, or a craving for food or alcohol or sex. Freeze yourself in this moment. What if you could access the awareness you have now *while the moment was actually happening*? At every single moment in your life you are making a choice to either act on a temporary mood such as anger, fear, or anxiety or to act on your Vision. Discipline is choosing your Vision.

"Why should I incorporate a strategy into my repertoire that curtails my freedom?" you may be thinking. Yes, I know this is hard to digest. Yet consider what discipline enables. You may feel free to cheat on your spouse while on a business trip, but how will this decision affect your long-term happiness? You may exercise your personal liberty by dropping out of college in your senior year and backpacking across the country with a few Kerouac books to keep you company, but what effect will it have on your long-term success? Your freedom may urge you to tell your brother to shove it when he asks for your forgiveness, but how will this affect your relationship with him?

Discipline sacrifices an emotion, a momentary impulse, a desire—for a greater cause. Yet I'm not going to try to hide the elephant in the room: it's true that discipline obstructs your freedom. Backpacking across the country with a few Kerouac novels actually doesn't sound too bad right now. Yet unfettered freedom is overrated. Why? Because it encourages you to do what you *feel* like doing in the moment—regardless of the consequences. As we discussed in Chapter 7, freedom is not free. Its price is the life direction your self-imposed boundaries enable.

THE INTERNAL CONFLICT

I want you to step onto the balcony for a moment and observe yourself in your daily life. Do a mental scan of the last few years. Recall a moment when an emotion pulled you away from a deeper value or life goal. Remember feeling irritable and snapping at a family member, or feeling jealous and saying something to your partner you came to regret, or boasting to a friend and feeling later it wasn't you speaking but your insecurity.

Recall the internal dissonance between your mood and your higher Self in this moment. Feel once again your burning desire to act out your mood. Remember the voice playing like a broken record inside your head, saying "If I don't protect myself, who will? They had *no right* to talk to me like that. Let me just get this off my chest and be done with it!" Now shift your focus to the other voice that commands you to act based on love and other higher values rather than your mood. Listen to its wisdom as it says, "I'd better take a few breaths and give this some time. I need to calm down and figure out what's really important to me, and what I have to let go. I love this person, and don't want to say something I'll regret."

How you respond to these disparate voices creates your character. Instead of fighting against or denying these two voices, embrace each one and the inner tension they create. It's precisely this internal conflict in the protagonist that defines the "hero's journey" in your favorite books and movies. Edward Norton's path toward believing in racial harmony in *American History X* was riveting only because of his fight against his own racist preconceptions. How interesting would you have found Luke Skywalker's quest to learn the way of the Jedi if there were no Dark Side within himself to struggle against? The force of your Vision can be with you, but only if you first reassure yourself that it's OK to feel the entire range of emotions that rage within you, vying against each other in a bitter struggle to be heard.

These diverse emotions are your internal rank and file. You always have a choice in how you manage the platoon. You can lead with empathy and acknowledge the uniqueness of each soldier while guiding the troops in a specific direction. Alternatively, you can abdicate your leadership and give your emotions free reign, in which case they will fight a destructive internal war that will leave you battered, paralyzed, and in a state of denial.

Pick a situation and ask yourself whether you're keeping your emotions under control or letting the inmates run the asylum. If you're staying up until three in the morning emailing potential internet dates who live thousands of miles away and, like you, are hiding behind their computers rather than risking being vulnerable with someone in their zip code, or if you're once again shacking up on the third date and then wondering why he doesn't call, or if you're having a "social drink" every time you feel nervous at an event, ask yourself, "What's my Vision with respect to dating, or drinking, or winding down every evening?" Reflect on what you deeply value before you allow the intensity of your need for companionship, sex, or short-term relief to guide your decisions.

Discipline is not just doing what your Vision guides you to do. It's refraining from doing what your Vision guides you not to do. After taking time to reflect on how you *want* to be, how you *know* you can be, integrate your new thoughts into an inspiring Vision to guide you from this day forward. Create a goal in your Action Plan such as, "Check internet dating sites a maximum of two times per week and turn off the computer by 11 p.m." or "Go on at least ___ dates and spend at least ___ months with someone before allowing the relationship to progress physically," or "Drink a maximum of two drinks on the weekend, and one drink during the week." Review whether you are achieving your new goal daily until you internalize it.

Does this sound too nitpicky and detail oriented for you? While it's true that this approach focuses on the nuances of the words you use with yourself, it's also true that if you're unwilling to describe your desired destination in detail you will never know when you arrive. How can you reach a place you can't identify? Do you jump in the car to drive off for a three-day weekend and tell your kids, "This is going to be so much fun. We're going to have such a good time in the place whose name I can't remember"? Picture your kids looking bemused, nudging each other, and wanting to get out of the car. This is how *you* feel when the Visionary within you doesn't assume its leadership role and define a clear path for you (as Actionary) to follow.

STAND AND DELIVER

Discipline is the practice of internal leadership. Not discipline meaning, "I will follow my Vision when it's convenient or when it doesn't disturb others." Discipline meaning: "My Vision will guide me independent of what comes my way. Yet I will be open to adapting it if circumstances consistently prove it too rigid."

Pick a situation and ask yourself if you're exercising self-discipline. If your child acts up, before you react shift your mind to your Vision Statement entry—written when you were thinking about you at the end of your life thinking about you now—that guides you to use empathetic and nurturing forms of parenting. If an employee is slow on the uptake and quick to head downstairs when the clock strikes five, recall your Vision Statement entry that requires you to be patient, to treat your staff with respect, and to help them find their passion in their work.

Conjure up an image in your mind of a disciplined person. Do they do whatever they feel in the moment regardless of the consequences?

Hardly. Do they blow up at their children, employees, or anyone else who doesn't live up to their expectations? Not at all. Do they treat you however they want based on their emotion *du jour*? I doubt it. They are disciplined because they've learned how to master their emotions.

Discipline requires two very disparate skills: the ability to resist and the ability to obey. It requires you to resist the dictates of your fleeting moods and to obey the commands of your higher Self. The real question, then, is which master you will follow.

"This sounds too premeditated and boring," you may be thinking. "I can't be blamed for giving in to my animal instincts from time to time." Yes, I know what I'm asking you to do isn't easy. You may be quite comfortable living hand to mouth with your emotions. You may be accustomed to serving up your emotions hot and fresh right out of the skillet regardless of how they fit with what you value.

It's not a question of blame, but responsibility. You have been blessed with the ability to accomplish much more in your life, to live a more stable, lengthy, and dynamic existence than most other animals because of your larger, more developed brain and your mental capacity to think before you act. Discipline leverages this capacity and enhances what makes you uniquely human.

Exercising self-discipline means that when an emotion is compelling you to return yet another text message while your daughter waits for you to go outside and play, or to make another selfish comment and push someone who loves you even further away, or to take another bite although your body no longer needs it, you can preempt any negative behaviors by exclaiming, "I will not just act because I feel I *need* to do something. I will instead recognize that while addictive tendencies make me human, I do not have to transform them from an impulse into my reality."

Alternatively, you may be thinking, "This discipline thing isn't all it's cracked up to be. Why not just live and let live?" This is a good question. Why exercise self-discipline at all for that matter? Because we're civilized. What we call civilization is the discipline of a society. We enact laws and elect a government to set parameters on what we can and cannot do based on (in theory) values we all hold dear. We then entrust this government to use these parameters to control the passions, prejudices, and harmful tendencies of our fellow citizens. These laws, in an ideal society, provide us with feelings of security and safety.

Self-discipline is the creation of an inner civilization. It's an effort to provide yourself with the security of knowing your actions will not stray from predetermined parameters in the name of certain truths *you* hold self-evident. Just as the goal of a civilized nation is for its citizens to live harmoniously with one another, your self-discipline enables your emotions, thoughts, and motivations to live in harmony. Just as any citizen in a civilized society must accept that they will not always get their way, neither will your desire, anxiety, anger, or any other emotion always get its way—yet it must live in harmony with your thoughts and beliefs and accept your Vision Statement as its guiding constitution.

Discipline, in essence, is the alignment of the part of you that sets goals or makes commitments (the Visionary) with the part of you that delivers (the Actionary). Just as Fred and I were able to get Fred to drive past Ben & Jerry's and continue all the way to the gym, if we can get you to release yourself from your moods and habitual patterns and align your daily actions with your Vision—whether that means quitting smoking, or making time for your family, or keeping your cool when a coworker gets under your skin, or learning how to play the guitar—then this book will have served its purpose. Note I said "we." I need your help. Together, let's develop some strategies to help you (as Visionary) make realistic commitments that you (as Actionary) can keep.

BUILD YOUR TRACK RECORD

In the last chapter, you learned how to develop your capacity for risk by taking small risks that increase your self-esteem and, consequently, your ability to take larger risks. The same dynamic holds true with self-discipline. When you make a small commitment to yourself and keep it—whether by delivering on a mental promise or achieving a goal you've written down in your Action Plan—you build your self-trust. Your enhanced self-image expands your capacity to make and then deliver on larger commitments.

DEVELOPING YOUR CAPACITY TO MAKE AND DELIVER ON COMMITMENTS

When you make a commitment to your Self, you are both the person doing the promising (you as Visionary) and the person carrying out the promise (you as Actionary). Both people are waiting to see if you can build your life around your declarations. When you deliver, the part of you that made the promise (the Visionary) increases its trust in the part of you that delivered (the Actionary) and vice versa.

The word confidence comes from the Latin roots *com* ("with") and *fidere* ("trust"). You have confidence in another person when you have "trust with" them. Similarly, you have self-confidence when you have trust with yourself. The good news is you already have a track record of making and keeping successful commitments and building "trust with" yourself. I'm willing to bet you've already honored a few tacit promises to yourself, such as: to put on clothes before you leave the house, to not steal your neighbor's hubcaps, to not pick your nose while giving a presentation, and to not stand up in the middle of a movie at a crowded theater and sing at the top of your lungs, "I just gotta be me!"

You take these self-declarations for granted because you perceive them as critical to your survival. Yet if you can make commitments at the basic self-preservation level, there's no reason you can't also make larger commitments driven by your higher values that further define the range of options your inner Actionary can choose from.

THE POWER OF YOUR WORD

The written word holds a lot of power. During the Korean War the Chinese, with marked success, turned many American prisoners against the U.S. government by forcing them to write down the problems with capitalism. This brainwashing was so successful that some American POWs were recorded giving long tirades repudiating capitalism on

Chinese national radio. When you write something down, you believe it with more conviction than when you just think it or say it.

Build your capacity to deliver on your word by writing down a few things you want to change in your life. Start small. Make a small commitment for a short period, such as a week. Here are a few examples of commitments I made to myself (and wrote down) last year:

- Try to volunteer at least once per week teaching self-sufficiency skills to low-income youth
- Try to go for a long walk in nature at least once per week
- Try not to work after 7 p.m. on weekdays

Sometimes you're not 100 percent sure you have the willingness or ability to achieve a goal. This creates a dilemma: write it down and it may reduce your self-esteem if you don't accomplish it; don't write it down and you might forget it and lose the opportunity to *build* the willingness or ability to achieve it. I recommend putting these "auditioning goals" onto paper—because they pave the way to more compelling goals in the future—and prefacing them with the word "Try," as I have above. This strategy enables you to steer your life in a new direction without making a promise you might break. I know this strategy works because I learned it the hard way.

Living in Africa for four years yielded an interesting side effect in my life. In a rural society with no telephones to call people when you're running late, a lack of punctuality was as much a part of the culture as the local dish of mashed cassava and beans I grew to love. Traveling from A to B was not as predictable as in America; to pass someone on the street and not stop to greet them is considered deftly rude in Kenyan culture, so imagine a small rural town where you know everyone and you get the idea.

When I first arrived in Kenya, I would show up punctually for a meeting with a few hundred parents for a school project at ten in the morning. I was greeted upon arrival by the sheep and the cows. After arriving on time on three or four occasions and waiting an hour and a half for everyone to arrive, I took the "If you can't beat 'em, join 'em" approach, and began to show up ninety minutes late as a matter of routine. This single decision more than any other prevented me from becoming frustrated and bitter toward the local culture, and enabled me to feel accepted and enjoy my time in Africa.

My newfound skill at arriving late for meetings did not win over many hearts after my return to America. It became the most difficult habit I've ever had to shake. No matter how hard I tried, I just couldn't be on time anymore.

Then I changed my commitment. Instead of "Be on time for every work and social meeting," I changed it to "Try to be on time." The problem with my initial commitment was if I was late by ten minutes, which happened routinely, I felt I had broken it and got down on myself, which exacerbated the problem. I had become accustomed in Africa to stopping and talking at length with people spontaneously, and couldn't adjust to abruptly disregarding others who weren't in the preconceived plan.

I finally realized I had to plan for contingencies and unforeseen interactions. My new Action Plan goal became "Try to be fifteen minutes early for every meeting with another human being—and bring a book." I'm still often ten or fifteen minutes behind my plan—yet there before the other person, or just a few minutes after.

I'm the greatest beneficiary of my punctuality. I get a small break in my day to just breathe and relax or to read something that keeps me on the cutting edge of my work. Arriving on time also builds up my leverage and negotiating power. I've noticed when the other person is late, they often feel they have to "make up" for not being punctual, and are more willing to concede on key issues than they would be otherwise.

THE TRUST MANTRA

Here's a strategy to help you make successful commitments and build trust in your relationships (with yourself and others) that guides every successful leader I've ever coached. I call it the Trust Mantra: *Underpromise and overdeliver, not the opposite.*

If you want to lose forty pounds in one year, make a commitment to either:

- Lose at least twenty pounds by the end of the year; or
- Try to lose forty pounds by the end of the year

If you want to make time to work on your paintings at least three times per week, write either:

- Paint at least twice per week; or
- Try to paint at least three times per week

If you want to stop drinking entirely, write:

- Have at most one drink every __ (number of weeks or months)

In each of these situations, you can still achieve your higher goal by underpromising. In fact, you will feel a higher sense of accomplishment when you surpass your commitment (overdeliver). Once you achieve your initial goal you can raise the stakes and—with your renewed self-confidence illuminating the way—set a higher goal.

In which area of your life do you feel frustrated because you're not living up to your expectations? Getting yourself to exercise? Calling your parents more often? Taking your partner out more and making them feel special? Spending more time with your kids? Have you reached the point where you say to yourself, "I'm just not going to say too much anymore. It's better not to set myself up for disappointment."

One of our foremost pioneers of self-reliant thinking, Ralph Waldo Emerson, wrote: "Trust thyself: every heart vibrates to that iron string." Have you lost faith in your capacity to deliver? If so, know this for certain: your lack of self-trust is spilling into other areas of your life. It's diminishing your self-esteem and your ability to build healthy, sustainable relationships.

You can rebuild your self-trust—starting now. Make a small commitment you instinctively feel you can deliver on, or reach a little higher and preface your commitment with the word "Try." Be careful with the words you use. Making commitments to yourself again after not delivering in the past is like reuniting with an ex after a breakup: both people (in your case, the Visionary and Actionary within you) are waiting for the other shoe to drop.

MAKE IT HAPPEN:

It's time for the Actionary to undergo its quarterly performance review. Hold a meeting between your internal Visionary and Actionary. To start the meeting, have the Visionary ask the Actionary, "How do you feel about your performance over the last few months?" Give the Actionary time to reflect on the results they've been bringing in before answering.

Then shift back to the Visionary again, who says, "Let's review our Vision Statement and Action Plan and see how we're doing." After assessing the Actionary's recent performance, create a few new strategies they can implement to improve how they perform in the future. If you feel it's appropriate, make changes to your Action Plan and/or Vision Statement accordingly.

DEATH BY CHOCOLATE

While these strategies will help, unless you lose your status as a human being you will still break some of your commitments. No matter what precautions you take, you will never reach a 100 percent delivery rate. Why? Because words are imperfect attempts to approximate reality. This is why the path to self-trust in the above diagram—like the risk-taking diagram in Chapter 9—is not linear, but a series of twists, turns, and detours. No matter how hard you try to order it, reality is a take-it-or-leave-it package filled with unexpected events and circumstances that often defies prediction. The struggle of a former client to deliver on his commitments recalls the essential humanness within all of us.

A burly man in his mid forties with straggly auburn hair and a strong southern accent lumbered up to me after a workshop on self-discipline. He looked down at the floor and stammered, "Tony, I just can't lose weight no matter how hard I try. I've just about given up on it now."

I asked him to share a few strategies he had used in the past to lose weight.

"I once put my mind to losing forty pounds over six months," Robert said. "For two months I went to the gym five times per week and gave up all desserts, and I lost fifteen pounds. I know that's hard to believe looking at me now. Then one day I broke down and had some chocolate cake, and didn't go to the gym. The cake was appropriately named 'Death by Chocolate.' I never did make it back to the gym after that day. I started eating desserts again and, well, here I am."

I listened quietly as Robert shook his head and grimaced. "At its core, this is an issue of self-trust," I shared. "Your self-esteem remained high as long as you delivered on the promise you made to yourself. The day you broke that promise and ate that first piece of cake is the day you lost all the self-confidence you worked so hard to gain."

Robert's plight is a reminder of why it's a good idea to be more flexible in the commitments you make than "Never eat dessert again until I've lost 40 pounds." Regardless of how you say or write it, however, there's no way around it: as long as you're human (i.e., for your foreseeable future) you'll break your commitments from time to time.

CHOOSE LEARNING OVER GUILT

What's the solution here? What can you do when, like Robert, you break a promise to your Self and eat that figurative piece of cake—which for you may be a cigarette, or not showing up to a class, or an emotional outburst? First, acknowledge that you didn't keep your word. Second, don't be hard on yourself. Third, reassess quickly and make a more realistic and achievable commitment.

Just like that—one, two, three, change. No guilt. No self-flagellation. Only learning. Not "Something must be wrong with me or I wouldn't have made this mistake." Not "I'm so disappointed in myself. I guess I just don't have what it takes." Instead: "What can I learn from my actions so I can be more effective the next time around?" Learn from the past, then let go of it and determine how you can do better in the future. Consider Nietzsche's wisdom:

> Never give way to remorse, but immediately say to yourself: that would merely mean adding a second stupidity to the first ... If you have done harm, see how you can do good.

Don't beat yourself up emotionally if you break a commitment. Feeling guilt is a "second stupidity" because it opens the door to all kinds of vices and dysfunctional behavior—many potentially even worse than where you were before you started making self-declarations in the first place! Whatever you did in the past—it's over! Move on! No amount of guilt will change one iota of what's already happened. It will, however, decrease your capacity to make the right choices in the future by tearing down your strength and self-esteem.

You may have a plethora of excuses to rationalize your breaches of self-discipline. These excuses are an internal defense mechanism to prevent you from falling prey to the destructive tentacles of guilt. Each time you stray from your path, you may create a new line of reasoning to justify your actions. "She shouldn't have provoked me," "It was only one cigarette," "It's not my fault if she takes everything so seriously. I was just having some fun." It's not only guilt that steers you in the wrong direction—it's also false reasoning designed to protect you from it. Replace both with an openness to learning and a relentless desire for truth. This is the only way to increase your chances of not doing in the future whatever you wish you didn't do in the past.

I know it's not easy to put this way of thinking into practice. You have a natural human tendency to get down on yourself whenever you meander off your path. No matter where you are in your life—including after not keeping your word or doing something you wish you hadn't—*just do the right thing now.* Nothing else is within your control. Learn from whatever transpired in the past, but then put it behind you and focus on the only power at your disposal: the power to create change in the present.

NO MATTER WHERE YOU ARE, MOVE TOWARD YOUR CENTER

Deeply rooted in Western culture (stemming from Catholicism and Judaism) is the idea that guilt is an effective way to motivate people. The conventional thinking instilled in you from childhood that enables others to use guilt to control you is: *feel badly enough about something and you'll stop doing it.* It only works for a time. Here's what actually happens: *feel badly enough about something and your self-esteem will decrease—which will in turn decrease your capacity to avoid whatever behavior you're feeling badly about.*

The alternative to guilt is self-love and learning. Self-love enhances your belief in your ability to learn and evolve, which removes the need for guilt. The next time you say, "How could I have done that? What's wrong with me?" recognize you are heading down the intimidate-myself-into-change-through-guilt path and step off it. Make a sharp turn toward your Vision—which hopefully includes loving yourself—and say, "I acted in the past based on the informational, psychological, emotional, and financial resources available to me. I now have new resources at my disposal—including the lessons I've learned—and will act differently in the future."

Bring forth in your mind someone you consider self-disciplined. Do they execute seamlessly? I don't think so. Does everything always fall into place for them? Although it may appear so, it doesn't. Even the people who seem the most in control of their lives falter from time to time. Consider a few relatively popular U.S. presidents and their monumental screwups. For JFK it was the Bay of Pigs; for LBJ it was Vietnam; for Bill Clinton it was Rwanda and Monica Lewinsky. The primary ingredient for self-discipline is not an innate ability to not mess up, but a stick-to-it-ness about getting back up, dusting yourself off, and trying again.

Every time you jump into the swirl of life, you extend from your center. When you lose your self-discipline you extend too far. To regain your center, locate it and then take a step in its direction. No matter where you are, just two simple steps: one, detect your center; two, move toward it. Your center is your Vision. The first step is to bring it into your mind or read your Vision Statement. The second step is to act in any way that's aligned with it. Note there is no step called "Feel Guilty" or "Doubt

Yourself." Just two mandatory steps: connect with the Visionary within and become the Actionary. Getting down on yourself is optional.

AMEND A COMMITMENT BEFORE BREAKING IT

"So what do I do?" Robert asked. "After all, I *did* eat the chocolate cake. How do I regain my self-trust?"

Discipline is impossible without self-trust. It's imperative, then, that any strategy for instituting self-discipline focuses on honoring your word—first with yourself and then with others. For this reason, I encourage you to *amend a commitment before breaking it*. Force yourself to sign a document every day for a week (or at least a few days) that authorizes you to amend any promise you make to yourself before dishonoring it. In other words, *change your Vision before you change your actions*. This is often called "managing expectations" when it involves a promise you've made to someone else. Yet to manage expectations with others, you must first learn how to manage expectations with yourself.

"It's critical not to break the promises you make to yourself," I shared with Robert. "This means that after you make a commitment you have two options. One is of course to deliver. The second is to change the commitment if you can't honor it. The next time you can't live up to a personal declaration—such as never to eat dessert—instead of breaking it, amend it so you can eat dessert no more than, say, twice a week. Yet don't eat dessert in that moment—that would be too easy. If you really feel you want to make this change, sit with your decision for a week to make sure it's aligned with what you deeply feel is right for you."

Robert first wrote, "Eat dessert no more than three times per week." By the third week, he changed it to once per week. He has been honoring this commitment for over four years. In fact, rarely does Robert now have dessert more than once per month. Robert has lost over fifty pounds and returned to a healthy weight. Why was Robert successful in achieving self-discipline? Because he increased his commitment gradually as he expanded his self-control rather than overreaching, coming up short, getting down on himself, and then giving it up entirely.

The Roman Stoic philosopher Lucius Seneca provided this insight: "Most powerful is he who has himself in his own power." While signing a document for a week may seem like overkill, it wasn't for Robert. It kept him firmly in his own power, and in control of his life direction. By amending his word before breaking it, he strengthened his self-trust. This small win led to much larger wins and set him on the path to self-discipline.

A COMMITMENT IS LIKE A NEGOTIABLE CONTRACT

A father tells his son he'll take him to the ball game on Sunday. On Friday, he realizes he'll never get his report in to his boss on Monday unless he skips the game and works all weekend. To understand the profound impact of discipline on your psyche, envision yourself as both the father and the son. If you don't inform your son before Sunday that you can't take him to the game, you (the son) will feel disappointed and will lose faith in you (the father). The next time you try to raise your son's hopes about another ball game, you (the son) will be hesitant to believe it will truly happen. If you want to keep your relationship with yourself in good standing, then, you have two alternatives. Either find a way to take your son to the game or tell him before Sunday that you'll take him to a park to throw the ball around for an hour and/or take him to a game another weekend.

If being successful is one of your goals, you must take care of your inner child by aligning your internal Visionary and Actionary. The ultrahuman part of you that feels scared and insecure and overwhelmed by that big intimidating world out there will start to *believe* in what you proclaim, will watch with keen eyes as you deliver a small win, and will increase its willingness to believe in something even greater.

This inner child is your fear, the tender part of you that shrieks when touched and crawls into its self-protective shell. Fostering its growth into a strong, fully-formed being that can stand on its own two feet is your life's greatest challenge. You rise to this challenge every time you stand and deliver. You enable her or him to believe it's *possible* to dare to dream because those dreams may actually materialize. This mindful, everyday process of committing what you can deliver and delivering on what you commit is the only path available to bestow your inner child with the necessary strength and confidence to conceive and then achieve great things in your life.

Gandhi once said, "Always aim at complete harmony of thought and word and deed." To achieve inner harmony and consistency, think of every commitment you make to yourself—and then to others—as a negotiable contract. By checking in with yourself for a week or at least a few days before amending a commitment, you purchase an insurance policy against having dessert, or taking a drink, or blowing up at your children when you've been hijacked by your emotions.

One of the key learnings of this chapter is that your inner Visionary and Actionary don't always naturally coalesce. Slow down and reconnect with what you value before making a decision and you will become more adept at coaxing them to reunite. Your effort to keep your actions within the parameters set by your Vision will not always bear fruit, yet will yield much greater results as you build your confidence in your ability to honor your commitments. The enhanced level of self-control you will feel when you honor your word will generate overwhelming feelings of self-realization, self-worth, self-trust, and, ultimately, self-respect.

Every time you keep your actions in line with your evolving Vision, you refine one of the most complex and critical skills in your repertoire—the ability to take a stand for something and then back it up—and become a person who exercises self-discipline. By teaching the Actionary how to act under the guidance of the Visionary within, you launch yourself on the only path available to create success—as you define it—in your life.

MAKE IT HAPPEN:

Think of a few habits you *don't yet have*—such as exercising, or volunteering, or abstaining from certain behaviors, or continuing your education, or going to yoga classes—that would help you become the person you know you can be. To acquire these habits, write down two or three commitments to your Self that you will honor over the next week. Preface your commitments with the word "Try" if necessary, and don't be overly ambitious in the beginning. Start small, gain some small wins, and build your "commitment track record."

Put your commitments in a place where you will see them every day—such as on a fluorescent card taped to your wall, refrigerator, or bathroom mirror. Alternatively, write them on a stick-it and put it on your computer monitor, or on an index card you keep in your purse or wallet. Check in with yourself on your progress a few times during the week. At the end of the week, reassess and either make new commitments or recommit to those you've already made. If you decide after a few weeks or a month to maintain any of your pledges for the entire year, put them in your Action Plan.

The Player and the Spectator

If youth knew; if age could.
—*Freud*

Have you ever watched a heron fly above the ocean and then suddenly plunge into the water, submerging itself in its quest for fish? Imagine you are flying above a lake and dive deep into the water, not for dinner but to reach the bottom. Once you arrive at the lake's floor, let your body become still. As the water settles and becomes clear, let your mind do the same. Sitting there, in the depths of the lake, is your true Self. When the lake is clear, you see to the bottom of who you truly are. You become calm, peaceful, and serene, just like the water.

Goethe once wrote, "It is easier to perceive error than to find truth, for the former lies on the surface and is easily seen, while the latter lies in the depth, where few are willing to search for it." Are you willing to take the plunge and search for truth, even though it will almost always elude you? Once you encounter even a glimpse of truth, all it will take is a tiny stone to fall into your lake to destroy the inner peace that accompanies it. The first ripple will lead to other, larger ripples, and soon the water will be stirred up and you will no longer be at peace.

When the water on the surface is agitated and rushing in different directions, you become like that water. When you feel anxious, upset, depressed, or afraid, return to the bottom of the lake and let the water settle. Then you will see clearly again. You will see others as they truly are—and yourself as you truly are. You will make decisions that emanate from your center.

You can think of your Vision and higher Self, which await you at the bottom of the lake, as the *spectator.* It observes the other part of you, the *player,* which coasts along the surface like the heron—acting and interacting its way through life. You assume both roles simultaneously: you are both the player and the spectator watching yourself play. You are the actor on stage and the observer focused intently on the actor from the balcony. When you take time out regularly to strengthen the spectator, the player learns to play smarter. The player becomes more directed, consistent, and effective.

Life is an intriguing paradox: you are the spectator during the most fragile, vulnerable periods of your life, and the player when you are the most able. As an infant and small child, you're the spectator. You observe everything around you with wondrous curiosity. Then you become the player for decades. You spin through life and act the days away. Over time, as you become older and weaker, the spectator takes over again, looks back on your life, and considers the player's moves.

Many people ignore the spectator's values and allow the player to do whatever it feels like in the moment. This is why when most people do the eightieth birthday exercise they find their day-to-day life so incongruent with their highest priorities.

By your eightieth birthday, it's too late. At this point, the spectator holds center stage by default as the player has grown weary. While you certainly do not have to "retire" the player when you turn eighty or any other age, neither should you ignore the spectator while you're in your prime.

There's tremendous irony in the human tendency to wait until the game is almost over to become the spectator and understand the player's motivations. As Emerson writes, "Experience is a comb which a man gets when he becomes bald." If you want to live a happy, successful, and meaningful life, you have to get off the field and talk to the spectator *now*, not after it's too late to do anything about what she or he tells you.

The relationship between the player and the spectator is paradoxical: the player must leave the field to build their comfort with the spectator, yet if the player doesn't have an initial faith in the spectator they won't seek out this meeting. In other words, you have to take time to dream to build your self-faith, yet you need self-faith to feel comfortable dreaming—and spending time with the spectator—in the first place. So we return to one of the most important lessons in this book: your success depends on your willingness to take a leap of faith and believe in the goodness and beauty within. This leap of faith builds your comfort with yourself, which enables you to dream and create a Vision for your life.

So bring your player and spectator together. Develop their relationship until it takes root and becomes sustainable. To reunite them, ask yourself questions such as:

- "How can I better actualize (player) what I deeply believe in (spectator)?"
- "What are my greatest dreams (spectator) and how can I live them every day (player)?"
- "Do I consistently take time (player) to be alone or do I avoid my Self (spectator)?"
- "Do I treat my family, friends, and partner (player) the way I deeply feel about them (spectator)?"
- "Do I have a job (player) that reflects my deepest values (spectator)?"

THE PLAYER AND THE SPECTATOR REVIEW FULL ALIGNMENT

Full Alignment is a book about how to integrate the spectator into the life of the player. It's about how to *live consciously*. It's a guide to enabling the player and spectator to live together in peaceful coexistence. This will only happen if you consistently take the player off the field to meet with the spectator so the player understands what the spectator values. You learned how to take this time off-line in *Chapter 1— Dream.*

In *Chapter 5—Believe* and *Chapter 6—Make Peace with Disapproval,* you discovered how critical it is for the spectator to believe in the player's abilities and vice versa. If the player doesn't have faith in the spectator, the player will not choose to spend time with him or her. When these meetings become frequent, the player builds a sufficient comfort level to ask the spectator a series of life questions.

You embarked on a journey into understanding these questions in *Chapter 2—The Timeless Power of Vision.* In *Chapter 3—The Confluence of Heart and Mind,* you considered the inner conflict raging within you that you must mediate to answer them. You learned how the player can record this conversation and apply the learnings to his or her daily life in *Chapter 4—Create Your Own Vision Statement.*

In *Chapter 8—The Source of Your Motivation,* you learned that when the player follows their instincts they can make bold moves that cause the spectator to rethink their values—a fact the player found particularly interesting. The player also liked the central theme of *Chapter 9—Develop Your Capacity for Risk*—that the team will only move downfield if the spectator gives the player some latitude to follow their instincts and try out some courageous moves.

A healthy relationship between the player and the spectator hinges on the player's capacity to commit actions consistent with what the spectator believes. In *Chapter 10—Design an Action Plan,* you learned a number of strategies to ensure that the player consistently checks in with the spectator to monitor the player's performance. The Vision Statement/Action Plan combination enables the player to continuously stay on track, a skill we referred to as discipline in *Chapter 11—Discipline: Cultivate the Actionary Within.*

Chapter 11 also reinforced that until the spectator—or Visionary—can make commitments the player—or Actionary—can deliver on, you won't earn trust from yourself or others. Finally, in the last chapter you learned how the player can call a time-out and reunite with the spectator even when under attack by the opposing team. These meetings enable the player to continuously learn from its challenges, maintain its poise, and face front and center no matter what transpires on the field.

STAYING THE COURSE

There are two essential lessons in *Full Alignment*. The first is that the spectator will only enjoy the game if you integrate their priorities into the player's movements throughout the whirlwind of life. The alternative—to wait until the disconnect between the spectator's values and the player's moves leaves you disillusioned and distraught—will slow your life to a standstill.

The second lesson is that you will never fully arrive. Complete Vision-Alignment is a feeling. While the feeling of being aligned can last for a long time, as with all other feelings sometimes you wake up and realize it's slipped away. On some days you realize your busy life has been driving you away from what you value and you need to return; on others you become aware it's *you* that's been changing. You haven't been willing to read the writing on the wall and shed the old skin that no longer covers you. This disconcerted, disoriented feeling is not negative; it's a signal that you need to slow down and become acquainted with the new feelings brewing within, and to embrace change.

You will notice two things about alignment over time: first, that you fall out of it much more quickly and easily than the painstaking effort you expend to achieve it. Second, that if you keep it in your mind as a continuous goal, its duration will increase over time as you become more skilled at maintaining it. Your constant, unswerving willingness to initiate a candid self-dialogue to assess where you are and then take a step toward your center (where alignment resides) will continuously regenerate the feeling of alignment and the feelings of success, happiness, and meaning that follow it wherever it goes.

The hundreds of strategies that fill the pages of this book are all different ways of moving toward a more aligned life. All have been building blocks to prepare you for one final commitment I want you to make before closing this book: to never stop reuniting the player and spectator, and coming up with new, unique, creative strategies during these meetings to integrate your life Vision into the choices you make every day. In so doing, you will keep your life continuously moving toward Full Alignment.

About The Author

Anthony Silard is President and CEO of The Executive Leadership Institute and The Center for Social Leadership. As a leadership development coach, Anthony has been the primary facilitator of multi-day leadership conferences for thousands of individuals and corporate and organizational executives over the past twelve years.

Anthony has been featured at the Presidential Summit for America's Future and on MSNBC, Voice of America, CNN, and over a hundred television stations and newspapers across America. He has lectured at Harvard, Georgetown, Stanford, the University of California at Berkeley, Howard University, George Washington University, and many other colleges throughout the country. A PBS documentary on his life and work has aired in over forty U.S. states. Anthony completed his Master's in Public Policy with a focus on Leadership at Harvard University and his BA at the University of California at Berkeley. He lives in Washington, D.C.

Finding Your Path to Alignment:
Alignment Workshops with Anthony Silard

If you are interested in participating in an alignment or leadership workshop with Anthony Silard, or in Anthony facilitating a workshop at your company, school, or organization, you can check for workshop updates/session topics and contact Anthony at *www.execleaders.com* (for individuals and companies) or *www.socialleaders.org* (for nonprofit organizations, universities, and schools).

The author will contribute 25 percent of the proceeds from Full Alignment *to nonprofit organizations to build their capacity for effective leadership.*

MAKE IT HAPPEN

MAKE IT HAPPEN

MAKE IT HAPPEN

MAKE IT HAPPEN

MAKE IT HAPPEN